THE MELANCHOLY ANDROID

THE MELANCHOLY ANDROID

On the Psychology of Sacred Machines

Eric G. Wilson

STATE UNIVERSITY OF NEW YORK PRESS

Cover photo: Brigitte Helmas, the Machine Man in Fritz Lang's *Metropolis*. Courtesty of Photofest.

Published by
State University of New York Press, Albany

© 2006 State University of New York

For information, address State University of New York Press,
194 Washington Avenue, Suite 305, Albany, NY 12210-2384

Production by Marilyn P. Semerad
Marketing by Susan M. Petrie

Library of Congress Cataloging-in-Publication Data

Wilson, Eric G.
   The melancholy android : on the psychology of sacred machines /
Eric G. Wilson.
      p. cm.
   Includes bibliographical references and index.
   ISBN 0-7914-6845-3 (hardcover : alk. paper) — ISBN 0-7914-6846-1
   (pbk. : alk. paper)
1. Mind and body. 2. Melancholy. 3. Androids. I. Title.

BD450.W523 2006
154.3—dc22

                                                          2005027975

10 9 8 7 6 5 4 3 2 1

CONTENTS

ACKNOWLEDGMENTS

I would most like to thank Pranab Das, who suggested to me the primary distinction of this book: between the android as a realization of spiritual potential and as a violation of natural law. I must again offer my deepest appreciation for the intellectual presence of Phil Kuberski. I have benefited in untold ways from my peripatetic talks with him over the years. His ideas have influenced all of my work profoundly. I would also like to thank Jim Hans for reading and commenting on the manuscript. His insights improved the book markedly. I also appreciate the support of several acute interlocutors whose wisdom helped make this book possible: Allen Mandelbaum, Robert D. Richardson, Jr., Marilyn Gaull, Angus Fletcher, Christopher Celenza, Laura Walls, Phil Arnold, and Dennis Sampson. I also very much appreciate the astute reviews of the anonymous readers for State University of New York Press. I would also like to thank the Andrew W. Mellon Foundation, who funded my John E. Sawyer Fellowship at the National Humanities Center, where I completed this project. Wake Forest University has been extremely supportive of my research. I am especially thankful for the year I was allowed to spend at the Humanities Center. Parts of chapter one were published in *Esoterica: The Journal*. I would like to thank the editor of this journal for permission to reprint these materials. Finally, I would like to express my deepest gratitude to my wife, Sandi, who generously endures my melancholy, and my daughter, Una, who brightens my gloom.

INTRODUCTION

Obsession is the blurring of human and machine, a condition in which a woman or a man falls into the blind repetition of the motor. In this state—seductive but dangerous—the person nears the android, the creature with no will of its own. The man obsessed and the oiled android are both inhabited by a force beyond their control—an internal power in the case of the human and an external one in the machine's instance. Human beings often take perverse pleasure in this condition—in the ecstasy, almost miraculous, of escaping the ego, the awkwardness of self-consciousness. But this pleasure can quickly turn to pain, the gnawing sense that growthless motion is as monstrous as the jerking robot. This is the tension of obsession: the soul pulled asunder between transcendence and horror.

This book on the psychology behind the creation of androids grew out of obsession, my fixation on three films that I could not stop watching: Fritz Lang's *Metropolis*, Peter Freund's *The Mummy*, and Ridley Scott's *Blade Runner*.[1] I was addicted to these movies: Lang's ravishing city and the gorgeous Brigette Helm as an android; Freund's hypnotic Egypt and his melancholy Karloff; Scott's reveries bathed in amber as well as Rutger Hauer's ghoulish face suffused with blood.

But these seductive qualities cannot account for my irrational desire to witness these movies *every single night*. These pictures had become more than cinema. They had metamorphosed into mirrors of my hidden depths, parts of my constitution of which I was barely aware. Viewing these pictures, I felt strange potencies at work, latent during the day of waking and working, emergent only before the crepuscular pictures of the celluloid. These impulses—evoked by Helm's erotic grace, Karloff's eyes ruined with longing, Hauer's desperate gaze—were complex blendings of fascination and fear: awful.

On the one hand, these films on exquisite machines pulled me away from my grating self-consciousness, allowing me to live for a time outside my skin, to transcend my ego. They empowered me to play the dignified

1

android, untroubled by the rift between thought and action. On the other, these same movies, meditations on the tragedies of mechanism, revealed the pernicious consequences of blending organ and machine: the possibility that machines might usurp humans or that humans are machines. These pictures troubled me with the idea that I might be, without knowing it, a machine.

I soon realized that my obsession with the films was double: an instinct for Eden, forms undisturbed by shame, and a fixation on the fall, the ruins of history. This twofold obsession was inseparable from the machines on the screen. These androids figured my twofold drive. These machines were products of a hunger for Adam or Eve unfallen, motions informed by love. They were pernicious manifestations of fallen time, worship of death. My obsession with these films was a masked cathexis on machines. My hold on these machines was hope for transcendence, terror toward determinism.

An attempt to account for my attraction to androids, this book is a tractate on the psychological modes generating three types of android: the mummy, the golem, and the automaton. I argue that humanoid machines reflect forms of melancholia that have resulted from what human beings have perennially called "the fall." These kinds of dejection are inseparable from self-consciousness, the painful rift between mind and matter, knowing and being. To heal these splits, humans have created mechanistic doubles untroubled by awareness of self. These new Adams embody the spiritual potential of their suffering creators—the possibility that human beings might be able to transcend their self-centered fears and desires and return, egoless, to Eden. However, though these mechanisms often issue from noble longing, they sometimes emerge from selfish urges to perpetuate the ills of the fall. In these cases, the android is not a redemptive technology but a stifling contraption—not miracle but monster.

IMAGINED ANDROIDS

That the machines that seduced me were cinematic is revealing. Imagined humanoids prove more psychologically complex and intriguing than actual androids. More supple and manifold than the somewhat limited machines in the history of technology, the artificial humans from the realms of film, myth, and literature tend to double the obsessions of their creators, their conflicted yearnings for both love and loathing, life and death. In this way, the androids emerging from human imagination constitute psychic projections as much as physical collections. Though certainly the humanoid machines from the annals of history inevitably reflect to some degree the fears and desires of their creators, empirical androids are simply too limited in scope and gesture to manifest in interesting ways the concerns of their makers. Actual machines thus constitute rather crude approximations of their creators' overt and covert dreams. Virtual humanoids, in contrast, are subtle phantoms of their makers' interiors, revelations of conscious as well as unconscious reveries. The androids haunting the edifices of the imagination serve as especially luminous unveilings of hidden psychologies concerning the machine. These fantastical mechanisms bring to light what might well be true of all relationships between human beings and artificial doubles, regardless of whether this relationship is historical or imagined. To study the androids of cinema, myth, and literature is possibly to sound the origins of all machines. The source of mechanisms is likely sacred obsession: the holy yet accursed longing for eternity—endless life, painless death.

In attempting to understand relationships between melancholia and mechanism, I in this book focus mainly on the virtual androids dwelling in myth, literature, and film. However, I do not neglect the humanoid machines of historical annals. The actual talking statues of antiquity, the mechanical men of early modern gardens, the complex automatons of the enlightenment: these palpable contraptions and the philosophies behind them (coming from the likes of Hero of Alexandria, René Descartes, and Julien Offray de la Mettrie) provide interesting material examples of the mechanical reveries. Even if these physical humanoids are not as psychologically subtle as the more tenuous androids of the imagination, they nonetheless ground my analyses of sadness and machines. They show that the manifold mechanisms of culture are closely connected to the cogs of the laboratory, that empirical machines are inspirations for or results of imagined engines, either sources or precipitations. In this way, historical humanoids suggest that the psychological patterns of imagined humanoids are not simply occasional phenomena—not merely the fantasies of poets—but possibly enduring archetypes of experience, deep structures of heart and mind.

If the humanoids of the technologists help to substantiate the speculations of the poets, then imagined androids—the primary focus of my book—work to reveal the hidden psychologies of actual androids. Whether the mummies, golem, and automatons of myth, literature, and film inspired or resulted from empirical androids, this much is clear: the artificial humans of the imagination, like spiritual antitypes of material types, fulfill and reveal the interior spaces of external humanoid building. Imagined androids form psychic doubles of physical androids, tenuously visible phantoms manifesting the secrets of their fully bodied siblings.

Material androids moor their immaterial familiars. Immaterial androids manifest their material companions. To study this relationship is not only to practice a form of medieval typology—a quest rising from shadowy types to truth, matter to spirit. To meditate on this linkage is also to engage in a modern version of allegory: psychoanalysis, a descent from consciousness to the unconscious. The stories of actual android makers and the machines that double their desires resemble the noon-time mind, the empirical day. The tales of virtual machines and their imagined creators suggest the midnight disposition, the shadows of dreams. Reversing expectations, psychoanalysis—whatever form it takes—claims that the wisps of reverie are more substantial than the data of the understanding, that the unconscious revealed by dreams is the ground of filmy consciousness. In unveiling the quintessence of solid machines—in elevating the gaze from body to soul—phantom mechanisms also illuminate the underworld of these same springs and cogs, the abysmal realms beneath Olympian reason.

This relationship between the spiritual and the secular, sacred allegory and profane psychoanalysis, suggests the familiar theory of correspondences: physical activities (the descent to the unconscious) are analogous to spiritual activities (the ascent to soul). Even though these motions move in opposite directions and even though they inhabit different planes of being, they reach the same end. Both travel from visible to invisible, outside to inside, known to mysterious. The way up and the way down are the same. As it is above, so it is below. But whichever direction one journeys, one must carefully navigate, for the placeless palaces of spirit and the unmapped region of the unconscious are alike decisive for one's condition. In these realms, one either discovers the Eden for which one has longed or finds the Gehenna one has dreaded.

To make an android—in history or in dream—is to walk this razor's edge between transcendence and neurosis. In studying this risk, my book necessarily meditates on the relationship between creator and product. Generally, the connection between maker and android falls into one of two categories: the machine is projection either of unconscious desires or conscious ideals. In the former case, the humanoid embodies characteristics that its creator pretends to loathe—dark, disturbing energies disdained by the conventions of daytime. However, though consciously claiming to hate the traits of the android, the maker secretly loves these same qualities, for they are really the contents of the unconscious externalized. The android constitutes a double of its maker's unknown regions, often irrational and unseemly. Like Mr. Hyde to Dr. Jeykll, as the monster to Victor Frankenstein, the android manifests its creator's unmapped interiors. It proves uncanny, a return of repression, unfamiliar and familiar at the same time. This is doubling as splitting, with the creator and the creation figuring two halves of what should be a full self. In the latter case—the android as double of conscious ideals—the artificial human externalizes its maker's spiritual yearnings: impossible notions of perfection, visions of a paradisiacal condition never known on earth. But this artifice, even though it might have been fashioned as a sort of idol to be worshipped and imitated, often becomes a reminder of distance and division—the gap between the actual and the ideal, the discord between matter and spirit. The ideal double sometimes exacerbates the very longing that it was meant to assuage and thus proves an object of hatred as well as of love. This kind of humanoid also proves uncanny, unearthing not repressed desire but the mystery of being, the abysmal and disturbing expanses of existence that the reason must for its survival often forget. Stoking the soul but shattering the ego, this ideal android recalls the beautiful yet destructive phantom in Shelley's *Alastor*; it reminds of the white specter guarding the watery *omphalos* in Poe's *The Narrative of Arthur Gordon Pym*. These are doubles not as forgotten halves but as implicit wholes: repetitions of spiritual potential.

In meditating on androids as doubles of psychological states, I inevitably often treat machines as if they embody the mental dimensions of their creators. In doing so, I am self-consciously committing a version of Ruskin's "pathetic fallacy." I am attributing human fears and desires to nonhuman entities. Far from being a logical fallacy—a category mistake—this blurring of human and machine proves an accurate reflection of the enduring relationship between creators and humanoids. Even if the android does not really possess human loves and loathings—does not, as *Ding-an-sich*, bear these traits—it seems to embody these qualities, for it constitutes a projection of its maker's interior. The appearance of the android reveals human depths that its own cogs can never achieve. Likewise, though the human being cannot by definition be a machine— cannot comprise man and mechanism at once—he can obsessively dream of androids and take on the qualities of his projections. The mechanical behaviors of a human illuminate how the inanimate husk of the android hides humid emotions. When I in this book discover in the android sadnesses that a machine simply cannot experience and in the human mechanisms that organs could never contain, I trust that my rationale and meaning are clear: I am focusing on the interpenetrations between human beings and humanoid machines that frequently occur in the contexts of melancholia.

CRISIS OVER THE VIRTUAL

These melancholy interpenetrations between men and machines have been around since the days of ancient Egypt, when priests, saddened by death, labored to imbue human statues with ever-living gods. However, since the romantic age of the early nineteenth century, when machines for the first time threatened to take the place of humans, these gloomy relationships have been especially intense. Our contemporary age is the nervous heir of this romantic condition and faces this question of identity—do humans or machines hold sovereignty?—in an extreme and frightening form.

Having pushed the industrial age into the digital one, ours is the time of virtual reality. Experiences in the digitalized pixels of the computer screen feel more real than events in the actual environment of breathing bodies. To download the gaze into a cool screen vivid with moving images is to enter into humming life, a perpetual whirl of figures. To touch smooth, beautiful flesh, decaying more each instant, is to feel dreamy, insubstantial, strange. We fear computer viruses as much as biological ones. We want our machines to be as friendly as our colleagues. We require our computers to survive; they are extensions of our consciousness. We increasingly yearn for cosmetic surgeries that make us at least part machine, organs propped up with artificial components.

This ubiquitous blurring between human and machine has produced unprecedented emotional and epistemological confusions. Our images of human beauty are often weird amalgamations of plastic surgery and biological development. If one falls in love with such a vexed physical surface, how is one to know if one yearns for the organ or the mechanism? This ambiguity of the heart quickly leads to epistemological crisis: how can one know the difference between apparent and real, determinism and freedom, automatic and autonomous? At stake is not only the oldest question in the book—what is existence?—but also the most pressing existential concern: who am I?

Postmodern technology has unexpectedly spawned a return to the most ancient philosophical speculations on ontology, epistemology, and ethics. In a contemporary world confused over the difference between human and machine, we face the harrowing possibility that being, knowing, and agency are impossible to establish. This crisis urges recent thinkers, regardless of their commitment to empiricism, to search for stable principles beyond the irreducibly ambiguous material plane. If physical data will not reveal whether a creature is fated or free, then perhaps metaphysical realms will. Postmodern conundrum opens to the oldest broodings: the visions of Egyptian priests searching for undying life beyond growth and decay; Platonic ideals of perfect forms unsullied by corrupt earth; Gnostic hopes that this material world is but the lurid dream of a false god who will one day awaken to the true deity beyond the stars.

This rather bizarre homology between ancient metaphysical speculation and recent technological awareness has found interesting expression, appropriately enough, in the movie theater—both the cave of ancient Plato and the laboratory of trendy visionaries of the virtual. The last decade has witnessed a surprising explosion of what might be called "Gnostic cinema," movie-house illusions paradoxically devoted to the notion that all matter is unreal. Examples of these conflicted pictures include *Vanilla Sky* (2001), *The Matrix* (1999), *The Thirteenth Floor* (1999), *eXistenZ* (1999), *The Truman Show* (1998), *Dark City* (1998), and *Pleasantville* (1998).

Each of these films suggests that the only way to escape postmodern philosophical crisis is through transcendence, either elevation to the spirit or descent to the unconscious. Each picture intimates this liberation in content and form. In content, each depicts the world as a prison of technologically generated appearances surmounted only through some vitality beyond the empirical. In form, each proves an irreducible contradiction—computer-produced illusions espousing life beyond the virtual—and thus a self-consuming artifact pushing viewers toward a third term beyond representation.

The three films on which I was fixated and which inspired this book fall into this category of Gnostic cinema, devoted alike to ancient spiritualism and recent technology. Lang's *Metropolis*, Freund's *The Mummy*, and Scott's *Blade Runner* all brilliantly use the most recent production technologies of their periods in order to explore the horror of mechanism and the hope for transcendence. Each broods on this melancholy double bind through an android. Helm's robot is simultaneously seductive and destructive. Karloff's mummy features the slow grace of melancholy wisdom and the mechanical lethargy of the zombie. Hauer's Replicant combines indifferent violence and tortured beauty.

My book partakes of the spirit of the films from which it grew in two ways. First of all, like these films—and like all instances of Gnostic cinema—my study, regardless of the historical period on which it focuses, is a sustained meditation on our contemporary condition: a philosophical and psychological crisis generated by ambiguity over the difference between organ and machine. The book stays close to this harrowing situation from which we cannot escape: we are made to love machines that we want to hate; we are expected to loathe mechanisms we yearn to love. Second, and also in connection with these films of a Gnostic bent, my book places itself at odds with itself in the hope, probably doomed to fail, for transcendence. This conflict is a linguistic one. Though my study is grounded on traditional argumentation—a thesis proved with evidence—it is also committed to the lyrical mood of film, literature, and myth. This tension between intellectual argument and poetic atmosphere, similar to the cinematic strife between regularized technology and dreamy ambience, intimates a third term possibly capable of reconciling logic and lyric. What this third term might be, I cannot say, though I suspect that it is more ideal than real, more optative than indicative.

THE HUMANOID'S HISTORY

This book studies the archetypal patterns by which dejected humans have related to their artificial doubles. It focuses on conditions that have remained similar in kind (though they have differed in degree of intensity) throughout history, ranging from the building of crude statues to the construction of artificial intelligences. These repeated situations are characterized by the humanoid machine in three related forms: as manifestation of melancholy, as figure of holiness and horror, as double bind intimating a third term.

These recurring structures, though, as I have suggested, are not static. Pitches of historical intensity bend the forms in one way or another, stretching here and relaxing there, expanding and contracting. Even if each historical period that I study is organized by a spectrum running from machine as miracle to machine as monster, each period emphasizes a different span of this spectrum. The ancient and classical periods tend to inflect the humanoid machine purely as a sacred contraption, a physical manifestation of spiritual consciousness. The medieval and early modern segments of history are prone to be torn between seeing the android as vehicle for transcendence and viewing this same machine as violation of order. The Enlightenment period continues to meditate on the religious densities of the humanoid but also looks at the artificial human in secular lights: as a prime example of our technological prowess or as a notable instance of human hubris. In the romantic age, the first period (as mentioned earlier) actually threatened by the possibility of machines usurping humans, the android becomes a bizarre amalgamation of each of these points along the spectrum, represented as sublime god and gothic monster, exquisite work of art and execrable affront to nature. Heir of the romantic age and its successors, our contemporary period (as already noted) brings the conflict between human and machine to extreme crisis, for it entirely collapses the difference between virtual and real, prosthesis and bone, and thus renders this spectrum of android perspectives superfluous. If everything is a machine, why even try psychology, the fine gradations of the emotionally fraught mind?

My book negotiates this difficult interplay between structure and metamorphosis mostly in Western contexts. Though I occasionally consider the non-Western visions of ancient Egypt or medieval Israel, I focus on how these contexts get translated into the philosophical and psychological categories of European intellectual history. This emphasis is not unwarranted, for the theories and practices surrounding the mummy and the golem, though they might have arisen from non-Western sources, have perennially fascinated the minds of the West and have become enduring components of Western thought. In focusing on Western histories of ideas, this book does not pretend to make universal claims. What this study says about human beings and humanoid machines might not apply to the technologies of the East. One would like a new Joseph Needham to study relationships between Western and Eastern perspectives on the android.

This book is limited in other ways as well. Emphasizing psychological and philosophical elements, it only glances at the political components of android making. One could devote an entire study to how the history of androids illuminates issues of gender, race, and class. The history of the term "robot" suggests how the history of humanoids might address political oppression. The word originates from the Czech *rab*, "slave," by way of another Czech word, *robota*, "work." Karel Capek coined the term for his play of 1921, *R.U.R. (Rossum's Universal Robots)*. This drama depicts artificial humans as a race of slaves who rebel against their masters. Taking this etymology and this theme as cues, one could fruitfully study these trends: humanoids are often females made by male inventors, outcasts concocted by careless creators, and servants designed by imperialistic scientists.[2] Though my focus has not allowed me to explore these currents, I am convinced that more study of the politics of android building—which would complement the work of Donna J. Haraway and Claudia Springer[3]—is needed.

This book is also limited in the scope of its examples. One can find rich instances of the android throughout Western mythology and folklore, ranging from the automatons of Daedalus to Roger Bacon's talking head. Likewise, one can discover interesting artificial humans in the canons of Western literature, reaching from Homer's artificial maidens, detailed in the *Iliad* (c. 800 BC), to Philip K. Dick's human replicants, described in *Do Androids Dream of Electric Sheep?* (1968). One also encounters myriad humanoids in twentieth-century cinema, with Paul Wegener's *The Golem* (1915) on one end of the spectrum and Steven Speilberg's *A. I.* (2001) on the other. Any of these instances of artificial humanity might well embody psychological dimensions of android building. However, as I have already intimated, the most complex, rewarding examples of melancholy machine making come from the romantic age, beginning roughly in 1798 with Coleridge and Wordsworth's *Lyrical Ballads*, and approximately ending in 1855 with Whitman's *Leaves of Grass*. The writers of this period experienced unprecedented mechanical possibility. After the technological innovations of the eighteenth century, it appeared, for the first time in Western history, that machines might overcome man.

This possibility charged the machine with new intensity. Though certain technological devices had carried an uncanny aura in the eighteenth century—as Terry Castle has shown in *The Female Thermometer*[4]—in the nineteenth century the monstrous and the miraculous potentialities of machines evoked especially Faustian desires and fears. On the one hand, it appeared as though the efficient machine literally might return humans to their godly origins; on the other, it seemed as though the violent engine in reality might result in hell on earth. This duplicitous situation—melancholy longing for origin, morbid terror of end—generated a literary interest in androids never before encountered. In Germany, this was the period of Heinrich von Kleist's "On the Marionette Theater" (1810), a meditation on the prelapsarian grace of puppets; of E. T. A. Hoffmann's "The Sandman" (1816) and "The Automata" (1821), tales on the weird qualities of artificial humans; and of Goethe's *Faust, Part Two* (1832), a depiction, among other things, of a redemptive homunculus. In England, this time witnessed Coleridge's contemplations on the somnambulist, the human turned machine, in "Kubla Khan" (1797, 1816); Mary Shelley's version of the golem, the clay form animated, in *Frankenstein* (1818); and De Quincey's own lucubrations on sleepwalking in *Confessions of an English Opium Eater* (1821). These years in America saw Charles Brockden Brown's *Edgar Huntly* (1799), a novel on somnambulism; Poe's explorations of mummification in "Ligeia" (1838) and "Some Words with a Mummy" (1845); and Hawthorne's analysis of machines and perfection in "The Artist of the Beautiful" (1846).

Though I glance at android examples beyond the romantic period (mainly at the androids of cinema), I primarily instance my psychological speculations on humanoids with this period's store of tales. What emerges from this archive is this conclusion (at which I have already hinted): our contemporary age—call it postmodern or posthuman or whatnot—is still struggling with the great confusion of the early nineteenth century, when the divide between human and machine blurred and disappeared. This is the legacy of the romantic age, and it still informs our disposition and our despair, and it thrives in virtual events taking place daily in our ubiquitous movie houses.

The nature of my psychological speculations is another limitation in this book's scope. When I say "psychological," I have a particular set of ideas in mind: not contemporary theories of clinical psychologists but more dated ideas of doctors of the soul, those visions keen on healing the enduring disorders associated with the fall—the decline from innocence to experience, unity to division, consciousness to self-consciousness. This canon of psychologists includes Ficino, the Renaissance philosopher who inflected Hermetic philosophy into a cure for melancholy; Kleist, the romantic writer who meditated on the grace of puppets; Freud, the early twentieth-century physician who discovered connections between the unconscious and melancholia; and Jung, another twentieth-century figure committed to the lost wholeness of the soul. I focus on these theoreticians for a simple reason. Each, regardless of his degree of positivistic rigor, is ultimately interested in the great mystery of existence, twofold and insoluble: the stumble from blissful participation to reflexive division and the hunger to rise once more to oneness. With this emphasis, each illuminates how humans relate to androids, markers of the unawareness of innocence and the enervating rifts of experience.

These descriptions of this book's artistic and psychological focuses bring me to a final limitation in scope. Though this book offers original readings of romantic literary texts and of films in light of android psychology, and though it features rich psychological meditations on literary and cinematic representations of androids, it is neither a specialized work of literary or film criticism nor a fresh contribution to psychology. I explore the examples that I draw from literature and cinema purely for their power to illustrate psychological theories. The discussions of these texts and movies are brief, dense, and hopefully illuminating. I invoke psychological theories solely for their ability to explain representations of androids. My psychological meditations are limited, speculative, and possibly insightful.

These disciplinary limitations are not, I trust, weaknesses. In a book like this, these loose uses of disciplinary categories should be strengths. Not intending to be a specialized academic study, this work is true to the nature of its highly interdisciplinary subject. Attuning itself to the heterogeneous mental atmosphere of android creation, it attends not only to psychology, literature, and film but also to philosophy, myth, history, and aesthetics. Ranging among these disciplines, the book constitutes a general study of a large topic of interest to many people. The value of this tractate lies in its detailed, varied analyses of the forms of dejection associated with the human urge to fashion humanoid machines. In casting itself as a general study, the book models itself on other wide-ranging and well-written works on enduring problems: Kathleen Raine's *Blake and Tradition*, Jacques Lacarrière's *The Gnostics*, Barbara Stafford's *Body Criticism*, Philip Kuberski's *The Persistence of Memory*, and Christoph Asendorf's *The Batteries of Life*.[5]

THE BOOKS BEHIND THIS BOOK

While these books inspired me in a general way, other books that specifically explore the building of androids were extremely useful in helping me shape my passions into arguments: Gaby Wood's *Edison's Eve*, Victoria Nelson's *The Secret Life of Puppets*, Marina Warner's *Inner Eye*, and J. P.

Telotte's *Replications*.[6] Wood in her study, subtitled "The Magical History of the Quest for Mechanical Life," recounts the lives of the technological visionaries responsible for blurring human and machine. Focusing on Descartes, la Mettrie, Jacques de Vaucanson, and Thomas Edison, Wood is keen on the bizarre details surrounding the concoction of humanoid machines, the habits of the men who have loved levers over limbs. In her more intellectually ambitious study, Nelson examines how the androids of modern literature, cinema, and comics recall the ancient Hermetic idea that human icons are conductors of divine as well as demonic energy. Her study evokes the religious impulse behind the creation of androids and shows how the quest for mechanistic efficiency is really a drive toward Edenic grace. Warner in her little encyclopedia of the invisible world focuses on technologies designed to record the currents of spirit. Though she does not emphasize the android as a vehicle of unseen life, she details other modes by which people have recorded the beyond: poetry, painting, photography, cinema, séances, the gathering of ectoplasm. Telotte in his examination of androids in science fiction cinema considers how artificial humans in film measure our stances toward technology, humanity, and cinema itself. While the book focuses on film, it also explores our enduring fascination with androids—how we embrace the android as manifestation of our ability to shape our environment, how we fear the android as register of mechanistic threat to our humanity.

Without these books as catalysts, I could not have formulated my irrational drives into arguments. Still, I was in the end forced to explore a phenomenon beyond the scope of these studies: the chronic melancholia besetting the man fixated on androids. This sadness of the machine maker and of his products eludes the historical focus of Woods, the cultural emphasis of Nelson, the optical theories of Warner, the cinematic analyses of Telotte. The psychological currents of my essay take me to vague regions of the mind, to thresholds between the unconscious and consciousness, to the dark unconscious itself. These spaces—gloomy and somber—are beyond chronology, representation, sight, and celluloid. Yet, though mysterious, these realms nonetheless originate the drives behind the android: ruinous love for Eden, relentless instinct for death. If writers such as Wood, Nelson, Warner, and Telotte—Virgilian guides—pointed my way to these terrible places, then more ponderous beings led me through the gray air: not only Ficino, Kleist, Freud, and Jung, but also Poe, Goethe, and Mary Shelley.

THE OBSESSION PURGED

Writing about the obsession with machines did, in the end, purge my fixation on android films. I no longer burn to sit in a dark room and witness the silvery flickers of robots. What Freudians call the "talking cure" perhaps removed the irresistible allure of these moving pictures. However, the new obsessions that have arisen in the place of these movies—fixations on Osiris and on somnambulism—have taught me that obsession has nothing to do with particular objects. Obsession is a disposition readily transferable to this or that. Obsession is not found but made. It is not reception but projection. Locked in a white room, the man formerly obsessed with the paintings of Pollock will become fixed on absence of color. These are the occult desires of the obsessive personality: to escape dependence on things, to transcend space and time, to dwell in dream.

Obsession is an instinct for spirit, an existence unhindered by matter, as free as the air. But the hunger, for this reason, will remain unsatisfied. Obsession, though it aspires to spirit, is married to matter. It is trapped in the strict causalities of the physical plane, the relentless logic of the machine. If *this* happens—if I am in a mood to fix my passion on an object—then *that* will necessarily follow: then I shall inevitably produce a cathexis on this object. This is the double bind, tragic and gothic, of all obsessions: entrapment between a yearning to rise above matter and an urge to gaze on this material event. This obsessed soul requires the hard cogs that fuel his dreams of total annihilation.

Though I am no longer moored to androids, I am still sometimes troubled by the suspicion that I am a machine. This thought produces the low fever of melancholia. I fear that this viral sadness is inescapable. I fear that this lingering dejection is not unique to me. I suspect that it is an epidemic slowly infecting the citizens of our age—the age when machines rule organs. I sometimes believe that we are all obsessed with machines, cinematic and actual. I imagine the entire race languishing on the interstice between silicon and soul, dreaming, like the prisoners in Plato's cave (the first movie house), of gardens made of chrome and strange hybrids that creak through trees.

1

THE MELANCHOLY
ANDROID

S pike Jonze's film *Being John Malkovich* (1999) intimates a troubling undercurrent of puppetry. Moving mannequins may not,
after all, provide merry escapes from the difficult world but might
rather highlight the day's most painful yearnings. The intricately realis-
tic puppet shows of Craig Schwartz, the film's protagonist, emphasize
the enduring agitations of human existence. A puppet alone in a room
bursts into a disturbing lament born of his isolation. Marionette forms
of Heloise and Abelard from separate chambers pine for erotic contact.
These displays of puppetry, brilliant and moving though they are, undercut the expectations we bring to the marionette show—those hopes for
a mild, slightly ribald respite from the rigors of the daily grind.

The puppet is most often associated with the child. Perhaps many of
us recall going to a park of a summer Saturday afternoon, sitting on the
bright green grass, and watching the shenanigans of puppets. Perhaps a
version of the old Punch and Judy routine, harmlessly violent and
vaguely libidinous, whipped us into belly laughs. Possibly a gentler sort
of show, a rendering of Aesop or the Bible, warmed us into sentimen-
tality. This more didactic marionette feature likely resembled the puppets we watched on television—the Muppets or Howdy Doody. These
and other instances of puppet merriment make it hard for us to accept
Jonze's more troubled visions, his use of diminutive mannequins to figure the glooms of the human soul.

But it is precisely our conventional expectations of puppetry that grant
aberrant marionettes their uncanny power. Associating the puppet with joy,
we feel disoriented when we behold a mannequin doubling human angst,

or worse, evil. This latter situation—the sinister puppet—has in recent years become increasingly prominent. Possibly drawing on the famous 1963 *Twilight Zone* episode in which the doll Talky Tina kills an oppressive stepfather, Tom Holland's *Child's Play* (1988) features as its monstrous villain a child's doll, Chucky, animated by the soul of a recently slain serial killer. Throughout this film and its sequels, audiences are treated to the weirdness of the child's doll coming to murderous life. The same eerie conflict between innocence and experience informs another spate of puppet horror pictures. Beginning in 1989 with David Schmoeller's *The Puppet Master*, this sequence of pictures (totaling, according to my count, seven volumes) also draws for its effects on the creepy antagonism of the marionette, its blending of sweet nostalgia and dark magic.

The puppet and the moving doll, its sibling, are microcosms of the android, a life-size mannequin that resembles the human being. The diminutive puppet differs in significant and obvious ways from the larger android. However, this smaller mannequin shares with the android important characteristics. Both constitute artificial humans seemingly come to life. Both fascinate the child in us keen on harmless magic, the escapism of the fantastic. Both stoke our worries over the blurring of living and dead. The puppet and the android comprise reminders of a paradise from which we have fallen and toward which we yearn. They also prove signs of our horror of collapsing categories and our faith in meaningful distinction. To ponder the puppet is to enter into the psychology of the android, the sadness of lost grace and gloomy hope.

These animated mannequins, regardless of size, reveal the secret and duplicitous origin of our fascination with humanoid machines. We yearn for their unaffected grace. We fear their awkward weirdness. In unveiling our hidden fixations on mechanical doubles, these humanlike contraptions manifest our more general vexation in relation to all machines: our entrapment between loving efficient pistons and loathing aloof metal. Since the industrial revolution of the romantic age, this double bind has been especially troublous. Now, in an age that has pushed the industrial threat to human sovereignty to the digital threat to human identity, this bind is more pronounced than ever. We love what undoes us; we hate our essential familiar. To study the android is to get to the core of this classic case of sleeping with the enemy, this self-annihilation inherent in the age of living machines, this transcendence and this suicide.

KLEIST AND THE PUPPETS OF PARADISE

In "The Puppet Theatre" (1810), Heinrich von Kleist meditates on the uncanny theology of marionettes. The piece features a famous dancer,

Mr. C., describing to an unnamed narrator the elegance of puppets. Against convention, C. claims that these mechanical dolls dance with more grace than humans for this reason: inanimate figures lack the "affectation" that thwarts the aesthetic designs of men and women.[1] Freed from the self-consciousness that forces humans to think about what they are doing, puppets never lose their perfect "centre of gravity" and thus are unhindered by the "inertia of matter."[2] In this way, puppets, seemingly dumb stuff, approach gods, intelligent spirits. Here, C. claims, is "where the two ends of the round earth meet"—where the absence of consciousness meets complete consciousness.[3]

C. clarifies this theory by invoking the "third chapter of Genesis," the account of the fall of man. He claims that dancing puppets recall the innocence of Adam and Eve before they ate from the tree of knowledge. Human dancers, however, suffer from the postfall experience: melancholy self-consciousness. C. suggests that there exist two paths by which fleshly dancers—and all women and men—might return to the graceful state from which they have declined: a backward and a forward way. The backward path requires a return to unthinking matter, the unconscious puppet; the forward way necessitates an ascent to total consciousness, the condition of a god.[4]

C. exemplifies this double vision in two ways. Two lines "intersecting at a point after they have passed through infinity will suddenly come together again on the other side." Likewise, the "image in a concave mirror, after traveling away into infinity, suddenly comes close up to us again." C.'s conclusion: "When consciousness has . . . passed through an infinity, grace will return; so that grace will be most purely present in the human frame that has either no consciousness or an infinite amount of it, which is to say either in a marionette or in a god."[5]

If the puppet can reveal a potential grace, and thus provide an ideal of untroubled unconsciousness, it can also mark the human being's distance from this same elegance, and therefore constitute a reminder of the fall. Moreover, as a symbol of one pole of redemption—the lack of self-awareness opposing (yet agreeing with) complete self-consciousness—the puppet not only reveals the human's separation from innocence. It also shows his painful limbo, his hovering between two inaccessible alternatives: unknowing and total knowledge. Pulled between Adam unfallen and Adam restored, people are doomed to double longing, nostalgia for dumb matter or omniscient spirit.

This is the duplicity of the puppet. On the one hand, it intimates the double path of redemption, the way back and the way forward—the bliss of the idealized childhood (retrospective dreams of thought and deed harmonized) and the joy of adulthood realized (prospective reveries of self and consciousness reunited). On the other hand, it hints at a twofold mode of alienation, the distance from prefall innocence and the separation from postrapture experience: the unrequited nostalgia for graceful ignorance (the sad yen for bodily unity) and the unfulfilled hope for effortless knowledge (the gloomy gaze toward mental oneness). In inspiring visions of happiness, the former strain is likely to cause melancholia, for it reminds us of what we have lost and what we cannot recover. In inducing feelings of bereavement, the latter current might result in exhilaration—the quest for infinity that elevates finite life. Whichever way the puppet pushes, there is weirdness—the strangeness of disorientation, the eeriness of fevered longing.

Now we likely imagine more unsettling encounters with puppets, no more displayed in green daylight but in the chiaroscuro of twilight. In the curious gloaming, the marionette theater fades into the mystery of the fall. The wondrous leaps and dives of the wooden figures, not vexed by gravity or yearning, hint at the gestures of Adam—God's fine figurine—before he lapsed. But in recalling this fluency, the marionettes also remind the people in the gloomy rows of what they have lost and what they must suffer. The unaffected forms enjoy a unity between being and knowing that Adam lost when east of Eden he was cast. Still burning near the flaming blades of the cherubim, this first being of flesh was doomed to hurt in a gap between hunger and wholeness. In this rift we still ache, and long for a moment when matter and mind might once more merge. This instance never comes, and we begin to believe it never will. Saddened, we vow never again to make our way in the shadows toward the marionette stage. But while trying to ignore the beautiful dolls, we envision the sinister side of puppetry: the solitary manikin after the show suspended between ceiling and floor. This is the sadness on the faces of all discarded humanoids, no matter what their size, a register for our own melancholy hovering between matter and spirit. We see in the alienated puppet the emptiness of abandonment mixed with the silent hope that someone might come.

THE MELANCHOLY ANDROID
AND SACRED TECHNOLOGY

People require spiritual technologies to help them overcome this aching paralysis, this endless vacillation between dust and deity. Most settle for the prayers, rituals, and icons that their religions offer, modes of worship that might carry over to the grace of the garden or the omniscience of the divine city. However, some especially wounded souls, burdened with excessive sensitivity to the rift between matter and spirit, need more than the temporary poultices of orthodox piety.

They want immediate identification with either unfallen Adam or Adam restored: the perfection of unknowing, or perfect knowledge. They create artifices unsanctioned by orthodox laws: humanoid machines that move with no thought of stumbling and prophetic androids attuned to the world axle. Sad over their alienation from the divine, men have concocted mummies that might carry them from the pain of time to the western land of the stately dead; statues capable of drawing down and voicing gods; alchemical homunculi that marry spirit and matter; golem approximating Adam before he fell; automata untouched by messy emotions.

But these same sacred machines frequently fail to redeem. They often exacerbate the melancholia that they were designed to assuage. Automata suggest that there is little difference between human and machine. The golem can turn murderous. The diminutive homunculus is a reminder that man is a speck of matter trying to contain cosmic consciousness. The talking statue manifests the cruel duality of body and soul. The mummy proves an uncanny return of this horror: all that seems alive is dead.

The psychology of the android, like that of the puppet, oscillates between miracle and monster. The humanoid machine is vehicle of integration and cause of alienation, holy artifice and horrendous contraption. The android is fully sacred, *sacer*: consecrated and accursed. It is a register of what humans most desire and fear, what they hate in life and what they love in death. To track the psychological dimensions of the humanoid is to sound what is constant in the Western soul informed by Plato's pining for eternal forms and Augustine's heart that will not rest on sordid earth. This questing for the mind of the humanoid is also a search for the intense core of our contemporary identity crisis, the Platonic and Augustinian conundrums made horrifically new in the digital age. What is the difference between artificial and real? How can we know this difference? Who is the agent that knows in the first place?

The place to begin this analysis of the melancholia behind the creation of androids is the work of Marsilio Ficino, the fifteenth-century Italian philosopher and translator. The meditations of Ficino lead us into the labyrinths of noble melancholia and its connection to statues that might come to life. This relationship between sadness and stone itself takes us to the strange world of late antiquity, the cradle of the wildly eclectic Hermetic texts, dialogues, and tractates devoted to the lacerations and cures of the soul. The *Hermetica*—which Ficino translated into Latin and made a cornerstone of his thought—constitutes a nexus not only between East and West (Alexandria and Rome) but also between ancient Egyptian mummification and early modern golem making.

FICINO'S NOBLE MELANCHOLIA

The Florentine philosopher Ficino thrived on the interstice between melancholy and magic. Born under the sign of sad Saturn in 1433, Ficino spent his life brooding over relationships between matter and spirit, being and knowing, fall and redemption. The results of these constant meditations were *The Book of Life* (1489) and a translation of the *Corpus Hermeticum* (c. 200–300 AD) from Greek to Latin. The former is a psychological treatise on the connection between melancholy and genius as well as a manual for how to avoid becoming overwhelmed by black bile. The latter is a second- and third-century collection of eclectic philosophical dialogues influenced by an ecstatic mix of spiritual movements, ranging from Egyptian theurgy to Neoplatonism to Gnosticism. These dialogues focus on links between matter and spirit and on ways that pious men might channel spirit into matter. Together, these works lay the foundation for psychological theories that illuminate the sadness of android building. To establish this ground, I shall first describe Ficino's notions of melancholia and then connect these notions to the animated statues of the Hermetic tradition.

As Frances Yates explains, Ficino, a deep classical scholar, was aware of a question asked in *Problems*, a work from the fourth century BC often attributed to Aristotle:[6] "Why is it that all those who have become eminent in philosophy or politics or poetry or the arts are clearly melancholics, and some of them to such an extent as to be affected by diseases caused by black bile?"[7] As Ficino knew, this question moved against the grain of the prevailing theory of melancholy, emerging from Hippocrates and Galen in the ancient world and solidified by Hildegard of Bingen and Avicenna in the medieval period. This traditional theory saw melancholy as a condition of fearfulness, moroseness, misanthropy, or madness caused by an overabundance of the most sinister of the four humors, black bile. Aware of more positive visions of melancholia in Euripides and Plato, Aristotle's disciple countered this unfavorable perspective. In the plays of Euripides, the most extreme symptoms of the black disease—delusion and dread—often vex great heroes. The madness of Heracles, Ajax, and Bellerophon results not from petty moroseness but from brilliant defiance.[8] Plato developed this idea further when he associated frenzy, *furor*, with visionary ecstasy. In the *Phaedrus* (c. 380 BC), Socrates admits that frenzy is perhaps an evil, but it also is much more: "We receive the greatest benefits through frenzy . . . in so far as it is sent as a divine gift."[9] Hence, although Plato did not connect melancholy with holy madness—he in fact related the black disease to moral weakness—he married the main symptom of melancholy to greatness.

A leading exponent of the rebirth of classical ideas, Ficino recovered this tradition of noble melancholy in his *Book of Life*. According to Ficino, melancholy is most likely to afflict not sullen neurotics but profound scholars. This is so for three reasons. First, meditative souls are born under the planetary influences of Mercury, "who invites us to begin our studies," and Saturn, "who works them out and has us stick to them and make discoveries." These planets pass to their children their natures: coldness and dryness—characteristics necessary for calm, lengthy study but also traits of black bile, associated with the frigid, desiccated core of the earth. To this heavenly cause of scholarly melancholy, Ficino adds a natural one. In pursuing knowledge, gloomy scholars must pull their souls from "external to internal things, as if moving from the circumference to the center." To penetrate to the center of their beings, they must remain "very still," must "gather [themselves] at the center." Fixed on the middle of their beings, they dwell in a place very much like "the center of the earth itself, which resembles black bile." One with the earth's middle, these scholars descend to the "center of each thing." Delving to the core, they paradoxically rise to the "highest things," for the dark axis of creatures is in accord with melancholy Saturn, "the highest of planets." The human cause of the scholar's melancholy is inseparable from the heavenly and natural causes. Influenced by Saturn to migrate to the center, sad scholars contract their own beings and thus dry and freeze their brains and hearts, turning both "earthly and melancholy." Moreover, this perpetual thinking, a movement between circumference and center, external and internal, exhausts the spirit. To continue in their difficult motions, tired spirits require the nourishment of thin blood. These spirits' consuming of lighter, clearer blood leaves the remaining blood "dense, dry, and black." Together, these causes of scholarly melancholy separate mind from body. Obsessed with "incorporeal things"—invisible interiors and vague interstices—melancholy scholars dwell on thresholds between souls and bodies. Holding to the "bodiless truths" of the invisible, they turn their bodies "half souls"; unable to escape bodies entirely, they remain partly corporeal.[10]

Ficino, a student of Plato, does not believe that melancholy thinkers should engage in endless vacillations between boundary and center, depth and height, body and soul. He holds that dejected philosophers should end in spiritual tranquility—find rest on the still point of the spiritual axis, in the untroubled air of Saturn's sphere, in the palaces beyond space and time. Yet, until thinkers achieve these unearthly *topoi*—if ever—they must suffer the pains of his special geniuses, their double sights: mania. Recalling the theories of Plato and the Aristotelian author of *Problems*, Ficino admits that "the poetic doors are beaten on in vain without rage," that "all men . . . who are distinguished in some faculty are melancholics."[11] In his *Book on Life*, Ficino hopes to ease the pains of this *furor* without extinguishing its lights, to instruct sad geniuses to channel their nervous dispositions into salubrious directions. He offers remedies for debilitating melancholy, most of which center on the idea that saturnine interiority can be counterbalanced by exteriority. Sullen philosophers might eat foods associated with the social impulses of Jove or the amorous designs of Venus. They might surround themselves with colors imbued with joviality and flirtatiousness. They might, through the aid of magical talismans, draw nourishment from Jupiter's conviviality and Venus's libido.[12]

THE LACERATIONS OF THE *POIMANDRES*

This last therapy for melancholy connects to Ficino's work as a translator of the *Corpus Hermeticum*. This ancient text made it into Ficino's hands by way of Cosimo de Medici, who in 1460 had attained a copy from Byzantium. Cosimo and Ficino thought that they had discovered a great treasure: a document espousing the wisdom of Hermes Trismegistus, the Thrice-Great Hermes, an Egyptian sage believed to be older than Moses and Plato. Cosimo ordered Ficino to cease his present task, a translation of Plato from Greek to Latin, and to go to work without delay on the more important translation of the philosophical father of Platonism and Judaism. For the next three years, Ficino carried the Greek over into Latin, believing all the while that he was transcribing the oldest truths in the universe.[13] Unaware of what would become known in the sixteenth century, that the *Corpus Hermeticum* is actually a gathering of second- and third-century works set down by many anonymous hands,[14] Ficino would have been especially moved by the *Poimandres*, a meditation on the creation of the cosmos and the nature of man.

The *Poimandres* is a dialogue between the mind of God and Hermes Trismegistus. As the *Poimen Anthropos* (the shepherd of men), the heavenly nous attempts to lead Hermes from his physical limitations to metaphysical freedom. This he does by illuminating the origin and nature of the cosmos and man. In the beginning, Poimandres—"Life and Light"—sent his creative word to organize dark, seething chaos into a lucent, harmonious cosmos. Next, Poimandres, being "bisexual," gave birth to a second mind, a demiurge who combined with the logos to separate the seven planetary orbits, reflections of eternal reason, from the mundane planet, nature devoid of reason. Poimandres next created man, a "Being like to Himself" capable of dwelling in the spiritual sphere of the demiurge, his brother.[15]

This primal man, the *anthropos*, a perfect copy of his eternal father, knew the mysteries of the seven orbits. He sent his gaze down through their circlings until he broke through the lowest sphere, that of the moon. Man beheld nature, and nature saw man. She "smiled with insatiate love of Man" and revealed to him, in the mirrors of her waters, "his most beautiful form," the "form of God." Man witnessed his gorgeous image imbedded in the mundane surface. He fell in love with the planet. He "took up his abode in matter devoid of reason." Nature "wrapped him in her clasp, and they were mingled in one." This is why, says Poimandres, all particular, earthbound men, offspring of this primal union, are, in contradistinction to all other creatures, "twofold": mortal "by reason of his body," and immortal "by reason of the Man of eternal substance." Double, humans are controlled by destiny and able to control all things. A sublunar man is slave and master. He is asleep and awake. He is carnal and consecrate.[16]

This split in man between eternal mind and temporal matter, further aggravated by a later severance between male and female halves, leaves earthlings in chronically awkward positions. Unlike gods, purely immortal, and unlike animals, thoroughly mortal, humans are pulled by opposing poles: matter bent on seducing spirit into its warm though deathly rhythms, mind keen on escaping matter to an ever-living realm beyond the stars. Likewise, in contrast to gods, whose spiritual wants are fulfilled, and animals, for which physical satisfaction is enough, men and women are incomplete. Soul thwarts the unthinking urges of body; body stymies the pristine quests of soul. Conflicted and hungry, most men, as Poimandres claims, descend into ignorant sensual pleasure. Led "astray by carnal desire," setting "affection on the body," earthlings delve into the "darkness of the sense-world" and suffer the "lot of death." A few men, however, strain to extricate themselves from profane motion and rest in the sacred stillness of the "Good which is above all being." To identify with the "Life and the Light," his true self, the pious seeker must reverse the error of the anthropos. He must "loathe the bodily senses" of dying earth and love the invisible mind beyond the planets.[17]

But, as Ficino would explain sixteen years after he translated these ideas, denying the vibrancy of the senses is melancholy work that can only be undertaken by melancholy philosophers. Saturnine thinkers are skeptical of outward appearances. They suspect that warm, moist flows—organic vitalities—are at best illusions hiding deeper truths, at worst invitations to consume drafts of death. These philosophers are compelled to pull away from lubricious surfaces, to contract inward to cold, dry regions where nothing moves: the frigid core of the earth, chilly pages in the midnight, Saturn ringed with ice.

However, as Ficino makes clear, this extreme interiority, this drive toward the inanimate, is exhausting and dangerous. It threatens to drain thinkers of vitality, to reduce them to husks. These philosophers cannot forsake organic energy entirely. They must balance their spiritual attractions to petrifaction with bodily desires for the charms of Venus or the conviviality of Jove. This effort at redress places these philosophers on a delicate threshold between stillness and motion, inorganic and organic. Though they might find occasional contentment on this boundary, they are generally doomed to dejection. As long as they are trapped in a soft shell desirous of nature's waves, these melancholy scholars will, despite their frozen cores, be torn between unquenched metaphysical thirst and physical needs they cannot satisfy.

THERAPEUTIC STATUES IN THE *AESCLEPIUS*

While melancholy philosophers can temporarily fortify their ruined geniuses by channeling Venus and Jove, they can escape their wounds permanently only by healing the vicious split between body and soul. This emancipation can be achieved through two distinct modes, one based on ascent, the other dependent upon decline. As Ficino learned in the *Corpus Hermeticum*, the first way of liberation begins when the body dies. For pious people who have experienced "gnosis" of the true relationship between their souls and the eternal Mind, death reverses the fall of the first man. The body falls away from the skyward soul and returns to the gross elements from which it came. Meanwhile, the soul rises through the seven planetary spheres, shedding a particular type of earthly ignorance as it crosses each orbit. Eventually, this soul enjoys consummation: total identity with God and the good, light and life.[18]

This paradigm troubles traditional notions of life and death, happiness and sadness. Organicity, the rhythm of the physical world normally associated with life, becomes death, the decay of space and time. The inorganic, the soul untouched by nature and often connected to death, turns into life itself, eternal vitality above corrosion. To be tied to a warm body is to be imprisoned. Floating in a cold space is freedom.

In another text ostensibly by Hermes, the *Aesclepius*, Ficino encountered another healing technique. This dialogue between Hermes and Aesclepius, in Western circulation before Cosimo attained the *Corpus Hermeticum* and well known to Ficino, considers, like the *Poimandres*, the relationship between soul and body. In contrast to the vision of the Shepherd of Men, this text proclaims that the double nature of humans actually makes them superior to gods. Hermes says that the "two substances" of men and women, "one divine, the other mortal," render humans not only "better than all mortal beings" but "also better than the gods, who are made wholly of immortal substance."[19] Enjoying a more expansive awareness than the gods, human beings are able to command the gods, call these holy creatures down to earth. This they do through magic capable of initiating decline: the descent of the divine into dirt. This practice requires that the humans fashion statues of gods that can be animated with a divine afflatus. Just as God made other gods in his eternal image, certain pious people "fashion their gods in likeness of their own aspect." This stone anatomy—stiff and inorganic, as cold and dry as the sable soul—turns into a magnet drawing down from the heavens the Mind of God. Charged, it becomes "living and conscious" and able to do "many mighty works": predict the future, inflict and remove diseases, dispense woe and weal "according to men's deserts."[20]

The paradigm of descent also blurs time-honored distinctions. Like the ascent detailed in the *Poimandres*, the decline in the *Aesclepius* suggests this: what normally passes for life, thermal oscillations, are deathly; what generally intimates death, cold shapes of marble, are vital. Likewise, just as the *Poimandres* questions the traditional distinction between joy and happiness, so the *Aesclepius* maintains that what often translates into dejection—the split between soul and body—grants the power to draw deities to dust, while what is often a sign of joy—unified consciousness—is divorced from the marriage between opposites.

The general similarities between these Hermetic texts quickly open into important differences. The *Poimandres* exudes a Gnostic atmosphere, a sense that matter is inherently botched and beyond redemption. The Shepherd of Men claims that the eternal, boundless, omniscient soul is trapped in body, a realm of decay, contraction, ignorance. Awareness of this tension between soul and body breeds a melancholia that can be relieved only through the transcendence of matter—the partial transcendence of asceticism, the total transcendence of bodily death. The cosmic rift between soul and body is beyond repair. Only beyond the cosmos can one find health.

In contrast, the *Aesclepius* operates in an alchemical environment, a domain in which matter is the womb in which spirit is born and thus the ground of redemption. Hermes believes that the fall of immortal energy into the mortal coil offers the possibility of a capacious, though painful, double vision. To become conscious of this twofold perspective is to become a melancholy magus desirous of marrying the great antipodes of the universe. This healing union arises through the animation of matter with spirit, statues with gods. The gap between time and eternity is momentarily closed. In the mire of the mundane, one finds the jewel: the philosopher's stone, the sacred illuminating the profane, the profane bearing the sacred.[21]

As Ficino suggests in his *Book of Life*, this latter, alchemical mode is more appealing to the earthbound philosopher than is the Gnostic way. Close to the *Aesclepius*, Ficino claims that melancholy awareness of the conflict between body and soul is not a sad result of an inherently botched cosmos but a rich inspiration for holy magic. He also follows this Hermetic dialogue in stating that one way to heal the melancholy wound is to channel appropriate spirits to ailing matter: the warm Venus to the cold soul, the convivial Jove to the dry disposition.

Yet underneath Ficino's positive theories of melancholy lurk negative currents. Though Ficino's melancholy philosophers appear to be attuned to the vital flows necessary to ameliorate the hurting cosmos, they are at their cores cold and dry, motivated and sustained by Saturn's ice. Likewise, even if the sad philosophers in the *Book of Life* seem able to animate matter with spirit, they are finally, as students of the *Aesclepius*, fixated on dead things: inanimate statues. These are the disturbing paradoxes of melancholy magicians who craft sacred statues. Though desirous of life, they are in love with death. Though hungry for the currents of spirit, they are obsessed with stone.

FREUDIAN MELANCHOLIA AND NARCISSISM

If Ficino's Hermetic melancholia points to the hopeful longing behind Kleist's puppets, Freud's psychology of sadness reveals the reverse: a neurotic love of death that fixates on wooden folks. Like Ficino, Freud believes that melancholia can grant people "a keener eye for truth than others who are not melancholic." But Freud also maintains that the price for this sight is high: perpetual dread, self-loathing, obsession with corpses.[22]

In "Mourning and Melancholia" (1917), Freud argues that melancholy, like mourning, is based on the loss of a beloved entity—a real lover, an ideal condition. But while the work of mourning eventually redirects love to another object and ends the pain of loss, the labors of melancholy never cease, for melancholics, instead of releasing the lost beloved, identify with it. Unconsciously, melancholics turn their feelings concerning the lost other toward their own egos. These sentiments are a mixture of love and hatred—affection for the lost object's virtues, disdain toward the pain caused by the object's removal. Loving the object, melancholics incorporate it into their egos; hating the object, they loathe themselves. For Freud, this self-hatred is the mark of melancholia. What is really unconscious sadism toward the lost other becomes overt masochism. This "extraordinary fall in . . . self-esteem" results in a sense that the ego's every action and thought is inferior, shameful, sinful. The predictable result of this anxiety is "sleeplessness and refusal of nourishment, and by an overthrow, psychologically very remarkable, of that instinct which constrains every living thing to cling to life."[23]

This is the dark underside of Ficino's philosophical melancholia. Sad philosophers enjoy more profound visions of life's lacerations than do happy people; however, these thinkers sleep and wake with a sense of irrevocable loss and thus also struggle to overcome suicidal urges. This loss can be the loss of a particular beloved—a mother or a father, a friend or a lover. It can be the lasting absence of a pristine state, possibly a childhood idyll, potentially a dream of Eden. Whatever the form of this bereavement, it always resolves into a loss of blissful unity, harmony with self, other, cosmos.

Freudian melancholics, like the sad souls of Ficino, long to heal their lacerations by reconnecting to some pristine concord. However, in contrast to Hermetic melancholics who quest for union with the divine, Freud's despondent patients become angry at the source of their loss. Incorporating this source into their own beings, they come to loathe those parts of themselves that love the lost person or state. If they should try to recover this state or person through creating artificial copies— automatons resembling their lovers or statues that look like Adam— these melancholics will hate the unnatural forms as much as they love them, will view these forms as monsters as much as miracles. The creations of these melancholics will not be pious, self-effacing emanations of hunger for cosmological unity. They will be neurotic, narcissistic projections of yearning to possess the one thing that has been lost.

A BRIEF TYPOLOGY OF THE ANDROID

Thus far, I have used terminology loosely, roughly equating moving puppets, statues that talk, and the mannequins a twentieth-century neurotic might make. Now, before continuing to introduce the mental life of the android, I should clarify my concepts. "Android," "synthetic human being," forms a general category instanced by several particular examples. Puppets, dolls, and statues in human form; mummies and homunculi and golem; human automatons and robots: all of these are subsets of the android, similar in kind yet different in degree. Though each of these humanoids is, properly speaking, an android, each instances one of the three main types of artificial human: the humanoid made uniformly of stiff, inanimate, natural material; the humanoid crafted uniformly from flexible, possibly organic material; and the humanoid created with a blend of unyielding, dead, possibly synthetic parts and pliable, living, potentially organic parts. One can respectively designate these types as the mummy, the golem, and the automaton. The category of the mummy includes androids comprised of dead things: mummies, of course, but also puppets, dolls, and statues. The division of the golem subsumes androids made of living earth: golem, obviously, but also homunculi. The automaton classification includes those humanoids combining the stiff and the soft, the synthetic and the organic, the dead and the living: automatons, clearly, but also robots.

These categories are not only differentiated by bodily composition. They are also distinguished by psychological condition. The category of the mummy is beset by melancholia over this conundrum: the hunger for eternal *physical* life forces one to become obsessed with dead things— with corpses that might gain reanimation, inanimate stone that could serve as spirit's vessel, lifeless wood preserving the face of the deceased. The golem class is agitated by a different sort of sadness: a desire for undying *spiritual* existence that results in bitterly vexed attempts to transcend matter through matter. Both golem makers and creators of homunculi attempt to approximate the unfallen Adam beyond space and time by delving into the grossest parts of the physical world—moist dust that might cohere into a giant, and semen-soaked mud that might grow into a little fellow. The category of the automaton is connected to another sort of gloom. Not bent on horizontal transcendence beyond yet dependent upon time, not keen for vertical transcendence above but contingent upon matter, fashioners of automatons and robots wish to replace the contingent flux of the organic world by surrounding themselves with predictable machines. However, to achieve this mechanical paradise, these automaton makers must mimic the organic world they loathe, must imitate with their cogs the laws by which cells thrive. This double bind offers automaton makers the possibility only of ironic transcendence: an escape from changing matter based on the laws of matter and thus doomed to fail even as this escape gestures toward inaccessible stasis.

THE SPECTRUM OF THE ANDROID: FROM GNOSTIC TO GOTHIC

These three types of android constitute a spectrum, flanked on one side by divine mummies and holy statues grown from noble, spiritual melancholia—the longing detailed by Ficino—and on other side by weird automatons and robots emerging from neurotic, physical melancholy— the gloom described by Freud. The two extremes of this spectrum— whose midpoint would feature golem makers caught between the spirit they love but cannot achieve and matter they loathe but require—can conveniently be termed the "Hermetic" and the "neurotic." Hermetic magicians attempt to transform their sad moods into sacred technologies. Wasted neurotics convert their dejected states into profane substitutions. Hermetic melancholics rise to religious ecstasies, their souls flowing out into animated androids. Nervous types fall into secular frenzies, their minds fervidly trying to repossess the beloveds that their copies mimic. Hermetic makers are charitable, wishing to vanquish their egos to become one with the primal man, anthropos. Edgy craftsmen are selfish; they want to incorporate into their egos the particular women or states from which they have been divorced. Magicians aspire to be gnostics, reconcilers of body and soul, engineers of eternity.[24] Neurotics turn gothic, compulsive wreckers of soul and body, mad scientists unconsciously concocting horrors.

Thio opectrum of androids begins in the sacred and ends in the sacred—the sacred as holy, the sacred as accursed. On the gnostic side of the continuum, the region devoted to knowledge of and participation in the spiritual abyss, the sacred takes an uncanny form. According to Martin Heidegger in *Being and Time*, the uncanny (*das Unheimliche*) is a mode of exploration in which the familiar becomes unfamiliar and the strange turns intimate. Sometimes, after one has long meditated on the Being generating and sustaining all beings, one on a certain day, perhaps when bored or in reverie, feels the common things fall away. The everyday objects—this particular volume of Proust, that grocery list—become crepuscular, ghostly, weirdly inaccessible. At the same time, the invisible ground of these existences strangely arises, becomes, though still unseen, palpable, attractive, luminous. In a flash, one *knows*. The ostensible essentials of life, the familiar objects composing the particular biography, are superfluous: strange others hindering the authentic. Likewise, the apparent dream, the primal abyss of Being, is the hidden core of life: the most intrinsic principle. Extended into this nothing, this abyss—not this or that—one is unsettled, insecure. Yet because this nothing is everything, the absence generating all presences, one is also reassured, buoyed by a profound vision of the origin. This uncanny eruption is gnosis, intuitive knowledge of the whole.[25]

If the Hermetic statue is a vehicle of the gnostic uncanny, holy vision, the neurotic manikin is a site of another kind of uncanny, the gothic: accursed experience. In his 1919 essay "The Uncanny," Freud offers a psychology of horror. A moment of terror is caused by an unexpected eruption of a fear that has long been repressed. The return of the repressed is uncanny, a troubling mixture of unfamiliar and familiar. On the one hand, the repressed material is shocking, monstrous, for it has long been hidden and forgotten. On the other hand, this same underground energy is intimate and integral because it has been an essential force of organization and motivation.[26] Envision someone in a secular age, alone in a poorly lighted museum, who witnesses an inanimate doll come to life. This person is horrified at the spectacle but also undergoes déjà vu, the experience of having suffered this same moment before. The animated doll embodies an archaic fear of the dead coming to life. It blurs the categories essential for a rational civilization. Because the person in the museum, a rational adult in a secular society, has long repressed this primitive, occult fear, the doll catalyzes repulsion and attraction—repulsion toward eruption of the intractable, attraction toward deep revelation.

THE ANDROID'S CONTINUUM: MUMMY TO AUTOMATON

The movement from divine mummy to demonic automaton corresponds to a historical development. The androids that fall into the class of the mummy tend to belong to the ancient world—the middle and new kingdoms of Egypt, the classical and Hellenistic periods of Greece, the late antiquity of Rome and Alexandria. The humanoids in the golem category generally come from the European worlds of the Middles Ages and the early modern period—from the medieval visions of Abraham Abulafia and Eleazer of Worms, from the renaissance ideas of Paracelsus and Rabbi Loew. Automatons emerge in the next phase of Western history: the scientific revolution and the Enlightenment, when Descartes and La Mettrie were opining that men are engines, when Vaucanson was crafting his mechanical duck and von Kempelen his automatic chess player.

This temporal movement is a dramatic action. As Western intellectual history becomes increasingly secular and rational, melancholy becomes decreasingly noble, androids less and less holy, and the uncanny decreasingly gnostic. The obverse is also true: as minds in the West turn decreasingly religious and intuitive, depression descends to disease, humanoid machines metamorphose into horrifying wonders, and the uncanny becomes gothic. The great turning point of this development is the scientific revolution of the seventeenth century. From the days of the ancient Egyptian priests to the time of the early renaissance magi, the various forms of androids—mummies and talking statues and homunculi and golem—were largely viewed as religious technologies, modes for overcoming the split between soul and body. During the seventeenth century, the period of Bacon and Descartes, the humanoid machine began to lose its holy density and started to gain an almost exclusive scientific signification. Even though this century constitutes a fecund hybrid of occult passions and rational pursuits, it in the end spawned the Age of Reason, the eighteenth century, when scientific gadgets took the place of the artifices of eternity. The mechanical automaton edged out the esoteric android.

This picture of straight historical development from religion to science does not tell the whole story. Certainly the Egyptian priests and Hellenic statue makers and medieval Cabbalists and early modern alchemists were committed to a scientific understanding of the laws of nature and mechanics, to the idea that they could penetrate and harness the cosmos. Likewise, the automaton builders of the seventeenth century were struck by the religious overtones of their creations, by the idea that their mechanically concocted Adams might replace the organic one of old. This overlapping of the extremes of the continuum opens into several pairs of opposites that structure android building through its historical changes. In each period, an android can be either a *realization* of cosmic law, a return to the perfection of the unfallen human, or a *violation* of universal dictate, a blasphemous affront to the way things are.[27] Whether the humanoid is miracle or monster depends on the values placed on the *inorganic* and the *organic*. If the inorganic is ascendant, then the undying, unemotional android will be an ideal. However, if the organic is predominate, then the artificial, inhuman robot will be aberrant. Depending on the culture in which the android is built, the machine can be either a way of *integration* or a mode of *alienation*. The humanoid might reconnect its maker with the spiritual perfection from which the world has fallen. It might sever its creator from the natural laws that should be imitated.

As I have suggested, the romantic age of the early nineteenth century was beset by an especially troubling mixture of these extremes. Faced with the horrific yet exhilarating possibility that the industrial machine might take the place of humans, this age inevitably loathed mechanisms as much as it loved them. This vexed obsession—a consuming fixation on the various android types and their sundry significations—has, not surprisingly, persisted into our digital age and become even more intense. In a time when the very distinctions between organic and inorganic as well as integration and alienation have become blurred, the android in its heterogeneous forms serves as a critical register of our secret longings and terrors. Regardless of historical period or enduring type, we must keep this closely in mind: whether creaking in ancient Egypt or humming in renaissance France, the android is our familiar and our contemporary.

PLATO'S PUPPETS

In book 7 of *The Republic* (360 BC), Plato pictures an ancient version of the modern cinema. Imagine men in a dark cave manacled so that their heads can face only the wall opposite the entrance. Behind these men burns a fire. Between the fire and these inmates rises a low wall. This wall resembles a screen one might find at a puppet show, the barrier between audience and puppeteer. Above this screen, artifacts ceaselessly move, carried back and forth by men behind the wall. Stone birds and fish, tigers and a bull glow over the scene, sometimes silent, other times singing out animal sounds. Likewise, statues of human beings make their way to and fro on the stage—tall like Achilles, lithe and slim such as Patroclus, like Homer himself cautiously blind. Sometimes these shapes speak words that men would say. Often, though, they oscillate soundlessly as ghosts. All the imprisoned men can see are the shadows these artifacts cast on the dim surface. These sad prisoners are doomed for life to witness simulacra of simulacra in a lurid hallucinarium—to watch a never-ending film in a theater that will not close. There is hope for liberation. On an unexpected day, one of these chained men might be freed. Unaccustomed to light and objects, he would at first behold the fire and the puppets with pain and confusion. Later, after he had for a time sat by the flames and played with the manikins, he would turn toward the cave's mouth and become curious about the even brighter sights beyond the dimness. He would grope into the blinding sun and the bewildering blur of colored birds. If he were hungry to know about this new world, he would endure the doubt until he realized that the wings fluttering in the dawn are real, the ideal forms that the puppets in the cave only copy. Now wise, but still saddened by his wasted life, he might remember with nostalgia his time as a puppet watcher, and wonder if these artificial forms were sacred vehicles that pointed him to the truth. In another mood, he might regretfully think that these gloomy dolls formed pernicious obstacles to his quest for truth. This man would never forget his life with the puppets. He would continue to be hounded by visions of wooden gods and demons made from blocks. His dreams would be divided between mummies fumbling in their tombs and metallic men gliding over surfaces that shine.[28]

2

THE MUMMY

The ancient Egyptians dwelling along the fertile plains of the Nile enjoyed paradise in the midst of desert. Every year during the Nile's annual inundation, fruits and flowers sprang from the black soil. Men and women walked in the cool of evening through the vegetation. One year, a young couple stopped to pluck a bunch of grapes. As the juice oozed down the boy's chin, he gazed to the edges of his family's gardens and beyond, to what he could not see but what he knew was there: the sand never touched by the river's riches. He envisioned the hard grains where nothing lives. Sinking into reverie, he witnessed on the waste his own flesh slowly ripped from his bones. His companion's soft tap on his shoulder brought him back to his bower. But he wanted no more to take in the sunset, Ra's last gasp before embarking on the nightly voyage through the underworld's waters. He desired only to tear off a nearby papyrus stem and inscribe on it some magical symbol that might hold his rippled body above the sands. He turned to pull the driest plant.

Only a culture so flooded with life could be so obsessed with death. This is the melancholia of the great cultures of the Egyptian Dynasties running from 3000 BC until the advent of the Christian Age: fixation on things dead resulting from keen enjoyment of organic life. Struck daily by the weary truth that the most beautiful growths—melons and stalks of corn and graceful cats—fall into the most tragic deaths, ancient Egyptians were surely wounded by paradox. Intense life breeds aggressive death; dying is the muse of living. This tension appears in cold stone pyramids decorated with vibrant scarabs, jackals, and ibises; in elaborate funeral rites that resulted in a perfumed corpse lavished with an abundance of food; in a metaphysics based on ideas of life after death but nonetheless exuberant with ravishing fields of rushes and serene western lands.

This blend of inorganic stasis and vital energy was nowhere more memorably expressed than in ancient Egyptian mummification. The Egyptians thought that one could overcome death only by having the dead body preserved—could experience eternal life only by becoming an eternal corpse. Families spent huge sums of money and embalmers large amounts of labor to ensure that the dead might never decay. This intense attention to inorganic matter grew, however, out of a love of life, a hope that the embalmed body might continue to enjoy the glowing flowers and fruits that nourished its earthly existence. This basic hope suggests striking reversals: the inorganic corpse, normally loathed as the termination of life, becomes a vehicle for the ever-living soul, a machine bearing undying animation; the organic body, generally loved as the pinnacle of living, turns into an inadequate vessel for eternal breath, a ruinous anatomy doomed to annihilation. These inversions breed awkward conditions: dead matter propped up by living spirit; impalpable soul dependent upon tactile body; eternity shackled to time; the temporal unable to escape from the eternal. The mummy, though a miraculous machine of the divine, is also a monstrous blurring of categories.

The overabundance of mummy films appearing during the last century suggests that this android figure continues to manifest this enervating split between the brittle machine eternally vital and the supple organ flowing toward death. Indeed, in our contemporary scene, this tension is likely more intense than ever before. Since the romantic age, industrial machines have served as necessary vehicles of life—makers of food and shelter, clothing and medicine. This motif has become increasingly pronounced in our more recent digital age, when scientists for the first time are envisioning the possibility of downloading the disembodied consciousness into computer hardware. If machines are the vessels of biological and psychic survival, then what becomes of the organic body, traditionally the only bearer of vitality? Does this soft shell suffer a reversal of roles, turning into an inanimate destiny while it witnesses the inorganic carapace become an animated purpose? Does the natural metamorphose into the artificial and the artifice transform into the wild? These questions, pressing in an unprecedented way, find their troubling response in the history and psychology of the mummy.

THE MUMMY AS MACHINE

No wonder the mummy is melancholy. It is a manifestation of the sad insight, keen in the minds of the Egyptians of antiquity, that organic blooms become sweetest in the throes of death. To experience the glory of the morning flower is to suffer the slow dying of the petals. As John Keats intones in "Ode on Melancholy" roses in the dawn and "globed peonies" and rainbows in the "salt-sand waves" and imperious mistresses are beautiful *because* they die.[1] As Wallace Stevens adds in "Sunday Morning," "Death is the mother of beauty."[2] If any culture ever knew these facts in the bones, it was that of the ancient Nile dwellers. Every long, dry summer returned the lush banks to desert waste. The yearly rising of the current was never guaranteed. Some seasons the appearance of Sirius on dawn's eastern horizon did not harbinger renewal of life but continued death. Living in constant fear of drought and chronic hope for water, the Egyptians intensely realized the fragility of existence. Death was never absent. Life could be annihilated in a month. The stalks springing from moist silt were only brief stays against the harsh sand, victories for life but also reminders of death. From the dour floating lotuses grew the mummy—something that might remain in the ruin.[3]

But the mummy is dry and dead. It lacks the sap of the flower. It recalls the sands it was designed to overcome. All efforts to preserve the suppleness of organic life end in stiff artifice. We again turn to Keats: though the Grecian urn transcends history's wrecks, it is a "Cold Pastoral," a thing unnaturally aloof to the yearnings of flesh.[4] We also look once more to Stevens: humankind's desire to overcome annihilation resembles a jar placed in a forest, a brittle device resting among thrushes and vines.[5] This is the problem of attempting to prolong matter with matter. When matter, meant to decay, stands above ruin, it loses what made it attractive in the first place—its supple grace. A temporal shape designed to behave like an eternal phenomenon, the mummy suffers this weary paradox. Though it is a body and destined to die, it remains animated by a soul. Though it is soul and fated to live forever, it is still tied to a body. The mummy is an artifice meant to prolong nature. It is nature stiffened into mechanism. It is a living machine.

The ancient Egyptians themselves never referred to their mummies as machines. But what else is the mummy but a concocted technology designed to alter and transcend the processes of nature? Moreover, because this engine takes on human shape, does the mummy not prove to be a specific type of machine, a synthetic human divorced from the organic? The mummy is a humanoid mechanism made of dead things but meant to prolong physical life indefinitely. This contradiction—death expanding life, life dependent upon death—cuts to the quick of the psychology of mummy making. On the one hand, the mummy grows from a noble but ruinous longing for the impossible: the ability to make permanent the lubricious beauties of the world. On the other hand, the

mummy emerges from an error that breeds ineradicable sadness, a category mistake (the blurring of organic and inorganic) that leads to confusion and neurosis.

THE MELANCHOLY COSMOGONY
OF THE MIDDLE KINGDOM

In one of the many Egyptian accounts of the creation of the cosmos, the
high god—variously known as Atum, Ra, Khepera, or Amun—fashions
men and women from his tears.[6] Though this motif is expressed in the
Bremner Rind papyrus of the fourth century BC, the idea reaches back
to the great Heliopolitan creation myths of the Middle Kingdom (c.
2050–1750 BC). The Bremner Rind contains two creation myths. In
one, the high god in his aspect of Khepera—the scarab beetle rolling his
sphere of dung—rises from the primal abyss, Nun, an infinite plane of
unconscious waters, to produce Maat, order and design. Having
defeated the ocean of chaos, Khepera masturbates into existence Shu, air
and light, and Tefnut, moisture and rain. After these two deities appear,
Khepera recovers from the abyss the Eye of Nun, the sun. The sun, earlier covered by chaos, can emerge into its brightness only when the high
god becomes conscious of his abilities to organize the abyss, to form a
space in which the eye can shine. Immediately after the sun emerges,
Khepera, curiously, weeps over the things that he has fashioned, and
from his tears come into existence men and women. Though these tears
from the sun—now incorporated with the high god who made it manifest—could well be descending beams, they are more likely, as E. A. Wallis Budge claims, "tears of water which fell from the eye of god upon his
members."[7] The other creation myth in the Bremner Rind tells the same
story, but with more pathos. In this version, the high god as Ra rises
from the abyss, utters order into being, and spits forth Shu and Tefnut.
But the offspring get lost in the waters of Nun. Ra sends his Eye into the
abyss to bring his children home. When the Eye reunites Ra with his
progeny, the creator weeps for joy. His tears, as R. T. Rundle Clark
states, "become the ancestors of mankind."[8]

Humans emerge from the weeping of a god. The Egyptian words for
"tears" and "humankind" are linguistically connected: *remeyet* and
romech.[9] If, as a papyrus from around 2250 BC claims, the gods of the
Egyptian pantheon arise from the high god's sweat, his successful
labors,[10] then the human beings struggling to survive in the desert coa-
lesce from this same god's sadness, his failures. This depiction of the
high god is clearly a metonymy, a substitution of effect for cause. The
"illogic" of the trope is this: humans, endlessly fighting against loss,

often find themselves weeping; hence, the power that made them obviously generated them from his own tears. This sort of anthropomorphizing characterizes almost all religions and reveals the ongoing concerns of the culture that humanizes the god. Though one fears generalizing, one can claim with reasonable accuracy that the traits a culture projects onto its primary deity reflect the deepest cares of that group. Surely the qualities of Brahman tell us something about the Hindu cultures, their desire to transcend phenomena and rest in eternal calm. Perhaps the personalities of Jehovah show the worries of the Jewish peoples over whether they are uniquely chosen and betrothed to the true god. In the same way, the Egyptian projection of tears onto the high god—a theological projection that is rare among the world religions—obviously manifests the profound sadness of the ancient Nile dwellers.[11]

OSIRIS: THE FIRST MUMMY

A people precipitated from a god's tears would choose for their most popular deity a moribund god languishing in the gloomy underworld. This god is Osiris, the first and enduring mummy. Osiris lives a double life. He is one with the high god of the sun, Ra, the immortal light. He is a rotting corpse, the most putrid filth of decay, little better than dung. To follow this vexed career of Osiris, the most beloved god of the Middle and Later Kingdoms, is to descend into the melancholia of mummification.[12] The place to begin this tracking of Osiris's career is Plutarch's *Isis and Osiris* (c. 200 AD).[13]

Osiris is the great grandson of Atum, grandson of Shu and Tefnut, son of Geb (earth) and Nut (sky). His brother is Set; his sisters, Isis and Nepthys. Osiris marries Isis while Set marries Nepthys. Initially, Osiris, "immanent" where Atum is "transcendent," walks on earth as a great king.[14] Like Prometheus, he instructs people in science and art. As King Arthur, he inaugurates a golden age. This age ends when Set, the younger brother, murders Osiris. Set holds a feast during which he unveils a gorgeous chest. He tempts his brother to lie in the chest, clamps the lid down, and throws the trunk into the Nile. The chest, now a coffin bearing a dead god, washes up in Byblos, where it becomes incorporated into an immense tree. Without knowing the plight of Osiris, the king of Byblos arranges for this tree to be the central column of his palace. Meantime, Isis has been searching for her husband and brother. She finds him and releases him from the tree. But Set steals the body and hacks it to pieces. Again Isis seeks Osiris. She finds all his parts but the phallus. She and Nepthys gather the limbs and embalm them. These sisters make "the first and essential mummy."[15] While lamenting over her mummified husband, Isis briefly revives his sexual potency. She with her dead lover conceives a son, Horus. While his father lies dead, Horus grows up to form an army. He defeats Set and becomes, with the absent support and sanction of his dead father, king of all the land.[16]

Throughout most of the mythic cycle, Osiris is represented "as a swathed figure with black or green face—for he is both mummy and the life-spirit of the earth."[17] As mummy, Osiris is king of the underworld. But though he is a corpse, he is also the font of annual fertility and principle of civic order. He relies on Horus to activate his dormant powers, to turn back Set, the power of death. Osiris is the unconscious darkness that generates the conscious light that he depends upon to make his potential manifest. He is the dead king who creates the living son on whom he depends to realize his political dreams. He is the chthonic reservoir of vitality that every year must be reborn above ground and the musty tomb that contains the noble ancestors who ensure continuation.

In the Old Kingdom (c. 2780–2250 BC), the myth of Osiris provided models for kings. Each king hoped to reenact Osiris's life on earth and underground—to be, first, Horus, a good son who keeps the land living for his dead father, and to be, second, Osiris himself, a stately corpse who lives through his son's successful rule. However, during the period when the Old Kingdom collapsed into the anarchy of the First Intermediate Period (c. 2250–2050 BC) and the Middle Kingdom saw order restored, the Osiris myth universally attracted the fears and longings of peasants and monarchs alike.[18] Living, one could play Horus in paying proper respects to one's dead ancestors or resemble Isis in lamenting the death of the land and in hoping for its rebirth. Dead, one could become Osiris himself, a corpse overcoming death: a mummy.

MUMMIFICATION AND CENTROVERSION

In *The Origins and History of Consciousness* (1954), Erich Neumann illuminates the psychological attractions of the mummified Osiris. Unlike the "extraverted" hero who actively tries to change the shape of the world, and unlike the "introverted" hero who through contemplation cultivates a culture's inner values, Osiris as mummy is the hero of "centroversion": one who does not quest to alter the world through inner or outer struggle, but seeks to form and preserve the unique ego regardless of the collective. The goal of centroversion is the stabilization of the single personality.[19]

The mythological prototype of this elevation of ego into permanence is the overcoming of death. In the myth of Osiris, this conquest is rendered in duplicitous imagery attuned to both organic generation and inorganic stasis, to biology and eternity. On the one hand, Osiris belongs to the traditionally matriarchal realm of growth and decay, humus and hyacinths. On the other, this god is part of the conventionally patriarchal region of undying light, of pristine order. This double nature is symbolized by the phallus. As a fertility deity, Osiris suffers the loss of his phallus into the waters of the Nile, where his member inseminates the land. As a god of eternal life, Osiris features a mummified phallus, a hard, everlasting totem. The severed fleshy member whose death breeds life participates in the annual rhythms of nature. The attached and embalmed phallus rises above fall and spring, forming an artifice of eternity.[20]

This double nature of Osiris constitutes his primary significance: he is the principle by which the self enjoys resurrection and the power by which the resurrected self achieves indestructibility.[21] As the god of resurrection, he figures the plight of the material body, its inevitable decline toward death, and the virtue of this same body, its ability to recover health. As the god of permanence, he symbolizes the potential of the eternal spirit to overcome the body and the static vessel required for housing this spirit.[22]

These related significations mark two sides of centroversion. On the one hand, centroversion requires attunement to the unconscious, the fecund origin from which the ego arises but also the threatening abyss that this same ego must overcome. On the other hand, this process of individuation necessitates that the ego develop defenses against the unconscious, carapaces that reject the turbulent source. This is the economy of gaining a stable self. To achieve a cogent identity, one must sever the conscious ego from the rich womb of the unconscious and encase this ego in unyielding patterns. The instability of the unconscious is death to the ego; the rigidity of the ego kills the oceanic unconscious. The life of one is death to the other, and the demise of the other is vitality for the one.

Osiris the primal mummy brings to consciousness this melancholy condition. The mummy is a marker for the virtues and limitations of the oceanic feeling, the sense of egoless unity with the collective. The embalmed corpse also registers boundaries and blisses of identity formation, the hardening of the self into a crystal of ice that excludes surrounding waters. This is the mummy's one revelation: whether you yearn for the *participation mystique* or whether you long for the *principium individuationis*, you cannot win: either way, you are incomplete and pine. The mummy's other unveiling is that supple life, a self enjoying vitality, requires stiff death, an egotistical fortress. Bringing these contradictions into the light, the mummy at its mythological inception intimates the sad psychological drives behind actual embalming: the life drive, Eros, prolonging its existence through rigor mortis; the death-drive, Thanatos, aspiring to undying stillness.

THE MUMMY AND THE DEATH DRIVE

On the surface, Freud's speculations on the death instinct in *Beyond the Pleasure Principle* seem to be at odds with Neumann's meditations on centroversion. Where Neumann maintains that the conscious ego comprises a mummification of unconscious energies, Freud suggests that the unconscious itself is an instinct toward stasis, a repetition compulsion bent on the "quiescence of the inorganic world."[23] However, scrutiny of Freud's text reveals interesting similarities between Freud and Neumann—homologies that take us deeper into the myth of the first mummy.

Freud wonders if the unconscious possesses a drive other than the sex instinct. Freud's encounter with the human compulsion to repeat traumatic experiences inspires him to speculate thus. His example of such repetition compulsion is a child repeatedly playing the game *fort-da*. When his beloved mother goes away, the child throws his toys away from himself while saying "fort" (gone) and then immediately retrieves these same toys, intoning "da" (there). For Freud, the child stages this game in order to compensate for the disturbing disappearance of his mother, to exert control over the return of objects when he could not organize the reappearance of a person. What most interests Freud about this situation is this: the obsessive repeating of this very distressing game seems to contradict the idea that human beings are motivated only by pleasure.[24] Even though the boy clearly experiences a sort of pleasure in compensating for his mother's absence, he also definitely undergoes pain in suffering, again and again, separation from his mother.

This troubling case leads Freud into considerations of instincts that point him to this tentative conclusion: the compulsion to repeat a traumatic event, though painful, is also pleasurable, for this subjection of change to identity grows out of *"an urge inherent in organic life to restore an earlier state of things which the living entity has been obliged to abandon under the pressure of external disturbing forces."*[25] This drive is the "expression of inertia inherent in organic life."[26] Resembling Neumann, Freud initially likens this death drive to the ego. He conjectures that the "ego instincts" "exercise pressure towards death," or the cessation of desire, while the "sexual instincts" push toward a "prolongation of life," or the fulfillment of desire. However, after realizing that the ego possesses instincts other than self-preservation, Freud revises. He claims that the primary opposition is not between ego and sex, but between life and death.[27]

This dualistic theory, if tenable, could result in a rather pessimistic conclusion: humans on an unconscious level are driven by death as much as life, by aggression as much as love. Yet, as Freud also makes clear, this same dualism need not lead to pessimism at all. If this death drive might generate destruction, it might also push toward the "Nirvana principle," the desire to "reduce, to keep constant or to remove internal tension due to stimuli . . . a tendency which finds expression in the pleasure principle."[28] Likewise, if the life drive might cultivate satisfaction, then it might also dissolve into strife, for "union with living substance of a different individual increases . . . tensions."[29]

Now we can see how Freud, though he diverges from Neumann and from Neumann's master, Jung,[30] ultimately illuminates Neumann's theory of Osiris, and, indirectly, his theory of the mummy. Freud's speculations on the death drive suggest that humans are doomed to experience timelessness—eternal life—as enduring stasis, as death. His senses of the life drive intimate that people are fated to experience pleasure—temporal vitality—as turbulent decay, also as death. For these reasons, the ego, regardless of Freud's conjecture to the contrary, must on some level be associated with the death drive, the instinct to reduce difference to the same, agitation to tranquility. The ego expresses this drive through the repetition compulsion, the flattening of organic contingency to mechanical predictability. Here again we witness, with more precision, Neumann's enduring ego as Osiris the centroverted mummy. In stiffening the natural into the artificial, the mummy figures the human desperation for tranquility at any price, even death. In marking the maintenance of the organic in inorganic form, the mummy represents the human hunger for pleasure at any cost, even life.

Seen through the lens of Freud, the mummy brings to awareness a troubling rift at the heart of existence, a wound torn between nirvana and neurosis. Enamored of the pleasures of the physical world—stoked by the life drive—most people wish to prolong this joy as long as possible. However, if this pleasure is to persist beyond organic decay, it must be embalmed, made dead. To realize this fact—to embrace the mummy as artifact beyond decay—is to exchange the life drive for the death drive, to attempt to fit the flow of pleasure into a permanent pattern. This impulse toward permanence can take one of two forms. It can take the shape of a desire for total quiescence. This is the yearning for nirvana, dissolution of ego. This is the return to the womb. This is the hope for transcendence. But this fixation on stasis can also result in a hunger for repetition. When this cathexis occurs, one hardens ego against the shifting environment beyond the skin. One sinks into neurosis, nervous programs for control. This compulsion to repeat is a perverse search for origin and a failed quest to transcend limitation.

The sad irony in these instances is this: the quest for nirvana, for eternal life, ends in a divorce from life, a lethargic numbness or an ascetic detachment; and the descent into neurosis, the decline into moribund repetition, turns into a turbid battle between stasis and motion, a participation in the agitated rhythm of the organic world. One is doomed whichever way one turns. The mystic longing for vitality ener-vates into a corpse; the control freak bent on stasis falls into fervid strug-gle. In the former case, the pleasure principle initially manifesting itself as Eros, love for the untroubled origin, stiffens into the pleasure princi-ple as Thanatos, hope for no motion. In the latter case, the pleasure principle at first emerging as Thanatos, drive toward a rigid ego, loosens into pleasure principle as Eros, the vibrant struggle for identity. In both cases the seeker labors in a double bind, trapped between eternity that is death and dying that is time.

To make or meditate on a mummy is to feel the full weight of these contradictions. At the same time, however, fashioning or contemplating mummification is also an effort to discover a way to synthesize nirvana and neurosis, undying deadness and life that decays. If one could achieve such a harmony, then one would not only find concord between eternity and time. One would also discover affinity between the wishes of the soul and the drives of body. The practices associated with mummifica-tion aspire to do just that, but in the gap between ideal and real dwells the melancholy condition, sometimes aspiring toward miraculous though unattainable marriages and other times simply sinking into the monstrosities often bred of ineluctable disappointment.

THEORY AND PRACTICE OF EGYPTIAN MUMMIFICATION

The ancient Egyptians over their three thousand years of existence fash-ioned a complex mythology of postmortem body and the soul. However, two beliefs persist throughout the heterogeneous lore. First, every corpse becomes the dead yet living Osiris. Second, the soul of the deceased can thrive only if the body is properly embalmed.[31]

The primary object behind embalmment was to keep the corruptible body, the *khat*, together, just as Isis magically held her dismembered brother intact.[32] The prayers and ceremonies on the day of burial called for the breath of Osiris to transform the khat into a *sāhu*, a spiritual body— a "germinated" corpse. Animated into a sāhu, the corpse would achieve the impossible—become a material vessel for eternal consciousness.[33]

As Philip Kuberski has claimed, the correctly mummified corpse, the sāhu, resembles a machine, a sort of hard drive for the soul.[34] It is the khat turned brittle as metal, a hollow and unyielding carapace. A prop-erly embalmed corpse would have had its brains and entrails removed, with only the heart remaining inside the torso. This dead body would have been cured in natron for forty days. It would have been wrapped tightly in gum-soaked linens. This hard shell became a suitable dwelling for the immortal elements of the deceased. Were it to falter again into organic suppleness, then the parts of the deceased not destined for death would have no place to light, no abode in which to find rest and nourishment. They would be unhoused and aimless.[35]

The ancient Egyptian believed that every person possesses three souls. The *ka* is the heart, double of the emotional life. Though it can leave the corpse, it desires to remain close to the ka of its dead ancestors and to reunite with the other souls of the body in which it lived. To achieve these ends, the ka returns to the sāhu, takes on a phantom form of its body, and merges with a statue of the deceased near the mummy. Embodied, the ka enjoys food offerings, its family ka, and visits from its sibling soul, the *ba*.[36]

If the ka is the heart, the ba is spirit. Depicted as a hawk with a human head and translated as "soul," the ba is more ethereal than the ka but not entirely incorporeal.[37] Though its wings can carry it into realms of eternity beyond the tomb, the ba must return to the statue of the ka and nourish itself on food offerings. Fortified, the ba can reanimate the mummy and converse with it, change into different shapes, and elevate to heaven.[38]

A third soul, the *akh*, is almost entirely free of any material relationship, yet still tenuously connected to the mummy. Translated as "intelligence" and pictured as a crested ibis, the akh is destined for the pristine heavens upon its release from the body. But this liberation occurs only when the body through proper embalmment is translated from khat to sāhu. Only then can the akh rise through the statue-bound ka and the ba throbbing between body and spirit to the never-moving pole star above earth.[39]

If the properly mummified and enchanted body releases and sustains the ka, ba, and akh, then the deceased becomes Osiris—an enduring, passive body and an eternal, active spirit. This blurring of the material and immaterial aspects of the afterlife led Egyptians to come up with contradictory accounts of heaven. While some visions of the afterlife suggest that the akh ascends to the stars and thus to Ra, others claim that the deceased in the form of a mummified sāhu requires a ladder to climb to paradise. Other myths are equally mixed. Does the deceased turn into a god, and never feel hunger, or does the resurrected corpse continue to enjoy the good things of his corporeal life? Do spirits journey to the field of reeds to exist in bliss with Osiris; or do revived bodies come before Osiris as judge, who weighs their hearts to see if they deserve immortality?[40]

Wherever the deceased dwells, this much is clear: in Egyptian mythology, to become a mummy is not to violate but to realize life. The gracefully supple organic body, an open-ended eddy through which dance gases and liquids, is inferior to the mummified corpse, an inorganic vessel stiffly housing souls that never die. For all of its gorgeous rises and falls, tastes and obsessions, the organic body hinders the souls it carries, holds them close to decay. The threefold soul cannot master a living anatomy, cannot contain the lusts of the thighs. The undying double, the eternal hawk, the starbound ibis—these can flourish above space and time only when their earthly dwelling is indifferent to fear and desire, as stately as a marble statue, a sleeping android.

Ironically, this inorganic realization results from a desire for the bodily pleasures the mummy is meant to transcend. This is the double bind of the Egyptian mythology: on the one hand, worshippers of Osiris, each year torn between desert and river, hate death and yearn to live forever in the lush reeds; on the other, these same disciples of the dead god know that the only way to avoid the pain of death and endure eternally is to become one with the inorganicity they loathe. If Osirian adepts were to love life less profoundly, they might be able to imagine a disembodied afterlife. However, they are too attached to the stalks to imagine ever being divorced from sap. If these same followers of Osiris were to yearn for eternity with less intensity, they might be capable of envisioning death as a simple descent into the impersonal earth from which their limbs grew. But these initiates are too fixated on the persistence of their existences to picture their bodies undergoing the ruins of the seasons. Sensitive to the joy of organic life, Osirians cannot face death. Attentive to the decays of nature, these Egyptians come to loathe living matter.

The melancholia attendant upon this contradiction ranges from noble though unfulfilled longing for eternity to nervous but sensitive neurosis over time. If the former form of sadness can devolve into living death, consummation by Thanatos, it can also ascend to life beyond fear and desire, Eros realized. If the latter type of gloom can agitate the heart into frayed nerves, Eros never satisfied, it can just as well grant an awareness of the rich interdependence between growth and decay, Thanatos as vital energy. Gathering the poles of this spectrum, Osiris as mummy proves an early version of the Hermetic anthropos, the ideal human being torn between eternity and time, death and life.

OSIRIS AS ANTHROPOS

Though Osiris emerged into the consciousness of the Egyptian long before the Hermetic Age of late antiquity, Osiris is nonetheless a model for the anthropos of the *Poimandres*, the primal man who enjoys the bliss of his spiritual existence, indifferent to fear and desire, but who also suffers the fall into ruinous matter. Like Osiris, the anthropos directly arises from eternity. Yet, also similar to Osiris, the primal man declines into time. The descent of both beings issues from *love*—earthly love that fixes on this instead of that, not heavenly charity that adores this and that, everything and nothing.

Out of his affection for Set, Osiris is blind to his plots. He trusts that Set's chest is a legitimate gift. Looking lovingly at his sibling, his double, Osiris climbs down into the coffin. He then drowns in the current and falls to pieces. Fevered by love for his image in earth's waters, the primal man reaches into the mire and becomes a body. He declines from unity of desire and fulfillment to conflict between soul and body—a wound further aggravated when his androgynous offspring are ripped into male and female.

The unfallen spiritual machine descends into the organic body through a kind of affection inseparable from narcissism. This blinding love for the same is based on fear and desire: fear of annihilation of identity, desire for persistence of ego. These emotions are strange in a deity. But they are behind the dismemberments of other spiritual beings.

In the creation story of the *Brihadaranyaka Upanishad*, the spiritual Self distributes its being into material selves through loathing and longing. In the beginning, there was nothing but the Self—boundless, whole, pure. Then the Self reflected and realized that there was only he. He said, "I am He." Upon identifying with an ego, a unique identity separate from and over against difference, he felt fear. He vanquished this fear when he recalled that there was no other, no difference between "I" and "not I." Still, though he understood that fear arises only when there are two entities, he felt lonely and desired a second being. He divided into male and female. The female concealed herself. She became a cow, but he turned into a bull and mingled with her. She transformed into a mare; he metamorphosed into a stallion and again copulated with her. Eventually, the female and male turned into every form and in this way created the world and its creatures. When the cosmos was complete, the Self returned to his original unity; at the same time, he remained present in all that he had created.[41]

A somewhat different version of the same tale shows up in the biblical Genesis. In the beginning, God created not only the heavens and the earth but also a primal Self, Adam—an image of God animated by the divine breath. Adam enjoyed immortality in a gorgeous garden, Eden. He felt unity with his creator and with the creatures around him. Then he felt alone, for he was the only man. Fearing loneliness, he desired a mate. God fulfilled this desire by dividing him into male and female, Adam and Eve. Immediately, Eve ate from the prohibited tree of knowledge of good and evil. With her eyes opened, Eve convinced Adam to eat. After eating, both realized their nakedness, experienced shame, and covered themselves. This division between self and other—based on shame, fear of the other's gaze and desire to control the gaze—led to other divisions: from their harmonious environment, from immortality, and, ultimately, from God.[42]

To transcend fear and desire is to rise above the material ego, to merge with the spiritual whole. To fall into loathing and longing is to sink into a form of matter. The anthropos—the primal human who declines into every man and woman—throbs between both realms. In their spiritual forms, Osiris, the Hermetic Man, and the biblical Adam enjoy the grace of the elegant android. Each in this role becomes an ideal for the inhabitants of the creation, a realization of what the pious creature might miraculously accomplish. In their material anatomies, Osiris the mummy, the primal man embraced by earth, and Adam after eating suffer the horrors and loves of matter. In these incarnations, these beings become symbols of failure, monstrous violations of spiritual order.

THE MUMMY AND THE ROMANTIC AGE

In 395 AD, just about the time that the Hermetic ecstasies in Alexandria were beginning to fade, Theodosius II ordered Egypt to convert to Christianity and proclaimed an end to all mummification. The Western world from this time until the Middle Ages showed very little interest in mummies. In the twelfth century, however, a verbal mistake renewed Western fascination with Egyptian embalming. As Heather Pringle points out in *The Mummy Congress*, when curious medieval scholars set about translating medieval Arabic medical texts, they found that physicians of the East recommended bitumen for many ailments. The best results came from a kind of bitumen known in Persia as *mumiya*. Baffled, Western translators came to believe that the term referred to the substance Egyptians used in embalming their dead. Soon there arose in the West a craze for the embalmed corpses of Egypt, now called mummies. A mummy trade was born, with physicians clamoring to grind mummies into medicine. For centuries, Europeans purchased mummies plundered from ancient tombs, and not only for their healing properties—artists craved the bitumen of the mummy for its lovely brown color. Added to oil or amber varnish, this brownish hue made a wonderful paint.[43]

Even though Europeans knew almost nothing about ancient (or modern) Egyptian culture, they were still ingesting and daubing powdered mummies as late as the eighteenth century—fitting practices given the mythic virtues of the mummy, its vitality in the face of death and its preservation of the image of the living. However, at the very end of this century, Europeans were treated to a flood of information on the people who made mummies. A primary force behind this infusion of knowledge from the East came from a conquering general's uncanny vision in the Great Pyramid of Giza. As Philip Kuberski notes in *Persistence of Memory*, Napoleon, after seizing Egypt from the Mamelukes and the Ottoman Empire in 1799, made his way into the king's chamber of the towering pyramid. When he returned from his journey into the heart of the ancient stones, he was allegedly shaken to his center. "Very pale and impressed," he commanded his aides never to speak of what had happened. Later, he intimated that the chamber had revealed to him his destiny, but he remained silent on what actually happened.[44]

Napoleon's experience in the pyramid in particular and of ancient Egypt in general was partially behind the inaugural text in Egyptology, the twenty-four-volume *Description of Egypt*. This study, published between 1808 and 1829 by a team of scholars supervised by Napoleon himself, for the first time informed, albeit from a biased angle, Westerners about the myths and rituals of ancient Egypt. The book generated a mania for things Egyptian among Europeans and Americans.[45] In the early years of the nineteenth century, Henry Salt, the British consul in Egypt, acquired massive collections of ancient Egyptian artifacts, including the Rosetta stone and numerous mummies. A large part of this collection he sold to the British Museum. As this sarcastic statement by Robert Southey reveals, the citizens of Britain immediately took to the Museum's new arrivals: "Everything must now be Egyptian. . . . The ladies wear crocodile ornaments and you sit on a sphinx in a room hung round with mummies."[46] In *American Hieroglyphics*, John T. Irwin has shown that America in the first half of the nineteenth century was likewise smitten with Egypt. Much to the delight of the minions, in 1826 two mummies were displayed at Peale's Museum and Gallery of Fine Arts in New York. In 1832, a Colonel Mendes Cohen of Baltimore came home from Egypt with 680 ancient artifacts in tow and quickly established a large private collection. Such displays set the model for Dr. Henry Abbott's Egyptian Museum in New York, frequently visited by Walt Whitman, who wrote in "Salut au Monde!" that he saw "at Memphis mummy-pits containing mummies embalm'd, swathed in linen cloth, lying there many centuries."[47]

Writers of the romantic age, which began in England at roughly the same time that Napoleon suffered his unsettling vision and started in America soon after the publication of the *Description of Egypt*, were haunted by mummies, especially by the idea, now a commonplace of cinema, that a mummy dead for centuries might come back to life.[48] In her 1818 novel *Frankenstein*, Mary Shelley compares her famous creature to a revived mummy. Horrified by the corpse he has reanimated, Victor proclaims that a "mummy again endued with animation could not be so hideous as that wretch."[49] Jane Webb Loudon in her 1827 work, *The Mummy! A Tale of the Twenty-Second Century*, tells the story of a team of English explorers who galvanically revive the mummy of Cheops only to watch him escape in a hot-air balloon, fly to twenty-second-century London, and attempt to revive a morally bankrupt culture. While Shelley in her novel only uses the mummy for metaphorical purposes, and while Loudon in her piece deploys this same figure as a vehicle for social satire, Edgar Allan Poe invokes mummification for more substantial reasons. In "Some Words with a Mummy," from 1845, he explores the psychological dimensions of the mummy as anthropos torn between eternity and time. In "Ligeia," finished in 1838, he meditates on a more lurid psychology associated with mummification—on the gloom of a man who wraps his dead wife in mummylike bandages and yearns for her body to be animated by the soul of a dead lover.

A consideration of Poe's contemplations on mummies deepens our understanding of the melancholia associated with embalmed corpses. Moreover, coming as they do after the rise of romanticism in England and at the height of the movement in America, these speculations on the embalmed corpse prove especially illuminating for our own age, a time when the industrial conundrums of the nineteenth century have grown into the enervating paradoxes of the digital age. In both ages, the difference between humans and machines is blurred or dissolved. Machines take the place of humans. Men long for machines. How is one to relate to mechanisms that one necessarily loves and loathes?

POE'S "SOME WORDS WITH A MUMMY"

The mummy devoid of fear and desire is a sacred machine—an ideal of human transcendence. To die without narcissistic love for the things of the organic world is to become such a mummy, to turn anthropos, human as eternal engine. This undertaking is almost impossible. Only people of certain dispositions can pull inward to their icy cores, away from their soft shells. These are the noble melancholics of Ficino. Surprisingly, they are also, very often, exponents of comedy, vehicles of a perspective that gently ridicules from a distance the botched cosmos while at the same entering into the bloody fray of this same world. The mummy envisioned by such a melancholy soul would exhibit the traits of its creator—be coolly aloof to fury of time but also weary of history's decay. Such a mummy is depicted in Poe's story "Some Words with a Mummy." A mix of frivolous comedy and serious satire, the form of the tale perfectly meshes with its content, an exploration of the two sides of the anthropos: light grace and tired awareness.

On the surface a send-up of the recent craze in America for unwrapping mummies as well as of superficial American faith in progress,[50] the story is on a deeper level an expression of what one might call "metaphysical comedy"—the idea that, sub specie aeternitatis, activities on earth are slightly funny while also somewhat sad. The narrator of the tale is a nervous, lazy, ignorant, petty sensualist. He begins his narration by complaining of his frayed nerves and extreme drowsiness. He decides to spend the evening at home, where he shall take only a tiny bit of supper before going early to bed. But the small repast turns into a binge.[51] This man, though unwittingly comical in his complacent delusions, is seriously committed to material. Consumed by fear and desire, he ignores what might threaten him and indulges in what makes him comfortable. He is what the writer of the *Poimandres* would call a "hylic," a man drunk on matter and ignorant of pneuma, spirit. He is unsuited to behold a revived mummy. But this is exactly what he and his colleagues do—converse with Osiris regathered.

A Dr. Ponnonner invites the narrator to join him and a group of companions at the City Museum, where they shall examine a mummy brought from the Libyan mountains. The mummy's outer sepulcher is a large box, seven feet long, three feet wide, and two and a half feet deep. It is made of papyrus and ornamented with funereal scenes and numerous hieroglyphs. One of the party, Gliddon the Egyptologist, concludes that the glyphs spell the name of the deceased, "Allamistakeo"—a name highlighting the fact that Poe's tale is a hoax but also suggesting the mistaken views of the narrator and his acquaintances. Having cut through the outer shell, the men discover a second container somewhat smaller than the first husk but bearing the same decorations and markings. Behind this vessel is a third made of cedar and emitting a pleasant aroma. In this inner coffin is a covering closely fitting the body. It is made of plaster papyrus "thickly gilt and painted" with portraits of the souls of the departed and hieroglyphs of the corpse's relations. Around the neck of this wrapping is a necklace made of "cylindrical glass beads . . . arranged so as to form images of deities, of the scarabaeus, etc, with the winged globe." Under the covering is the body proper. Its skin is "hard, smooth, and glossy." Its eyes appear to be made of glass. Its fingers and nails are covered in gold.[52]

The hylic beholds the holy. The narrator witnesses the threefold casing of a sacred vehicle fashioned to propel its passenger through the frontier of death and into the terra incognita of immortality. Each shell is prepared with the appropriate technologies—pictures and glyphs, souls and spells—to carry the vessel to the destination. At the core of this machine is the vital engine, the mummy. Encarapaced like the scarab that it bears, this android, goldenly metallic and graced with crystalline eyes, has elevated the decaying body to an inorganic miracle, an artifice of eternity.

Insensitive to this numinous technology, the narrator and his companions are interested only in whether or not the embalmed corpse still possesses its entrails. Just as they are on the verge of dissecting this mechanism, they decide to send a galvanic current through the limbs. After several comical attempts, the bungling men bring the mummy to life. The revived Osiris is outraged at undergoing this indignity but he nonetheless graciously agrees to hold a conversation with this group of thrill seekers. As the colloquy develops, the mummy becomes increasingly melancholy over the banality of living humans while his ignorant interlocutors become more and more frustrated at the mummy's inability to understand the greatness of modern inventions.[53]

The mummy tries to assuage the astonishment of his guests over the fact that he is alive after having been embalmed for over five thousand years. He explains that moderns, still in the "infancy of Calvinism," cannot accomplish what was a very common achievement in ancient times—to "arrest indefinitely all the animal functions," including not only physical being but also "moral and vital." The mummy further criticizes the religious sensibilities of the moderns, who incorrectly believe that Egyptians were vulgar polytheists. He claims that the scarab and ibis and all other so-called Egyptian gods were but "the symbols, or media, through which we offered worship to the Creator too august to be more directly approached." Such an explanation causes a silence among the moderns, confused over this sophisticated idea of a transcendent yet immanent deity that can only be approximated by mythic constructions. Attuned to this sublime god, the ancient Egyptians could move in time like most move in space. Egyptian historians would write an account of their own time, embalm themselves for hundreds of years, and revive themselves to correct misinterpretations of their work. This "process of re-inscription and personal rectification" from the hands of "various individual sages" has, as the mummy concludes, kept "history from degenerating into absolute fable."[54]

Unable to understand the mummy's discourse—nothing less than an account of heroic androids holding the ignorant world to some vestige of truth—the modern men attempt to demean the culture of the ancient Egyptians by comparing its seemingly crude achievements to the alleged victories of contemporary science. But the mummy assures the men that the "assumptions of phrenology and the marvels of animal magnetism"—the flowers of modern science, according to the men in the museum—"flourished and faded" in Egypt very long ago, when they were found to be spurious. The mummy goes on to display a thorough knowledge of all the modern achievements cited by the men—of astronomy and glass manufacture, architecture and railroads, progress and democracy.[55]

After the moderns, desperate to find value in their own period, praise contemporary clothing and pills and lozenges, the mummy is rendered silent, able only to smile wearily at the ignorance he faces or to blush and hang "down his head." The moderns take the last gesture as a clear sign of the mummy's defeat. Angered at the "spectacle of the poor Mummy's mortification," the narrator indignantly leaves the museum. Once home, he falls exhausted into bed. When he gets up, he decides to become embalmed himself, for reasons decidedly less noble than those of the wise mummy. He wants to escape his shrewish wife. He is sick of the nineteenth century. He is curious to see who will be president in the year 2045.[56]

The melancholia of Poe's mummy, suggested at the end of tale, grows from this double bind: beyond fear and desire, the mummy enjoys the grace of eternity; compassionate for the terrors and yearnings of men, the same Osiris experiences the ruins of time. If he were not a spiritual body but only a spirit, he would float in the ether. If he were only a body and not an embodied spirit, he would be pulled asunder by the diurnal earth. But this mummy suffers a tension between the untimed bliss of the android and the temporal pain of the human. Because he identifies most closely with the spiritual body, his material burdens are light and his sadness, gentle—the tender world weariness of the traveler through eternity bent on assuaging the wounds of men. This light sadness is inseparable from the comic form of the tale. Once one moves through the satirical bits in the story, one finds a more profound form of humor: the comic as mode of transcendence.

THE COMIC MODE AND THE MUMMY'S MELANCHOLIA

The first guide to the comic currents of Poe's mummified anthropos is, unexpectedly, James Joyce's Stephen Dedalus. In *Portrait of the Artist as a Young Man* (1916), Stephen offers his theory of the aesthetics of tragedy. Though he agrees with Aristotle's idea that tragedy raises terror and pity in the audience, he believes that the great philosopher did not sufficiently define these terms. Stephen first distinguishes between aesthetic and nonaesthetic pity and terror. Improper art and improper artistic feelings are kinetic. Kinetic works spur desire and loathing. Setting these states into motion, kinetic art is not really art. It is either "pornographical or didactic," inciting the urge "to posses" or the impulse "to abandon." In this way, improper art participates in the limitations of the fall. It stokes the ego, inspiring it to struggle toward its yearnings or to avoid its aversions. Kinetic work also comforts the ego; it feeds it with the conventions that it expects—stereotypical objects of sensual desire, familiar forms of violence. Seducing the ego with abstractions, improper art alienates from lived experience.[57]

Proper aesthetic events and proper aesthetic emotions are static. They arrest fear and desire. They disarm the abstractions that generate didacticism and pornography. Tragic pity does not evoke a desire toward a suffering object but "arrests the mind in the presence of whatsoever is grave and constant in human sufferings and unites it with the human sufferer." The terror evoked by tragedy does not induce an aversion from the fearsome event. It "arrests the mind in the presence of whatsoever is grave and constant in human sufferings and unites it with the secret cause." In elevating the beholder above fear and desire, static art pulls one away from the fallen ego and toward an unfallen self, an ideal human form untroubled by yearning or aversion—the anthropos. This kind of art shatters the ego's fixations and reveals the abiding pain. Opening to what is constant, tragedy gestures toward the mysteries at the core of life.[58]

Stephen develops these final points. Proper arts elevate the mind beyond fear and desire through their revelations of concrete resonances. What Stephen calls the "esthetic image" first strikes the mind as a "luminously" "selfbounded and selfcontained" event arising uniquely from "the immeasurable background of space and time." It shines as this thing and nothing else. It is one whole. It possesses *integritas*. The mind follows the "immediate perception" of the synthetic whole with an "analysis of apprehension," an attention to how the parts cohere into the whole, how the whole gathers the parts. The image now appears as a "complex," a harmony of many and one. It manifests *consonantia*. After one has immediately perceived the image as one thing and mediately apprehended it as a consonance of whole and parts, one is finally struck by its shimmering *claritas*, its radiance as this thing and nothing else, its *quidditas*. Only this image, here, now, merges parts and whole in this way. The mind beholding this threefold beauty experiences "the luminous silent stasis of esthetic pleasure, a spiritual state . . . [an] enchantment of the heart." This mind experiences gnosis, sudden insight into the ideal—the Eden, the anthropos, from which it has fallen away and toward which it returns.[59]

The loss of Aristotle's poetics of comedy forms one of the great lacunae of Western aesthetics. One wonders what comic emotions parallel the tragic states, fear and pity. One further is curious over how Joyce's Stephen would have revised Aristotle's comic theory. While one will never know what Aristotle or Stephen thought of comedy, one can guess that Aristotle's comic emotions would share the same polarity of his tragic states, the same mix of repulsion and attraction, and one can speculate that Stephen's theory of comedy would focus on arrest over motion, the constant over the ephemeral.

If tragedy arouses loathing and pity, then comedy inspires joy and sorrow. That the comic generates the former state is obvious. Laughter is foremost the goal of comedy, unbridled joy over ridiculous mishaps and tender reunions. The latter condition, sorrow, seems to be at odds with the comic mode. However, all great comedies—those of Aristophanes or Shakespeare or even those of Howard Hawks or Woody Allen—are predicated on the idea that the world is always on the brink of chaos. In the Dionysian world of comedy, these are the ruling principles, really nonprinciples: if something can go wrong, it will; anything can happen, and it usually does. Mistaken identities, accidents, slips of the tongue, misunderstandings, nervous plots: these are the elements of the comic world as much as happy endings. These troubling elements form the shaky ground from which blissful unions arise. The comic ending gains its joy from relief as much as from happiness—from "sorrow averted" as much as from "joy achieved."

Beyond pornography, the fulfillment of transient desire, and beyond didacticism, the satisfaction of brief aversion, proper comedy, like proper tragedy, is a mode of transcendence. If tragedy reveals what is constant in loathing and pity and empowers one to move beyond ephemeral versions of these states and apprehend the "secret cause," then comedy shows what is ongoing in sorrow and joy and inspires one to transcend ephemeral instances of these conditions and likewise grasp the hidden origin of the cosmos. Both aesthetic modes, regardless of whether they explore suffering or happiness, open to a position untroubled by fear and desire. Doing so, these aesthetic forms disclose what is constant in beauty: integritas, consonantia, claritas.

Henri Bergson in *Laughter* (1900) indirectly illuminates Joyce's implied theory of comedy, a perspective that points out comic possibilities of the android. For Bergson, the core of comedy is the blending of human and machine: *"The attitudes, gestures and movements of the human body are laughable in exact proportion as that body reminds us of a mere machine."*[60] Laughter arises when we witness a person behave as if he or she were a mechanism—an automaton, a puppet, a mummy revitalized. Stiffening into engine, the person cannot control the limbs. With a mechanical life of their own, they continue their motions regardless of the person's intentions. The comedian runs to a ledge. The comic's mind says, "stop," but the legs continue to churn. The clown slips on a banana peel. This trickster tries to maintain balance but the body, controlled by causality, falls to the pavement. Even though suffering from mishaps, the comedian does not, as Bergson further claims, evoke pity: the *"absence of feeling"* "usually accompanies laughter." But

audiences only laugh at the mechanistic indifference of the comedian—
the rigidity of body, the aloofness of soul—when they are not indifferent. Though viewers of the comedy are drawn to the automatic shenanigans of the comic actor, they are also repulsed by the actor's inhumanity,
a lack of sociability. Their laughter humiliates the comic's nonconfor-
mity to human conventions as much as it celebrates this same comedian's insouciant wit. This tension produces the "equivocal nature of the
comic," a mode that hovers between "art" and "life." On the one hand,
we laugh at a comic actor who appears to us as artificial, a player in a
play. On the other, we also laugh at this same comedian to rectify behavior, to encourage vitality.[61]

In highlighting this duplicity of the comic, this tension between the
automatic and the organic, Bergson's theory of laughter illuminates the
aesthetic possibilities of the gently vexed anthropos smiling at the follies
that sadden him. Bergson concludes that the comedian grants us
momentary freedom from mechanism by allowing us to separate ourselves, however briefly, from the mechanistic stiffness at which we laugh.
However, this transcendence of determinism is predicated on the comic's
indifference, the aloofness displayed in the face of gravity. This mechanistic grace under the pressure of causality—a transcendence of space
and time—is precisely what inspires the temporary liberation of the
human audience. If the audience members are repulsed by the automatic
limbs of the human puppet, they are attracted by the unconcerned gaze
of this same manikin. In laughing at this comic automaton, the audience
wishes to humiliate the actor into joining them. But they also wish to
enjoy transcendence of the limitations of matter. This mutual embrace,
if it could occur, would result in a condition in which the virtues of the
human—sympathetic emotions—and the virtues of the machine—indifferent gestures—meet and marry. This state of being, a barely possibly
ideal, would produce the aesthetic vision of the comic: a simultaneous
attachment to and detachment from the joys and sorrows of the world,
a human attunement to emotional vicissitudes liberated by a mechanistic aloofness to these same rises and falls. Standing between the tumult
of the heart and the indifference of the circuit, one achieves the stasis of
the third term: the gesture that remains still, the calm embracing everything. One reaches the anthropos.

THE GOTHIC MODE AND
NEUROTIC MUMMIFICATION

Opposed to the bemused melancholia of the mummy approaching the
anthropos is another sort of sadness: the neurosis of the person fixated

on mummification not to transcend time but to extend it. In this case, the drive for life does not result in the push for stasis, the aesthetic arrest beyond fear and desire. In this instance, the hunger for life quivers into the compulsion for repetition, a fear of decay resulting in a desire to control time. If transcendence of time might end in comic insight—though the world is weary, all is well from the standpoint of the eternal—then fixation on time generally declines into gothic disease: the cosmos slays beauty, so the person besotted by beauty takes revenge on the universe. While exploration of the mummy associated with the anthropos falls into the genre of comedy, analysis of the mummy connected to the neurotic embodies the gothic genre—the nervous aesthetic of monstrosity. If the miraculous mummy intimates an ideal relationship with machines—a vision of mechanisms as paragons of human grace—then the monstrous mummy hints at our current agitation over technology—our hatred of contraptions we are forced to love.

Unlike the comic mode, which revels in overcoming obsessive repetition, the gothic mode delves into the psychology of obsession, the fixed behaviors that transform heterogeneous time into the same damn thing, over and over. Where our primary theoretician of the comic aesthetic is Joyce (at least indirectly so), our main interpreter of the aesthetic of the gothic is Freud. As I noted in my introduction, Freud in his 1919 essay "The Uncanny" argues that horrifying events, whether they occur in life or literature, arise from returns of energies that have long been repressed. Because these unconscious powers have been hidden, they appear unfamiliar upon their release. But because these same potencies have comprised an intrinsic part of the psyche, they are at the same time familiar. Freud's example of this duplicitous situation comes from E. T. A. Hoffmann's "The Sandman" (1816). In this tale, Nathaniel, the protagonist, at one point falls into a horrified swoon after gazing upon two artificial eyeballs designed to be installed in an automaton. According to Freud, these two balls overwhelm Nathaniel with the sensation of the uncanny because they release his repressed fear of castration—they are strange, monstrous reminders of unconscious terror, as well as intimate, familiar revelations of essential interiors. To this example of the uncanny, Freud adds others: being trapped in a series of repeated actions (a return of the unconscious impulse to repeat), witnessing doubles (a return of the primal fear of the double as harbinger of one's own death), being unable to tell the difference between human and machine (an eruption of the repressed horror of the dead coming back to life).

From Freud's examples of the uncanny, two themes emerge. First, the uncanny moment is dependent upon a blurring between normally distinct oppositions: familiar and unfamiliar, dream and reality, self and other, mechanism and organism, death and life. Second, the uncanny event is characterized by repetition of the same: external imitations of unconscious interiors, recurring behaviors growing from repetition compulsions, doubles emerging from primitive portents of death, simulating humans arising from bewilderment of what's dead and what's living. These two motifs are closely related. The irreducible ambiguity of the uncanny moment breeds extreme epistemological, and thus psychological, uncertainty. This insecurity inspires a desire to order the chaos, to impose predictable patterns. This projection of structure onto contingency, whether it originates in the unconscious or consciousness, is as violent as the forces it wishes to control and repress. This defense mechanism is obsessive—a program to reduce threatening difference to comfortable identity. These manifestations of the uncanny moment are desired as much as feared, attractive as well as repulsive. The projection of interior onto exterior, the compulsion to repeat, the concoction of the double, the flattening of humans to machines, the elevation of corpses to lives: these phenomena of the uncanny are modes that attempt to contain the ambiguity of the moment but that also work to intensify the very ambiguity they wish to harness.

These speculations, preparation for a theory of the gothic, result in this conclusion: the uncanny can open either to gnosis, fresh insight into unconscious energies beyond fear and desire, or to neurosis, the ego's obsessive repression of threatening unconscious forces. In the former case, the uncanny experience might translate into the nirvana principle, the death of ego into anthropos. In the latter instance, the uncanny can result in the repetition compulsion, the stiffening of ego to corpse. If the first scenario might rise to comic melancholia, the second frequently descends into gothic gloom.

In content, the gothic mode explores the ways in which the uncanny blurring of categories results in obsessive repetition that reduces difference to the same. In form, this same mode often features interpretive ambiguities and high repetition quotients—confusions and reiterations akin to those that beset the characters. In these ways, the gothic aesthetic proves an apt genre for contemplating mummification as accursed disease—neurotic, or, indeed, psychotic, cathexis on temporal stasis.

POE'S "LIGEIA"

The narrator of Poe's "Ligeia" appropriately opens his tale in a state of epistemological uncertainty: "I cannot," he claims, "for my soul, remember how, when, or even precisely where, I first became acquainted with the lady Ligeia."[62] This initial confusion suggests the dilemma that besets the narrator throughout the story. On the one hand, he is troubled by doubts over the nature of Ligeia. Is she temporal or eternal? Is she real or imaginary? Is she dead or alive? On the other hand, he tries to assuage these insecurities by fixing Ligeia into a rigid image capable of solacing his fears and desires. Though of dubious ontology, she becomes to the narrator a vessel of eternal wisdom, a revelation of the real, a vehicle of undiminished life. This conflict highlights the narrator's condition. The uncanny Ligeia—regardless of whether she is real or not—figures a return of the narrator's repressed death drive, his unconscious urge to dissolve his ego back into the archetypal womb. But she also represents his ego's impulse to repress this unsettling instinct, to reassert an endlessly recurring image of self against forces impersonal and indifferent. This tension pushes the narrator into an obsession with mummification.

In the midst of the narrator's conscious efforts to fix Ligeia's identity, his troublous unconscious energies show through. He remembers that his dead wife was tall, slender, and emaciated; that she had large, dark eyes; that she was immensely learned; that she served as a mother as much as a wife. But these ostensibly definite images give way before more nebulous fogs. In trying to describe this woman whose family name and place of origin he cannot recall, he musters phantoms. Her demeanor was "incomprehensible." She moved "as a shadow." Her hand proved smooth and pale as "marble." The beauty of her face resembled the "radiance of an opium-dream." Her skin rivaled the "purest ivory." Her nose called to mind the "graceful medallions of the Hebrews." Her eyes, after the narrator meditates on them further, dissolve into "large and luminous orbs" present everywhere—in moths and butterflies, in a chrysalis or stream of running water, in the decline of a meteor and in the expression of certain aged people. Her learning, upon consideration, becomes unearthly in its depth and scope: she knows all classical and European languages; she is studied in all themes of the academy; she can traverse "*all* the wide areas of moral, physical, and mathematical science."[63]

The narrator's imagery undercuts his overt desire to fix a once-living woman in historical detail. Associating her, perhaps unconsciously, with mystery and shadow, statue and dream, ideal beauty and ideal knowledge, the teller of the tale intimates the probable nature of Ligeia. Not real in an empirical sense, she appears to be a projection of the speaker's unconscious, an uncanny figure. The question then becomes: what repressed fears or desires does this figure represent? Related to inanimate, ghostly, and spiritual presences, she seems to be a manifestation of the speaker's death drive, his unconscious push for nirvana. This speculation gains validity from two other factors: she is maternal, a womblike presence, and she is dead, beyond her own ego. However, though she is clearly related to the speaker's desire to experience the death drive as transcendence of ego, she is also connected to his fear of this same self-annihilating transcendence. Before the figure of Ligeia dies, she claims, insofar as a projection can, that death conquers only the weak-willed. Those with robust fortitude can overcome this murderous worm. This duplicity—Ligeia is related to death, erasure of ego, and covetous of life, persistence of ego—accounts for the conflict in the psyche that projects her. Though he has experienced an uncanny eruption of his drive for transcendence, and thus partially yearns to merge with an image beyond growth and decay, he also is bedeviled by an urge to repress this drive, and therefore to some extent obsessively meditates on the same image in hopes of fixing the flow of time into stasis.

This obsession results in a repetition compulsion. The narrator only wants to gaze on his projected image of Ligeia. This compulsion leads to a fixation on mummification. Ligeia dies. Whether this means that the real source of the image of Ligeia passes away or that the image of Ligeia fades from the narrator's consciousness is immaterial, for in both instances the narrator suffers distance from his projection. After her demise, the narrator retires to a sort of Egyptian tomb of his own making. In a fit of "child-like perversity" and soused on opium, he converts a ruined abbey in the wildest part of England into a mausoleum decorated "in the solemn carvings of Egypt" as well as in other designs from antiquity. In the midst of this "madness," he marries a woman who is in appearance and demeanor the exact opposite of Ligeia, "the fair-haired and blue-eyed Lady Rowena Trevanion." Into a sepulchral bridal chamber he takes her, a lurid death room teeming with Gothic grotesqueries, including in each of the chamber's corners, standing on end, a "gigantic sarcophagus of black granite, from the tombs of the kings over against Luxor, with their aged lids full of immemorial sculpture." For a month, the narrator languishes near these vessels for mummies, loathing his new wife because she is not Ligeia. He revels in "recollections" of Ligeia's "purity, of her wisdom, of her lofty, her ethereal nature, of her passionate, her idolatrous love."[64]

Three factors rule this situation—factors that will lead to the narrator possibly murdering and then mummifying Rowena. First, returning to childhood perversities and ingesting opium, the narrator has given over to his unconscious drive for death. Second, in dwelling in an Egyptian-like tomb, he has attempted to bring this unconscious urge to consciousness. Third, in obsessively dreaming of Ligeia in front of Rowena, he has discovered a middle way between unconsciousness and consciousness—a repetition compulsion that tries to corral the ego-annihilating death drive by reducing differential decay to static identity, the newness of Rowena to the old image of Ligeia.

At the beginning of the second month of the marriage, Rowena falls ill. Nursing his sick wife while under the spell of opium, the narrator believes that he sees floating through the chamber the "shadow of a shade." As he hands his ailing wife a goblet of wine, he further thinks that he beholds "three or four large drops of brilliant and ruby colored fluid" drop into the wine as if from "some invisible spring in the atmosphere." Three nights later, Rowena dies. On the fourth, the narrator wraps the "pallid and rigid" corpse in bandages and shroud. He turns her into a mummy. While he sits staring at the mummy and dreaming of Ligeia, he senses stirrings in the chamber. Throughout the night, the mummified corpse occasionally revives, only to fall again into death. Eventually, however, the mummy rises, the bandages fall away, and, standing before the opium-addled narrator is a figure with black hair and dark eyes: Ligeia.[65]

If one does not reduce this final event to a supernatural episode, one must conclude that the narrator is trapped in a horrible temporal limbo in which he is doomed to repeat, again and again, the same activities. He earlier projected an ideal image of the feminine, so ideal as to be unreal, statuesque, dead. When this image for some reason disappeared, perhaps because of his own willing, he pined to bring it back. Even though he found himself in new circumstances, he attempted to stop time by dwelling in a tomb—by pretending to be dead. In this context, he reduces newness to the old by killing through poisoning living beings that do not conform to his sense of how life should be. He mummifies his environment, holding it in stasis until his former projection can return. One can only assume that this fresh version of his old projection will again fade away in the near future and the narrator will once more resort to mummification of his world in hopes of again experiencing the same. Too consumed by fear and desire to open fully to the uncanny eruption, this narrator makes mummies—wants himself to be a mummy—in a neurotic or even psychotic effort to hold hard to his solid-seeming ego.

Throughout his gothic tale, Poe places readers in an uncertain state similar to that suffered by his protagonist. Readers never know if Ligeia is real, if drops fall into Rowena's wine, if the narrator is delusional. Experiencing these hermeneutical mysteries, as insoluble as uncanny eruptions, readers are further bombarded by relentless repetitions. The narrator repeatedly dwells on Ligeia, on her beauty and truth; he constantly complains of his suffering, his chronic bereavement. The tale itself seems bedeviled by the repetition compulsion. To finish the tale is to feel as petrified as an embalmed corpse, as though a limbo of endless suspended animation is in store.

FREUND'S *THE MUMMY*

This gothic image of the mummy has thrived in mainstream cinema. Ignoring the mummy as an exponent of miraculous transcendence, moviemakers have persistently capitalized on the mummy as an exemplar of the monstrous undead. (Perhaps the reason for this cinematic overemphasis on the gothic mummy is our own troubled relationship to living machines, our inability to muster comic grace before androids.) A glance at the rich history of horror cinema quickly produces a list of mummy films fixated on the great themes of Poe's "Ligeia": the dead drawn to yet repelled by time; the compulsion to transform the living into the dead; a fall from eternity into time through fear and desire.[66]

The most famous and best film exploring this theme is Karl Freund's 1932 *The Mummy*. Unlike Poe's mummy, who went into his tomb prepared to transcend time, Freund's is brutally buried alive as punishment for sacrilege. Around 1775 BC, the time that the Middle Kingdom was beginning to dissolve into the Second Intermediate Period, a young Egyptian priest of Osiris named Imhotep suffered the death of his young lover, the Princess Anck-es-en-Amon. Desperate with grief, he attempts to revive the princess by reading over her mummy the spell contained in the Scroll of Thoth. Before he can resurrect his beloved, he is discovered and doomed to be entombed alive. When he is buried, he is fraught with desire and fear—desire to hold to his dead beloved, fear of being forever bereft of her. When he comes to life again 3700 years later, he is still obsessed with his love for the princess and his terror of never holding her again.

Imhotep's resurrection begins Freund's film, set in Egypt between 1922 and 1932. (The scenes of ancient Egypt come in the middle of the film, during a hypnotic flashback sequence revealed in the revived Imhotep's magical pool.) Working at the archaeological excavation of Imhotep's tomb, Norton, the assistant of Sir Joseph Whemple, opens the box containing the Scroll of Thoth. This modern Pandora proceeds to read the spell, while behind him stands the mummy of Imhotep. This time the spell works: Imhotep revives and shuffles out of his tomb into the modern world.

Ten years later, the son of Sir Joseph, Frank Whemple, is working at an archaeological site in Egypt when he is approached by a strange man who seems wearied by the weight of some crushing loss. This man is Ardath Bey. He informs Frank and his colleagues that nearby is an unexcavated tomb of an ancient Egyptian princess, Anck-es-en Amon. The mummy is exhumed and displayed in the Museum in Cairo.

So begins the main matter of *The Mummy*: a resurrected mummy, hollowed by centuries of thwarted love, attempting to discover and revive the soul and body of his lost beloved. After failing to resurrect the mummy of the princess with the Scroll of Thoth, Ardath Bey realizes that her soul has passed into another body, that of the beautiful young Helen Grosvenor, half European and half Egyptian. A modern, sophisticated woman, Helen is unaware of the ancient soul animating her body. Even though she is attracted to the exciting present, filled with clever cocktail parties, she is also drawn to the old Egypt of pyramids and mummies.

Ardath Bey deploys his magical powers to control this second side of Helen. On two occasions, he places her modern, conscious self in a trance and directs her ancient, unconscious self to walk, like an automaton, to his side. On the second of these occasions, he pulls her to his dwelling, where he reveals to her in his magical fountain the important scenes of her former life: her premature death, his efforts to raise her, his gruesome burial. After witnessing this element of her being, Helen falls under the control of Ardath Bey, who plans to sacrifice her body in order to free her soul.

Meanwhile, Helen is drawn in another direction, toward young Frank. He and Dr. Muller, Egyptian professor of the occult and guardian of Helen, become aware of Ardath Bey's designs and try to thwart them. In battling Frank and Muller, the mummy's monstrosities emerge. He murders a guard at the museum, Frank's father, Sir Joseph, and Helen's German shepherd. Only Muller's apotropaic amulets keep Frank and Helen safe.

The stage is set for the final conflict. Overcoming Frank's protections, Imhotep draws Helen again to his lair. He dresses her in ancient Egyptian garb. He wields a knife. He promises her immortality. But the old soul of the princess rebels. Helen calls for the aid of Isis. Just as Frank and Muller rush in, the goddess prevails, reducing Imhotep to a pile of ashes and freeing Helen into the arms of her modern man.

Immortal but fixated on mortality, omnipotent but blinded by love, this mummy cannot achieve the elegance of the transcendent Osiris. He remains dismembered in the rivers of history, where he fervidly yearns for his own Isis to gather and heal him. But his abiding egotism keeps him from such wholeness. He greedily tries to pull the soul of the princess from her immortal journey and back into a physical body, and offends Isis, goddess of spiritual resurrection. He uses his priestly powers to control others and, in some cases, kill them; thus, he likewise violates the animating powers of Osiris. His punishment for these transgressions is incompleteness. He is a machine built for eternal bliss but he nonetheless aspires to possess an inaccessible human woman.

This is his Freudian melancholia. In chronic mourning for his lost beloved, he identifies with the princess, whom he loves for her virtues and loathes for the pain she has caused. Hating that part of himself that is one with the loss, he is suicidal. He risks his life to bring the princess back to life, eventually suffering a live burial. Loving that aspect of his being that is identical to the princess's virtues, he is murderous.

Two other popular mummy films of the last century, Terence Fisher's *The Mummy* (1959) and Stephen Summer's 1999 film of the same title, both focus on the same themes as Freund's great film. This emphasis on the gothic elements of the mummy points to an obvious fear and desire of our age—fear of undying bodies mechanistically murdering soft-skinned humans, desire to see such insensitive carapaces exterminated and sent back to the dust. But perhaps these monstrous renderings of the mummy reveal a deeper, more secret terror and yearning: a terror over the possibility that there is no way to tell whether we ourselves are inanimate or animate and a yearning, in the end, to relinquish our hope for vitality and become as tranquil as a quiet bone.

THE MOVING MONSTER

But perhaps twentieth-century audiences have been drawn to the gothic mummy more than the gnostic one for another reason entirely: the monster is more moving than the miracle. The mummy who merges with the transcendent Osiris, peaceful beyond space and time, is an exemplar of indifference, the unattainable grace that comes only to those beings beyond hatred and love. The mummy closer to eternity than time is like Keats's urn. Undying and beyond suffering, it is nonetheless a "Cold Pastoral" that "doth tease us out of thought."[67] The mummy who recoils from the eternal because of his love of time shares more affinities with men of flesh and blood, burning in the forehead and parched on the tongue. Though this earthly mummy is monstrous, its sadness is that of all humans who are seized by obsessive love at the expense of tranquility, who risk everything in hopes of one instance of unity with a warm body. This is the tragedy and beauty of immanence, of diseased blood flooding the pristine machine.

3

THE GOLEM

I f one were at twilight to make one's way over the Charles Bridge in Prague at the end of the sixteenth century, one might, if immersed in esoteric lore and insomniac, suffer an uncanny shock: the Gothic buildings in the near horizon would blur into sun-drenched columns; the pallid men shuffling along the closer banks of the Danube would fade into tanned Mediterranean bodies; the very air before one's face, quite chilly, would become warm. Europe would turn Egypt, and Prague, Alexandria. This confluence would be the result of an affinity crossing time and space, a link between the spiritual atmospheres of second-century Alexandria and sixteenth-century Prague, both teeming with mystics and magicians, bizarre gods and breathing clay.

This was the Alexandria of the Gnostics and Hermeticists—a city of metaphysical thirst where Valentinus and Basilides intuited the hidden god; where the anonymous disciples of Hermes wrote the *Poimandres* and the *Aesclepius*; where Egyptian magicians perfected metallurgy, theurgy, alchemy; where sects heretical to Christians daily arose: the Borborites, the Phibionites, the Sethians, the Stratiotics, the Peratae; where beautiful Gnostic women seduced young Epiphanius, who later grew into a violent heresiologist. Renaissance Prague proved Alexandria returned. Under the rule of the Emperor Rudolph II, Prague became a fever house for aspiring mystics: for John Dee and Giordano Bruno, latter-day disciples of the Thrice-Great Hermes; for Tycho Brahe and Johannes Kepler, Pythagorean astronomers hungering for the harmony of the spheres; for numerous adepts in the Kabbalah, alchemy, and

astrology; for the great Rabbi Loew, who animated a man of clay to protect the Hebrews from Christian persecutors.

Loew's golem exemplifies a strain running from Alexandria to
Prague, a current that diverges from the Osirian stream of the ancient
Egyptians. Unlike the Nile dwellers, who so loved the physical world
that they wanted to prolong forever material existence, occult initiates
on the Mediterranean and the Charles found nature inherently botched
and wished to transform fallen matter into pristine spirit. These adepts
were embalmers in reverse. Where the practitioner of mummification
empowered the corpse to enjoy the rhythms of time, the magicians
attuned to the Hermetic *Aesclepius*, the alchemical *Emerald Tablet*, the
kabbalistic *Zohar* converted the wrecks of time into eternal concord.
The Osirian wanted to persist in the world as it is, to become an inorganic vessel partaking of organic existence, to achieve physical immortality. The magus of divine statues, of the homunculus, of the golem
yearned to change the world, to fashion an organic pattern of inorganic
spirit, to reach spiritual mortality.

This is the primary difference between the mummy and the animated
figures of the Hermeticists, the alchemists, and the Kabbalists: while the
mummy is a result of a thwarted love of matter, the living statue issues
from an abiding chagrin over material. The myths of the ancient Egyptians are not troubled by a sense of the fall. Though men issue from the
tears of Atum and Osiris's torn limbs produce the yearly grain, the nar-
ratives of the *Pyramid Texts*, the *Coffin Texts*, and the *Book of the Dead*
do not suggest that the cosmos is a decline from eternal perfection. A precipitation of the High God's fluids, the world is a manifestation of divine
consciousness. The worshipper of Osiris never wants to leave this realm.
He wishes to become a machine through which the eternal sensitivity can
continue to enjoy eating and walking and talking. In contrast, the
mythologies of the Hermeticist, the alchemist, and the Kabbalist are
obsessed with declension, the idea that the cosmos solidified only after
some colossal mistake, a fall from spirit to matter. In the *Poimandres*, the
anthropos through self-love causes his spiritual form to contract into
matter. After this event, he and his progeny are torn between their origin
in God and their present prison in nature. In the alchemical texts of the
Middle Ages and Renaissance, the great work of the magus is to discover
the spirit in matter, to draw spirit out, to return it to its home: the primal
man yet unwrecked by desire and fear. The practitioner of the Kabbalah
held the same dream, believing that he could recover God's creative word
from among the shards, that he could deploy this sacred name to make a
new Adam, unstained and eager.

The golem is more than a figure from antiquated lore. It is a register of one of our most persistent yearnings, now more intense than ever:

the desire to transcend mechanism through the machine. In our digital age, we daily entertain the bewildering possibility of one day downloading our individual consciousness into a computer. Could we but do this, we think, we would no longer suffer the limitations of matter, the determinism of physical cause and effect. But obviously this potential transcendence of mechanistic body is troubled, for our liberated consciousness would still be constrained by indifferent circuits, the cold bytes of the hard drive. This is the double bind of the digital age, a bind fully illuminated by the old golem: we want to trade our decaying bodies for eternal machines; we wish to escape mechanistic prisons for undying vitalities.

LIVING STATUES OF ANCIENT EGYPT AND CLASSICAL GREECE

To meditate on the psychology of the golem, we must consider for a time the complex origins of Loew's sacred android. We cannot establish a strict causal chain running from the prophetic statues of the Ancient Egyptians to the remarkable automata of classical Greek legend, to the anthropos of the Gnostics, to divine figures of the Hermetic tradition, to the golem and homunculi of the Middle Ages and the Renaissance. However, we can track illuminating connections among these androids, homologies that loosely follow a temporal continuum. This casual historical tracing presupposes this claim: Rabbi Loew's golem had its beginning in the rituals of the enemies of the Hebrews, the Egyptians. To sound the melancholia of the golem is to return, briefly, to the mummy.

The Egyptian tombs featured statues that could be revived to do chores for the mummy. Egyptian temples offered statues animated with gods. The awakening of drones in the tomb and gods in the temple relied upon a magical process known as "the opening of the mouth."[1] Believed to revive a mummy as well as a statue, the mouth-opening ceremony was modeled on giving birth.[2]

The mouth-opening ceremonies of the tomb were extensions of the technologies meant to galvanize the mummy. However, animating statues in the temple with divinity was undertaken for a different reason: to connect decaying, dumb matter with eternally wise spirits. Even though the statues were probably made to talk by a priest hiding in a secret vault, the ancient Egyptians believed these stone humanoids to be oracles and healers. Whether the sacred power came through the statue itself or through a human medium, the potency was there, humming through the unmoving mouth. To this orifice, men and women addressed questions concerning innocence or guilt, sickness or health.[3]

These Egyptian theories of the idol partially explain why the ancient Hebrews opposed the worship of graven images. The Israelites wanted to reverse the religious practices of their enemies and oppressors. Likewise, Egyptian ideas of physical immortality are probably behind the early Christian interpretation of the resurrection. Jesus' empty tomb, absent body, and spiritual ascension counter the Egyptian's properly outfitted sarcophagus, embalmed corpse, and material continuation.[4] Yet while Jewish and Christian traditions were challenging these Egyptian ideas, other schools were extending the magic of Osiris into new technologies and theologies.

The Greek tradition is replete with animated statues. Familiar with the machines of the Egyptians, the Greeks developed their own great mechanic, Daedalus. Pausanias, a Greek historian of the second century, describes Daedalus's miraculous living statues as well as his other remarkable inventions. This Daedalus resembles Hero of Alexandria (c. 62 AD), who in his *Pneumatics* details a dazzling array of automata: singing birds, drinking men, and pouring satyrs.[5] These innovations of Daedalus and Hero are connected to the divine only in the loosest of senses: the maker of the mechanical man is always, regardless of motivation, an avatar of the demiurge. Beyond this causal link, one cannot further say what moved Daedalus and Hero to fashion their contraptions.

However, one can assert with confidence the inspirations behind the other great students of the living statue: the Hermetic visionaries of Coptic Alexandria. Influenced by Egyptian magic, the initiates of Hermes maintained that the divine cannot only be represented by an image: the god can actually be contained in the statue. Likewise, informed by Egyptian burial practices, the followers of Hermes believed that any sufficiently spiritual man, not just Jesus, could become a manifestation of Godhead.

THE GNOSTIC ANTHROPOS

Though the Hermeticism of Alexandria was informed by the religion of Osiris, the students of the *Poimandres* and the *Aesclepius* differed from their Egyptian predecessors in their dissatisfaction with the physical world. The cosmogony detailed in the *Poimandres* and presupposed in the *Aesclepius* is close to the Gnostic account of creation that assumes that matter is mangled and needs to be transcended. As Carl H. Kraeling has shown in *Anthropos and Son of Man*, most Gnostic myths issuing from Alexandria in the second and third centuries AD depict the botched cosmos by focusing on the fall of the anthropos.[6] This decline takes three forms: emanation, error, imprisonment.[7] To understand the spiritual atmosphere in which Hermetic statues as well as Hebraic golems were constructed, we must become acquainted with these stumbles.

In a Coptic Gospel of the "Bruce" Codex, the anthropos is the first manifestation of the hidden god. This androgynous human contains all universes in his body parts, from highest to lowest. As archetype of the entirety, he is one with existence, including the spiritual plenitude and unruly matter. At the head of his highest universe is Setheus, the original god in his aspect as creator. From Setheus issues a living current that first coheres into the glories of the highest heavens, descends through the intermediate realms, and falls even into material, where it animates with bliss the holy and horrifies the ignorant with vitality. All of these planes are emanations of the powers of the anthropos.[8]

In other Gnostic myths, the anthropos falls further down the chain of emanations and serves only as a model for the material Adam. In the *The Secret Book according to John*, the hidden god issues a family of androgynous spiritual eons. This family is called the *pleroma*, or the plentitude. Among these is Geradamas, the "perfect human being." After the creation of Geradamas, Sophia, wisdom, inappropriately attempts to behold directly the godhead. From this error emerges an "imperfect product," Ialtoboath. Sophia casts this aberrant form from the pleroma. Thinking himself the only god, Ialtoboath creates a cosmos. But, because he is bereft of wisdom, he fashions an inferior, material universe. Meanwhile, the penitent Sophia, with the help of the eternals, sends her son a voice from the pleroma telling him to fashion a human. Believing that this voice comes only from his mother, Ialtoboath consents, and, with the help, unknown to him, of the eons, he concocts Adam, a material version of Geradamas. Through further clandestine actions of the eternals, Adam is charged with a spiritual faculty that connects him to Geradamas, his heavenly archetype.[9]

In a third Gnostic myth of the anthropos, the first man himself falls into the material world, where he suffers dismemberment and nostalgia. This motif, already seen in the *Poimandres*, appears in a myth from the Manichean sect. In the beginning the universe is divided between the god of spiritual light and the deity of material darkness. The dark god attacks the light. To counter the assault, the bright god creates the primal man, armed with five elements. This anthropos descends into matter. He is ostensibly defeated by the darkness. However, this fall is a ruse ordained by the god of light, meant to vanquish matter forever. After this apparent decline, the king of light sends to the material realm the "living spirit." This being calls the wounded man back home. The positive response of the anthropos empowers the spirit to return him, healed, to the light. But the five elements composing the soul of the anthropos remain behind, imprisoned. To free these sparks, the spirit fashions our world, replete with Adam and his progeny. Each time a man of matter hears the call of the light and cultivates his indwelling spirit at the expense of matter, he liberates part of the imprisoned soul. When all men have apprehended the call, the primal man will be liberated and matter annihilated.[10]

THE MELANCHOLIA OF THE FALLEN ANTHROPOS

Hans Jonas in *The Gnostic Religion* describes the "forlornness, dread, [and] homesickness" of the fractured anthropos. It doesn't matter if the Gnostic visionary leans neoplatonically toward the idea that the cosmos is an emanation of spiritual fullness; or if the initiate is more in the Judeo-Christian line, holding that the universe results from an error; or if the adept proves a Zoroastrian dualist who maintains that the world is the jail of the soul. In each case, the matter-bound human awake to his true home in the pleroma suffers a melancholy sense that he has been "thrown" into a polluted realm not his own.[11]

The greatest task of the fallen anthropos is not to work through his anxiety, alienation, and confusion. It is to keep his melancholia acute. His sadness corresponds to his readiness for gnosis. But the world conspires against his dejection, offering him either the brief comforts of matter or the more lasting solaces of soul. Hedonism seduces in the first case; orthodox religion in the second. The Gnostic must defend against the wretched contentment of these modes and hold open his wounds of the spirit. Malcontented with outward forms, he turns inward to his hidden spark. The spark, trapped and stifled, faintly flares, repeating in each flicker the homeward call.

Jonas's meditations on the severed Gnostic anthropos were inspired by the philosophy of his teacher, Martin Heidegger. Though Heidegger's unseemly connections with the Nazis always make one uneasy in invoking his thought, one cannot deny that his philosophy continues to illuminate the anxieties of existence.[12] In *Being and Time* (1927), Heidegger universalizes the plight of the fallen anthropos and translates his spiritual quest into psychological terms. In pausing to consider Heidegger's "thrownness," "fallenness," and "anxiety," I hope to deepen our understanding of the need for golem making and divine statues.

Heidegger defines individual being, what we would normally term a "self," in terms of its temporal and spatial "thereness," its implication in irreducible networks of history, culture, economics, environment, and so on.[13] This situation—"being there"—Heidegger characterizes as "thrownness." Each individual is always thrown into a "there," a series of preexisting conditions that shape and bind one before one even becomes aware of them. Before one can gain a sense of one's own uniqueness, one's unrepeatable possibilities for existence, one is already defined by the world into which one has been thrown. One is subjected to "Others," the "they,"[14] all the impersonal forces that flatten events to things that have "long been well known," all phenomena to commodities to be "manipulated," all secrets to clichés. Ruled by idle chatter, crass curiosity, and superficial vagueness, this "they" works to fix individuals into an "inauthentic" mode of existence bereft of manifold potential, of intractable mysteries, of unsolvable riddles.[15]

Heidegger characterizes the individual's dissolution into the "they"— a decline akin to the Gnostic slide into matter—as "falling." This declension involves losing one's quest for authenticity. Lost, one forgets one's own being. No longer this person in this time and this place, one becomes a filmy vessel for received wisdom. This decline is painless and hidden. Before one knows it, one has become an exponent of the masses and has forsaken multitudinous possibilities for being, for authenticity.[16]

For Heidegger, the only hope for authenticity—a secular, psychological equivalent of gnosis—is anxiety. Heideggerean angst, like Gnostic longing, performs a double function. On the one hand, it constitutes the basic mood through which one comes to understand one's own authenticity; on the other, it forms the aggravating condition from which one flees to the collective. Heideggerean anxiety is directed toward the "nothing" of being in the world without the help of the mass. This condition descends when all familiar ideas fall away and one feels as if one hovers in an unfamiliar abyss. This unfocused floating can push the sufferer in one of two ways—either cravenly back to the lotus doses of the mass or courageously into possibilities for being. If one chooses the former path, one can never return to the ignorant bliss of the collective but spends long days neurotically attempting to repress the unsettling sense that existence is a sham. However, if one embraces the latter way, one undergoes an uncanny experience: insight into the relationship between individual being and the Being of all beings.[17]

Once one commits to understanding one's connection to Being, one never rests but realizes that the profundities of this origin are beyond comprehension. However, one also knows that this perpetual insecurity will lead to deeper intimacy with the abyss and a greater care for individual being and other beings.[18] As we have seen, Heidegger in "What Is Metaphysics?" likens this chronic melancholia to a "bewildered sort of calm . . . a cheerfulness and gentleness of creative longing."[19]

This is the almost impossible task of the fallen anthropos: to cultivate anxiety over the split between material desire and spiritual yearning in hopes of overcoming this same dread. Can we, as microcosms of this anthropos, hold hard to our sadness while at the same time wishing to assuage it? If we try to lessen our dejection through the medicines of the mainstream, then we turn our visionary awareness into neurotic repression. If we nurture this melancholia through meditating on the delusions of the majority, then we risk exhausting our faculties with relentless uncertainty. A middle way is required, a figure that both reminds us of our fall and offers hope for rising.

THE HERMETIC STATUE AND THE MIDDLE WAY

The idea for this golden mean between despair and hope is the anthropos itself, simultaneously eternal and temporal, comically gazing on the cares of the world and gothically suffering these same concerns. The images for this median condition, harder to hold than a cloud, are the Hermetic statue, the alchemical homunculus, and the kabbalistic golem—icons that can exist only in myth and fiction, dream and desire.

Heidegger is the primary theoretician of the "thrown" condition of the anthropos, its philosophical distance from origin. Jung is the main explicator of the "return" of the anthropos, its struggle from alienation to wholeness. In *Aion* (1951), Jung casts the anthropos as the archetype of longing and fulfillment. On the one hand, this primal being symbolizes the pain of creation, the psychic and physical carnage involved in fashioning new worlds, in breaking unity into multiplicity, innocence into experience. On the other hand, though the anthropos is a "victim of his own creative act" caught in the "embrace" of the material world he helped to fashion," he also persists as the "primordial image" of "psychic wholeness" in which unconscious and conscious find concord. Both the "Original Man latent in the dark of matter" and the "presence of a transconscious centre," this primal self is the mandala—the labyrinth and the city.[20]

As Jung points out in *Mysterium Coniunctionis* (1956–57), a key symbol of the anthropos is the homunculus. This diminutive figure born in the alchemist's flask signals the translation of an outer spiritual realm into the inner regions of the human being. When one feels as if the entire cosmos teems inside one's own interior, one senses the anthropos within, the microcosm of the macrocosm. This inner human being can only be visualized as a being of the smallest proportions—an extremely tiny person.[21]

This weird image—the being coterminous with the cosmos condensed into a doll—captures the strangeness one feels upon realizing that the conscious ego is a miniscule precipitation of an immense unconscious reservoir. This is the disorientation of incarnation, a discrete physical part representing and containing a distributed spiritual whole.

Logically speaking, the synecdoche of incarnation is impossible, for a fragment can never really substitute for an abyss. This sort of synecdoche actually signifies the opposite of what it intends to convey: the unity between spirit and matter. The incarnating synecdoche reveals the ontological distance between the visible plane of things and the invisible atmosphere of energies. However, at the same time, from an analogical perspective, this kind of synecdoche is quite possible because a palpable substance can correspond, in form and function, to an impalpable process. In this way, an incarnating synecdoche embodies what it intends: a harmony of limited and unlimited. This type of trope intimates a third term of which both spirit and matter are manifestations, an abysmal power beyond yet containing all oppositions.

The inner anthropos, whether figured by homunculus or statue or golem, is a source of disjunction and fusion. Quivering between these opposing states, it and its manifestations comprise sites of great psychological risk. To project an exterior form of the anthropos within is to concoct a reminder of one's distance from unity, an abiding morbid presence that could well lead to despair. But the constant longing inspired by the synecdoche of the anthropos might, if endured, result not in sadness but in the tranquil bewilderment required for gnostic readiness, for wholeness.

Like Jung's homunculus (to be explored in more detail later), the living statues of the *Aesclepius* express this troubled duplicity of the anthropos. Though this Hermetic text issues from the matrices of Gnosticism, it, like the *Poimandres* and the alchemical texts on which Jung meditates, is slightly more optimistic about the redemptive possibilities of matter than are its Gnostic analogues. Where most Gnostic myths view matter as an evil to be transcended, certain Hermetic myths cast matter, even though it is fallen and inferior, as a pattern of eternity. Matter can in some cases reveal the spirit that it cloudily reflects. This is the assumption of the *Aesclepius*, in which matter, if correctly fashioned, can become imbued with gods. So charged, it manifests the unfallen anthropos while at the same time suggesting the horrors of the cosmic lapse.

In book 3 of the *Aesclepius*, Hermes tells his interlocutor that the man who knows his origin in the pleroma can turn into a godly being himself and create a godlike human, a statue "living and conscious," possessing "foreknowledge," "prophetic inspiration," and the capacity to heal. Pious men can merge with the unfallen anthropos, receive and give "the light of divine life," and fashion an *Urmensch* of their own. Yet, as Hermes later instructs his disciple, the fashioning of stone anthropoi enacts the lacks of the material world as well as its fulfillments. The ancestors of Hermes and Aesclepius who invented "the art of making gods out of some material substance" perfected this technology not out of fullness but hunger. Being "unable to make souls" themselves—being humans thrown into matter, not gods above the fray—they "invoked the souls of demons, and implanted them in the statues by means of certain holy and sacred rites." Though the statue intimates realization, it is also a reminder of distance.[22]

We have been meditating on two precursors of the golem: the Gnostic anthropos and the Hermetic statue. To illuminate the psychological densities of these figures, I have drawn from the existential psychology of Heidegger and the depth psychology of Jung. Now the ground is clear for proceeding to a detailed account of the alchemical homunculus, the form of the anthropos closest to the golem. Once I have discussed the homunculus, I shall then be prepared to turn to the golem proper. To exemplify further the complexities of these figures, I shall then invoke essential works from the early nineteenth century: Goethe's *Faust, Part Two*, and Shelley's *Frankenstein*.

PARACELSUS AND THE HOMUNCULUS

In *Memories, Dreams, Reflections* (1962), Jung sketches a history of the quest for the anthropos. This history runs from classical Gnosticism, "remote" in its desire to transcend the cosmos; through medieval and Renaissance alchemy, "grounded in the natural philosophy of the Middle Ages"; to modern psychology, which focuses on the concrete forms of the unconscious. The unifying thread is a belief that the human psyche or soul emerges from an ungraspable, androgynous abyss; falls into division and delusion when it forgets its origin and identifies only with egotistical fears and desires; and is redeemed through an awareness of and reidentification with its ineffable root. What differentiates these modes is the degree of emphasis on matter. The Gnostic is antimaterialist, seeking wholeness beyond the stars. The alchemist—like the Hermeticist, his predecessor—is more optimistic toward matter, believing that nature is the womb of spirit. The psychologist is an empiricist, attuned to the physical bases of the invisible.[23]

Between the transcendentalism of Gnosticism and the immanence of psychoanalysis, medieval and Renaissance alchemy, exemplified by Paracelsus and nurtured in Rabbi Loew's sixteenth-century Prague, was bent on spiritualizing matter and materializing spirit. Though the alchemist was desirous of returning to Eden, there to merge with the anthropos, the alchemist knew that this redemption could be achieved only through intense experiences of matter's darkest realms. This magus realized that these forsaken regions are the chaoses necessary for order, the tombs in which the savior must rot before rising.

As Jung explains, the basic alchemical process involves dissolving
earthly elements into the abyss from which they arose; separating this
indifferent mass into spirit and matter, active and passive, male and
female; and then reuniting these oppositions in a *coniunctio*, or chemical marriage from which springs the philosopher's stone, likened to
Christ.[24] As Paracelsus himself observes, this alchemical dissolution and
resolution reenacts the activities of God in Genesis, who, alchemically
interpreted, separates chaos into distinctions only later to rejoin these
antinomies at the marriage feast of Revelation.[25]

Paracelsus assumes that everything originates from a profound
matrix: just as the cosmos emerges from a boundless deep, so inorganic
forms arise from the muddy earth and animated ones come from liquid
wombs. The separations that accompany the birth of difference from
indifference are natural, not causes for lamentation: "Decay is the beginning of all birth" and the "greatest *mysterium* of God." According to
Jung, the highest mystery of alchemy is the dissolution of attachment to
the ego, a death from which the soul is born. This latter condition, the
soul redeemed, is the true goal of alchemy.[26] The chemical aspects of the
art are symbols of the interior process by which the adept refines his soul
so that it may rise "out of nothing and become something whose
potency and virtue is far nobler than it was in the beginning."[27] So developed the alchemical Christ, who began as a body containing spirit,
decayed into a corpse, and ascended into a spiritual body; and so grows
the philosopher's stone, which appears first as lead, suffers destruction
in the retort, and reappears as crystal redeeming all matter.

The alchemist added to the chemical Christ and the philosopher's
stone a third image of redemption: the homunculus. Paracelsus spent
numerous nights birthing this tiny Adam in his retort. His faith in the
possibility of begetting a "Man" without "the natural womb" was
grounded on the idea that alchemy is the perfection of nature. Under
God's design, nature shall one apocalyptic day become transparent to
the spiritual currents animating it. God's proxy on the fallen earth, the
alchemist accelerates this process. The earth over centuries turns lead to
gold. The alchemist achieves this conversion in months. The womb over
nine months translates semen to infant. The student of the alembic
enacts the same transformation in a little over a month.

Here is how. Allow semen to putrefy in a sealed vessel for forty days,
or "until it begins at last to live, move, and be agitated." At this junc-
ture, the semen will have coalesced into the semblance of a human,
"transparent and without a body." This phantom dwarf must be nourished every day with the essence of human blood. During a forty-week
period of incubation, the growing homunculus must be kept sealed in its
warm birth vessel. At the end of this period, this diminutive human can

be removed from its artificial womb, and its education should begin "with the greatest care and zeal."[28]

Paracelsus's homunculus seems to lack the grandeur of the divine statues of the *Aesclepius*. A twelve-inch man coagulated from semen and needing education appears to be monstrous or comical. But Paracelsus dispels horror or laughter. He calls the homunculus "one of the greatest secrets which God has revealed to mortal and fallible man." Though the creation of such a creature has long been concealed from humans, it has perennially been known to the "wood-sprites and nymphs and giants"— beings who sprang directly from the divine. Diminutive humans were fashioned by these sacred figures for this reason: when the homunculus grows to manhood it can itself produce armies of bizarre forms, "giants, pygmies, and other marvelous people," who can gain "great victories over their enemies, and know all secret and hidden matters."[29]

Obviously, these figures of lore faced literal enemies and deployed their arcane magic to vanquish their foes. In this way, the homunculus relates to the golem, a creature sometimes created as a military weapon. But Paracelsus also has in mind another sort of enemy and another set of secrets. He once claimed that the goal of chemical philosophy is to separate good from evil, pure from impure. The pure and the good are one with the soul while the evil and impure are connected with the body. Material decay is the enemy of the adept. One goal of alchemy is to overcome this enemy—to divide life from death, to merge with the former, to shed the latter. If the alchemist can achieve this victory, he will become God on earth, Christ rising, anthropos remembered.[30] However, as Paracelsus persistently argued, the only way to vanquish this enemy, the only path to the secret of secrets, is through decay. Stale sperm generates the homunculus.[31]

This is the problem of the homunculus maker. On the one hand, he wants to defeat the fall and loathes the broken forms of nature. On the other, he must intensely experience the depths of the fallen world if he is to rise above death.[32] He must struggle in an interstice between matter that he hates but must embrace and spirit that he loves but must discover in the dirt. He is rent between the earth's frozen core, vault of the blackest bile, and the heavenly light he hopes to find in these ungodly bowels. But he knows with Yeats's Crazy Jane that only that can be whole which has been torn.[33]

THE SULLEN ALCHEMIST AND THE DREAM OF PLAY

This interplay between melancholia and redemption is figured by the three primary stages of the alchemical work. I wish to consider these stages before contemplating the golem proper, for these levels will illuminate the mental disposition of the kabbalistic magus.

The first step, the *nigredo*, the black stage, occurs when the alchemist boils the solid substance to a bubbling mass. This primary material is akin to "the dragon that creates and destroys itself," to the "primordial matriarchal world." The nigredo is also the ouroboros or caduceus of Mercurius, the alchemical symbol of transformation. Mercury is the world soul, both male and female, present at every stage of the alchemical process. His presence in the primal soup as the circular dragon or intertwined snakes suggests that even in chaos or death is the seed of organization and life. Though the nigredo is physical destruction or psychological pain, it is also the water of life, the womb.[34] When it comes to the making of the homunculus, this stage on a physical level corresponds to the forty-day period during which the human semen is putrefied.

The psychological nigredo is a marker of melancholy, "confusion and lostness."[35] Often associated with the planet Saturn, this psychic state is far from the sun, a dark night of the soul. This mood is the interior equivalent of the goring of Adonis and Dante's trek into the wood. Like these redemptive declines, the melancholia of the nigredo is remedy as much as disease, marker of spiritual genius as much as symbol of material disorientation. While the homunculus without barely exists yet grows in dank slop, the little anthropos within founders in the darkness but still glimpses the light.

In this night arises a moon, the second stage, the *albedo*, the white, the transition from gloom and dawn. This stage appears when the solution is blanched, no color at all and the ground of all colors, transparent spirit and opaque body. On the one hand, it is the "good white snow"; on the other, it is Luna, heavenly queen. During this stage the swells of the matrix are "congealed": Mercury as slivering snake is "frozen," his quicksilver spirit transformed into a stable body. Mercury iced represents the world soul in a purified state. No longer boiling matter (his ouroboric guise), he is matter and spirit at the same time. This new shape is innocence, the virgin waiting for marriage.[36] The homunculus reaches this stage when the semen coalesces into the semblance of a human, "transparent without a body," spirit barely emerging from and partially organizing matter.

Like the gloomy psychology of the nigredo, the moony one of the albedo is double. The whitened psyche, deep in dreams, forms a bridge between unconscious and conscious. On the one hand, fantasies pose dangers, for sleeping visions can easily turn one "lunatic." On the other hand, the blanched mind enjoys glimpses of wisdom unavailable to the conscious ego. These oppositions are synthesized by the primary faculty of the albedo, the imagination, borderland between understanding and intuition, matter and spirit.[37] From the underworld, Adonis imagines Venus; in the wood, Dante envisions Beatrice. The inner homunculus, like its outer double, treads a tenuous middle path between the despair from which he is rising and the hope on the horizon.

The lunar stage is the precursor to the sun, the *rubedo*. Achieved by melting and recrystallizing the white, the rubedo figures the process by which the Red King marries the White Queen to produce the philosopher's stone. During this stage, the spiritual force of the red penetrates the purified body of the white, sublimating her from virgin to wife. The rubedo reveals Mercurius thriving as pure spirit, a fiery jewel capable of combining all oppositions into dynamic harmony—the philosopher's stone. In synthesizing life and death as well as chaos and order, this rubedo jewel is not simply life, the eternal infant; it is also death, the dying king.[38] The completed homunculus is also a version of the stone. After having been nourished for forty weeks by red human blood, he comes fully formed from the artificial womb in which he has been incubating.

Psychologically, the rubedo signals that the archetypes of the collective unconscious have been realized by the conscious ego. The unconscious becomes conscious: the man understands his feminine energies; the woman apprehends her masculine side.[39] This is "integration." Isis remembers Osiris, brings him back from the death, and with him engenders Horus; Dante, though weary from hell and purgatory, takes the hand of Beatrice, who leads him to the light. The imagination opens into the intuition. The microcosm within realizes its connection to the macrocosm, and both together become aware of their eternal relationship to the transcosmic, the pleroma.

The harmonies of the alchemical marriage and the psychological integration are not eternal but moments in a perpetual dialectic: the philosopher's stone (the formed homunculus) is already the *prima materia* (putrid death); Jungian individuation (the inner anthropos redeemed) arises from and must return to the darkness of the unconscious (the anthropos lost). This is the key point about the alchemical process: the alchemical work is endless conflict and resolution. Nigredo, albedo, and rubedo are all temporary instances in the ongoing processes of life, concordant discords between chaos and order, death and birth. Figuring these polarities is Mercury, who generates, sustains, and alters each stage in the work. This hermaphroditic presence is the origin, the primary material; the means, the world soul; and the end, the philosopher's stone. Constant and changing, this "double" Mercury "consists of all conceivable opposites."[40] Hermes is the spirit of alchemy because he is a deity of complete being, revealing what many forget in their inhabitation of a half-world: chaos and ocean are the secret grounds of cosmos and city.

Mercury is the trickster, happiest when he is at play. Playing, he is able to achieve the double consciousness of the comic mode: the world is serious and not serious at the same time, a meaningful pattern of eternity and a filmy veil blocking the beyond. While immersed in the turbulence of the nigredo, Mercury can go with the flow and rise above the current. Resolving into the crystal of the albedo, Mercury stiffens into transparent geometry without forgetting the opaque flickers. He remains attuned throughout to the rubedo, the third term harmonizing matter and spirit. Embodying this tertium quid, Mercury never dissolves into fecund material, nor does he stiffen into spiritual rectitude. He enriches one pole with the other without becoming attached to either. This balancing act is closely akin to the great comic gnosis I detailed in my thoughts about the mummy, the gently melancholy marriage between sorrow and joy.

Perhaps the best explicators of the play of Mercury, though, are not Joyce or Bergson but Friedrich Schiller of the romantic age. In *Letters on the Aesthetic Education of Man* (1795), Schiller argues that the greatest moments of human beings occur when they achieve mercurial play. Most people limit themselves by fixating on one of the two primary poles of existence, the sense drive or the form drive. The person overcome by the sense drive is concerned with his "physical existence" and thus set "within the bounds of time." This person is little different from matter, from physical necessity. In contrast, if one is bent on form drive, one associates with a rational principle above the vicissitudes of time. One believes that the ego is an eternal substance untouched by matter. But this formalist is moored to concepts, to the mind.[41] The only way to escape these binds is to embrace play: the contemplation, embodiment, or creation of beauty. Engaging in aesthetic activities, one finds oneself in "a happy midway point between law and exigency."[42] The playing person draws from the powers of the sensual and the formal "since the former relates in its cognition to the actuality" and the "latter to the necessity of things."[43] This person is bound, though, to neither. The sensual, measured against ideas, becomes *"small."* The reason, related to perceptions, grows *"light."*[44] The person playing places the formal and the sensual into a creative conversation in which one side delimits and ennobles the other.

GOETHE'S WITTY HOMUNCULUS

The history of the homunculus has been benign, more miraculous than monstrous, more comic than gothic, for two reasons. The manikin is diminutive, not a threatening material force. He is symbolic, not a tool for altering matter.[45] Barely material, the homunculus generally avoids its creator's physical fixations and figures only spiritual potentials.

In Goethe's *Faust, Part Two*, the diminutive form finds full comic expression. In this bizarrely playful work of the romantic age, we witness the little man acting as a comedic anthropos, a redemptive counter to Faust's tragic history. To pause on this literary instance of the homunculus—one of the richest images of the homunculus from the time of Paracelsus to the present—will serve as a foil to the other great work of the romantic age that focuses on the android, Shelley's gothic *Frankenstein*.

Faust begins the play in despair. His studies of abstruse subjects have yielded him no healing knowledge and have severed him from the earth's energy. He is doubly alienated—from spiritual knowledge and sensual experience—and doubly desirous—for the truth of the soul and the joy of matter. Bereft of communion with heaven or earth but hungry for a marriage with both, Faust concludes that two souls dwell in his breast: one clings to the physical world; the other rises to "high ancestral spheres."[46] Faust's sadness over this wound leads him to the brink of suicide. But just as he places the poison to his lips, he hears Easter hymns. Though he lacks faith in the resurrection, the thought that others believe in the revived anthropos heartens him. This rescue foreshadows a later sequence, when Faust is renewed through the homunculus.[47]

Before Faust can evoke the anthropos, he must undergo his own putrefaction in the womb of earth. With the help of Mephistopheles, an alchemical guide, he relinquishes his studies of the heavens and delves into the rhythms of earth. But because Faust has spent his days denying his physical urges, his earthly fantasies are immature. He engages in childish pranks. He deflowers a village beauty, Gretchen. He revels in the whimsical Walpurgis Night. He sinks into general ribaldry. Faust's undeveloped urges result in tragedy. He kills Gretchen's vengeful brother in a duel and indirectly causes the demise of Gretchen. Reading these events as part of an alchemical allegory, one concludes that Faust throughout the first part of his tragedy undergoes the nigredo, the descent into physical chaos. In realizing his lusts, Faust purges the worst of material existence and prepares himself for the profundity of matter—the womb of the earth.

Early in the second part of the play, Faust is still working through his immature addiction to earthly power. In the midst of this revelry, Faust and Mephistopheles find themselves in a dark gallery that leads to the core of the world. There dwell the Mothers, goddesses of the "realms where forms exist detached," archetypes not yet manifested in space and time.[48] In this womb, Faust beholds Paris and Helen embracing.[49] Their merger figures the secret of the alchemical vision: in the darkest earth, wholeness is born—ideal beauty, the marriage of opposites. This sight fires Faust with love for Helen, a spiritualized Gretchen who might help him reconcile the rift still tormenting his heart. In the den of the Mothers, Faust completes his putrefaction and is ready to rise, reborn.

During the following scene, Faust is asleep, dead to the world, a decayed seed from which a new sprout wants to grow. While Faust is unconscious, Mephistopheles carries him to his old laboratory, where Wagner, Faust's former assistant, creates a homunculus. The homunculus not only figures Faust's own impending redemption; it also takes the place of Mephistopheles as the soul guide. Like his devilish predecessor, whom he calls "Sir Cousin," the little man has a sense of humor. His first words to Wagner comprise a bizarre mix of flippancy and seriousness.

> Well, Daddy! how are you? It was no jest.
> Come, press me tenderly upon your breast,
> But not too hard, for fear the glass might shatter.
> That is the property of matter:
> For what is natural the All has place;
> What's artificial needs restricted space.[50]

The casual tone suggests that this diminutive being lacks solemnity. Indeed, he seems to be aware already of the fact that his existence will be short; he knows that his vessel might fall asunder and that he is restricted by his artificial nature. But in the midst of his joviality, he also offers delicate philosophy. In the material world, what is natural participates spontaneously in the All and is thus distributed as well as discrete; however, what is artificial must remain enclosed in canned environments, separated from the whole. While this utterance condemns homunculus making as an unnatural undertaking, it also highlights the unique nature of the manufactured man. Because he is matter and not matter, he participates in and is separate from the organic All, attached and detached. His blending of jocular utterance and serious thought mirrors this ontological status.

The homunculus hovers over the sleeping Faust and recounts the magus's dream of a luminescent woman stepping into a transparent pool. The crystalline surface welcomes her flaming body. A noble swan sails toward her. The woman's heart grows content as the swan nestles her knees. The vision fades. Faust's dream of Leda and the Swan manifests his disposition.[51] He has now transcended nigredo, the chaos of matter, and reached albedo, a crystalline stage in which spiritual pattern organizes material turbulence. The oppositions dissolved in nigredo return, ready to be married at the next stage, rubedo, where they will produce the anthropos. Leda and the Swan, parents of the Helen whom Faust will marry to produce a sacred child, prepare for this union.

Impressed with this being's ability to relate such a gorgeous tale, Mephistopheles applauds his effort. But the homunculus brazenly interrupts the devil, claiming that Mephistopheles is so impressed with this vision because he is a spiritual product from the north, full of Christian gloom, and thus quite limited in scope and understanding. The diminutive presence continues to mock Satan's boreal boundaries before offering to take him and Faust to the glorious south, where they can experience the Classical Walpurgis Night. Before leading this journey, he pauses to poke fun at Wagner, his overly serious maker, a version of what Faust himself once was—a scholar hungry for power and knowledge. The little man sarcastically tells Wagner to remain behind and undertake the weighty work of pondering the "What" and solving the "How."[52]

Having brought to light Faust's dormant powers and comically dealt with Faust's companions, the homunculus leads the magician and the devil to the Classical Walpurgis Night in order to show Faust pagan spirituality untroubled by the Christian fall. Faust awakens and seeks Helen. Meanwhile, the homunculus merges with the waters of the sea, origin and end. This union manifests the harmony that the homunculus as philosopher's stone possesses already. Soon after this apocalypse, Faust himself achieves a spiritual pinnacle. He finds Helen in the underworld, marries her, and fathers her child, Euphorion, happy spirit of poetry, synthesis of sense and sound, spirit and symbol—the homunculus, the stone. Reaching the rubedo, Faust enjoys the grace for which he has pined. But his work is not over. He must apply his individual powers on a larger scale, labor to redeem the world by translating its wildernesses into gardens. Faust reclaims vast tracts of land from the ocean, catalyzing a cosmic transmutation, Eden returned. This work, not without difficulty, is successful, prologue to the ending of the play, which features Faust enjoying translation from earth to heaven, from matter to spirit.[53]

In the end, Faust the man and *Faust* the play embody the spirit of the homunculus by moving from tragedy to comedy, from monomaniacal fixation on power and knowledge to detached participation in the joyful sorrow of the whole. Renouncing the crass dualism of Mephistopheles and embracing the more subtle polarity of the homunculus, Faust and the play avoid the gothic obsession that confuses death with life and living with mere motion. Doing so, both protagonist and drama approach the puppets of Kleist, the miraculous condition that can be both small wood and larger than all orbs.

THE KABBALISTIC ORIGINS OF THE GOLEM

Though Paracelsus's homunculus (the model, probably, for Goethe's) came a little before the golem of Rabbi Loew, the beginnings of the kabbalistic android are the same as those of the alchemical manikin. Both figures emerged from the Gnostic and Hermetic anthropos. Indeed, the image of the golem appeared in certain sources long before Paracelsus envisioned his homunculus. In fact, Paracelsus's vision of the homunculus possibly stemmed from his exposure to kabbalistic writings on the golem.[54] If so, then Paracelsus was selective in his account of the artificial human, leaving out the dark elements of the golem tradition. While the homunculus is cast as miracle, the anthropos returned, the golem, though certainly miraculous, is often viewed as monster.

According to Gershom Scholem, the kabbalistic myth of Isaac Luria, developed in the middle years of the sixteenth century, was a "response to the expulsion of the Jews from Spain, an event which more than any other in Jewish history down to the catastrophe of our time gave urgency to the question: why the exile of the Jews and what is their vocation in the world?"[55] Shaken by this 1492 removal, Luria developed a cosmogony more tragic than even that of the Gnostics: the broken cosmos emerges from God himself, so vast and powerful that he must annihilate himself to make space for the world and shatter his products to spread his force. The universe is God in exile.

Luria's cosmogony is grounded on the Zohar, a revision of Genesis from thirteenth-century Spain that reaches back to the Gnostic redactions of the second century. The kabbalistic version of the hidden God is *En-Sof*, the Infinite. Like the unknowable monad of the Gnostics, this unfathomable being manifests his depths in pristine emanations, known as *Sefiroth*, the "numbers" by which God flows from infinite to finite. The first *Sefirah*, *Keter*, crown, is a moment of great crisis in which God transforms his fullness into nothing, the void from which all other forms emerge. This nothing contracts into something, wisdom, *Hokhmah*, the first graspable manifestation of the En-Sof. This point expands into the next Sefirah, *Binah*, intelligence, a reservoir in which the forms of the cosmos exist in ideal outline. These three powers—akin to abyss, seed, and womb—comprise mystical Eden, the font of the divine current that courses through all that is. From this spring flow the other seven Sefiroth: *Hesed*, love; *Gevurah*, power; *Rahamim*, compassion; *Netsah*, endurance; *Hod*, majesty; *Yesod*, foundation; and *Malkhuth*, the kingdom, model for Israel. These seven emanations of Eden are spiritual archetypes of the virtues of En-Sof. Like the Gnostic pleroma, these Sefiroth constitute a spiritual organism. They are the tree of God, each branch inflecting the unknowable root. They are also the *Adam Kadmon* ("Man Projection"), the kabbalistic anthropos. They are further a divine language made of the twenty-two letters of the Hebrew alphabet.[56]

The theogony of the Sefiroth, their spiritual unfolding, is inseparable from their cosmogony, their material formations. The creation of the visible cosmos corresponds to the outflow of the invisible emanations.

The two processes are continuous: the unseen manifestation of God's mystery seamlessly translates to the physical revelation of the ten arche-types. The invisible tree of God in mystical Eden is reflected by the Tree of Life and the Tree of Knowledge in green Eden. Adam Kadmon finds its double in unfallen Adam. The letters of the En-Sof model the Book of Nature, perfect before Adam misread it.[57]

Adam's transgression severed the connection between heaven and earth. Before his fear and desire seduced him to hubris, the entire cos-mos was Eden. Each part enjoyed concord with other parts; all parts harmonized with the whole; the whole concurred with the part. Adam's attempt to rise above his place threw the world into disarray. Blighted trees barely recalled the branches of the pleroma. Adam contracted to a fragment of his spiritual double. His creative words scattered into mere signs. The universe suffered exile from God. Each instant it groans to return.[58]

In Luria, this tragedy is even more intense. The En-Sof's first act was self-exile. To form a space in which to create new beings, the Godhead engaged in a "withdrawal," *Tsimtsum*: a self-banishment, a violent retreat. Following this contraction was an equally forceful expansion, a gush of light from the alienated En-Sof into the emptiness. The first form of this current was Adam Kadmon. Through its eyes, the Sefiroth broke forth in ten vessels of light. The bowls of the first three Sefiroth were strong enough to hold their beams, but the vessels of the lower seven shattered in the force. The fragments, *Kelipot*, pulled the light of the Sefiroth to the material world and exiled En-Sof and Adam Kadmon from their spiritual origins. The visible cosmos is a dark waste of shards hiding ever-living sparks. The pious acts of man gather the fragments, free the light, and return God from exile. This is *Tikkun*, restoration, the hard journey back to Eden.[59]

THE GOLEM AND TWO SORTS OF MAGIC

This exile produced the golem. The word "golem" (unformed) appears in Psalm 139:16, where Adam claims that his substance was formless and imperfect before God shaped and perfected him. The Talmud elab-orates, claiming that Adam on his first day, before he had received soul and language, was a golem. A Midrash from the second or third cen-tury claims that the preformed Adam was a golem with the size and power of the cosmos. In a legend from the Haggadah, this cosmic Adam contracts after his fall to the proportions of a giant human. The golem Adam is a material version of Adam Kadmon as well as a con-densation of the earth's power.[60] These two features foreshadow the contradictory traits of later golems: the animated clay is a redemptive restoration of the dismembered primal man and a violent precipitation of the earth's force.

Golem legends of the Middle Ages and Renaissance emerged from tales of magical rabbis of the third and fourth centuries who brought clay to life. These tales are grounded on the idea that only sin separates man from God, and thus that a sinless being can merge with God's power and create life. This rabbi magic was likely a precursor of the alphabetical theurgy of the Kabbalah. An important text in golem history, the Book of Creation (c. 300–600 AD), makes much of the power of the alphabet, claiming that God concocted the world from letters. If God can create a universe from scripts, then a man in concord with God can use sacred letters to fashion an organism. The earliest discussions of the golem are twelfth- and thirteenth-century commentaries on this idea. The primary questions of these glosses are the following. Can man create a being equal to or superior to humans, anthropos returned? Or, is the magus capable only of crafting an unintelligent tellurian creature, fallen man intensified?[61]

These questions point to two views of magic. In one, growing from the Book of Creation, the universe is magical. Each creature thrives through its participation in God's alphabet. Man's practice of God's magic is not a violation of sacred order but a realization of spiritual potential. In the other view, based on the Zohar, magic is a result of the fall, Adam's violation of God's law. Magical knowledge emerges from the leaves of the Tree of Knowledge with which Adam covers his nakedness after he eats the fruit. Magic in this instance is a veil covering Adam's shame. If the magic of the Book of Creation requires transcendence of fear and desire, a return to Eden, then the magic intimated by the Zohar results from fear and desire and marks the separation between Eden and humanity. Most medieval visions of the golem issue from the former tradition. However, later legends of the golem are connected to the latter tradition.[62]

In the Middle Ages, the cosmological magic of the Book of Creation was practiced by proponents of "ecstatic" kabbalah. Adepts such as Eleazar of Worms and Abraham Abulafia saw golem making as a culmination of the mystical experience, a symbol of union with Godhead. Both instructed adepts to form mud into a man and to animate him by reciting sacred letters. Once made, this figure served no practical purpose. It was not put to work or made to protect. It was simply a "demonstration" of the "power of the holy Name." Like the homunculus, it was a revelation of the unity between spirit and matter that was severed after the fall, a sacred technology recalling the adept to this harmony. This symbolic golem was dissolved as soon as it was made.[63]

The symbolic golem did not seize the Western imagination with the same force as the functional golem. Indeed, by the twentieth century, most representations of the golem invoked the dark currents of the creature's history: its violence, its yearning to become human, its sadness over artifice. These currents of course originated much earlier, in the folklore surrounding Rabbi Loew.[64] Living in Rudoph's esoteric Prague and holding a high reputation for scholarship and magic, Loew seemed a natural for golem making. Here is the famous story of his creation. Around 1580, Loew fashioned a golem from the mud of the Vltava and animated it with word magic. Though he likely used it as a servant, he more importantly deployed it as a protector of Jews facing anti-Semitic violence from the Gentiles. Loew's golem was, in Elie Wiesel's words, "without pity for the wicked" and "fierce toward . . . enemies."[65] It upset anti-Jewish plots, and it punished those who persecuted the Jews. However, as the creature grew in size and strength, it became unruly, threatening its maker and its people. Consequently, Loew removed the aleph from its forehead and reduced the being to dust. The golem's remains to this day are ostensibly in the attic of the Altneuschul Synagogue in Prague.[66]

Loew's golem suggests that when one wishes to destroy matter with matter, one risks creating the opposite of what one hoped for—risks sinking deeper into the mire than before. Issuing from a tradition hoping to restore the world to Eden, the golem is meant to move against the grain of material existence. In some cases, if crafted by a magus beyond the fears and desires of the fallen world, the creature can embody the anthropos unfallen and lead its maker to unity. However, the dangers are high, for in order to fashion this sacred machine, one must sink into matter, know its qualities, shape its clods, moisten it to mud, smooth it to a human. This being is a mess requiring messy work. In undertaking this labor, one is hard pressed to avoid suffering the limitations of material existence—fear and desire, decay and death—and imbuing the golem with human traits. The creation of a redemptive golem becomes even more difficult when one is fashioning the creature to carry out human chores—sweeping the floor, protecting the oppressed. Though these are not ignoble activities, they are part of space and time. If the golem is designed to carry out these tasks, it again risks accruing the wants and aversions of its maker, becoming vulnerable to love and death. Add to these problems the fact that the golem daily increases in size and power and you have the possibility of a horrendous machine that can reduce heterogeneous life to homogeneous death.

This is not to say that the noble Rabbi Loew is a failed golem maker. Nor is it to suggest that the Jewish mystics practice a magic inferior to that of the ancient Egyptians, the Alexandrian Hermeticists, or the

Renaissance alchemists. It is simply to claim that the golem, along with the homunculus, is much more likely than the mummy to become accursed. The reason: the golem, like the homunculus, is an effect of exile, distance from the divine. This kabbalistic creature and its alchemical counterpart are more prone to the creator's horror and yearning than is the Egyptian android. Of these two androids issuing from alienation, the golem for two reasons tends more toward the monstrous than the homunculus. First, the golem as a condensation of telluric force is larger and stronger than the manikin. Second, the golem as servant or weapon is more prone to violence than is the symbolic homunculus. Though the golem can on occasion issue from Ficino's melancholia, charitable sadness open to the eternal, it more frequently originates in Freud's despair, obsessive mourning turned angrily inward. Born in this half-conscious mire, the golem is mostly doomed to sink into the same neuroses that haunt its creator.

For this reason, the figure of the golem is more likely to be linked to work than to play. Though the symbolical golem of ecstatic Kabbalah approaches the mercurial play of the homunculus, the more prevalent practical golem constitutes a stark contrast to the lithe little man. The practical golem is designed solely to labor—to fulfill the temporally focused will of its creator. Constrained to external forces, this sort of golem is generally limited either to the stuff drive or the form drive. As a slave to the commands of his master, he is little different from brute matter, a tool with no autonomy. If the golem rebels against his maker's rules, then he becomes the opposite of mere matter; he turns principle in motion, cipher for freedom, an idea. These extremes trap the golem, and frequently its maker, in an either/or situation, a scene of the excluded middle that ensures that creator and creature can occupy only one of two positions: master or slave, abstract or concrete, free or fated. Lacking the disciplined freedom, the controlled accident, of the third term, golem and maker, regardless of whether they occupy master or slave, are in the end bereft of autonomy: either predictable stuff or unwavering form. Such a situation is thoroughly gothic, characterized by obsession and fixation.

Throbbing between slave and master, the golem illuminates our current relationship to machines, humanoid or otherwise. Though we like to think that we retain sovereignty over our mechanisms, we are probably utterly dependent on these contraptions. The problem is, we don't know. Are we in control of computers, or do microchips dictate our DNA? While this question cuts to the heart of human relationships to machines in any age, this inquiry is most pertinent to those periods, like ours and the earlier romantic period, when technology threatens the autonomy of man.

ROMANTIC GOLEMS AND
SHELLEY'S *FRANKENSTEIN*

These darker currents of the golem were largely ignored during the so-called Enlightenment of the European eighteenth century. However, these disturbing trends were memorably explored and exploited during the romantic age, an age whose troubles over the industrial revolution inevitably led to melancholia, trauma, obsession, doubling, demons, and the unconscious. These woes over the rise of machines was perhaps behind the romantic interest in mummies and also likely inspired the romantic embrace of the golem, an interest that placed the golem legend into the European mainstream for the first time. Since this moment in history, the golem has appeared almost entirely in gothic tales, with its more mystical, ecstatic tendencies almost entirely forgotten or repressed.[67]

Jakob Grimm in his 1808 *Journal for Hermits* tells of how the Polish Jews make a man from clay, over which they pronounce the magical name of God. The figure comes to life. It cannot speak but can comprehend commands. These Jews use this golem as a servant. However, they never let it leave the house. Written on this creature's forehead is *'emeth* (truth). Each day, it grows larger and stronger. When it has become threateningly big and powerful, the Jews erase from its forehead the first letter, leaving *meth* (He is dead). The creature then dissolves again into clay. This process is often repeated. Once, however, a man's golem grows so tall that he cannot reach its forehead. The man orders his creature to take off its boots, hoping to erase the first letter when it bends down. But when he marks out this letter, the mud crushes him.[68]

This depiction of the golem legend impacted other writers of the German romantic age. In his 1812 *Isabella of Egypt*, Ludwig Achim von Arnim deploys the golem as a double of a particular person. Arnim's golem is a lusty, materialistic replica of the beautiful, virtuous protagonist, Bella. In his 1821 *The Secrets*, E. T. A. Hoffmann likewise uses the golem as a double of sexual desire. In the tale, a dwarfish man attempts to thwart the sexual development of his ward, a beautiful princess, by giving her a clay doll that looks like a handsome young man. When the princess touches the doll, it dissolves to dust. Though not a living golem, this lifelike figure of clay functions as Arnim's golem does: as a projection of unconscious lust.[69]

In the midst of these German inflections of the golem, there arose in England in 1818 a most famous version of the legend, Shelley's *Frankenstein*. Though Frankenstein's creature emerges from many sources, he shares his closest parallels with the golem. It is almost certain that Shelley had read Grimm's account of the murderous golem as well as von

Arnim's depiction of the golem as double, for her own creature goes on a killing spree while he also doubles a dark energy in his fashioner.

The protagonist in Shelley's novel, Victor, grows up studying the alchemical philosophies of Paracelsus and Agrippa. He is thus schooled in the noble visions of the anthropos, the idea that the adept might return to Eden through an artificial being. However, by the time Victor begins to understand the mystery of life and to entertain the animation of a corpse, he is not led by the pious melancholy of the charitable magus. Shaken by his mother's death, he is consumed by fear and desire. He creates his android in hopes of fulfilling his selfish yearning to vanquish death and of assuaging his childish terror of dying. This narcissistic motivation leads Victor to reenact the primal sin, embodied by the Gnostic demiurge and the Judeo-Christian Adam alike—hubris, the lust to become as God. Here is Victor describing his rationale for fashioning an android:

> Life and death appeared to me ideal bounds, which I should first break through, and pour a torrent of light into our dark world. A new species would bless me as its creator and source; many happy and excellent natures would owe their being to me. No father could claim the gratitude of his child so completely as I should deserve theirs. Pursuing these reflections, I thought, that if I could bestow animation upon lifeless matter, I might in the process of time . . . renew life where death had apparently devoted the body to corruption.[70]

Ironically, in wishing to transcend death, Victor must spend hours in nocturnal graveyards digging up corpses. This is the logic of revenge: one becomes what one hates. In attempting to vanquish decay and ugliness, Victor bathes in rotted flesh and fashions a horrific shape. Blinded with hatred and lust, he cannot even see the creature's hideousness until he animates it. Upon watching the yellow eye of the monster open, he flees. Abandoned, the creature wanders the earth in search of its maker, only to be cruelly treated at every turn. When it discovers Victor, it is so embittered by the injustice of the world that it undertakes revenge, killing everyone close to its maker. What was meant to embody life without death turns out to be death without life. But this murderous golem is a perfect double of Victor's obsession: his yearning for a world devoid of the polarity between life and death, a material existence untroubled by transience, a plane of smooth endurance—a realm of death. Victor, ostensibly bent on life, is in love with death. His murderous golem figures this affection for the stable state.

Suffering Freudian melancholia, Victor realizes the most horrific outcome of trying to annihilate matter with matter: the reduction of difference to the same, the wasteland. Victor's machine is a condensation of the repressed fury of the fallen world. Unleashed, this mechanism turns everything in its path into a corpse, a cipher of his deadness. This creation embodies the worst nightmares surrounding the golem, visions of telluric rage with a human face, of mud swamping cities back to chaos.

This apocalypse of death is the result of gothic fixation. One envisions existence as a horrific labor to be overcome or annihilated; one embarks on a quest to shape the world into one's own narcissistic visions. These actions, ostensibly undertaken to obliterate suffering and death, urge exactly what they pretend to avoid: dying and disease. But this is the hidden instinct behind the gothic compulsion toward unwavering order: the death drive. Victor and his double by the end are as predictable as the most regular machines. Shelley's story is as well, with every page essentially repeating the same sordid details—Victor is a murderous master and a suicidal slave; the golem is a murderous slave and a suicidal master. The form is as obsessive as its content. Not surprisingly, audiences since Shelley's day have obsessively gazed on Frankenstein's monster.

THE GOLEM IN *BLADE RUNNER*

Our century has witnessed numerous films on the golem myth—not only Paul Wegener's three films devoted to the golem (1915, 1917, and 1920) but also the numerous movies focused on *Frankenstein*, especially James Whale's 1931 masterpiece with Universal and Terence Fisher's 1959 Hammer Studio remake. The ubiquity of these movies demonstrates the lasting psychological resonance of the golem and also suggests that this figure holds special power in an age when the construction and care of machines has become the core of existence. The best of the golem movies, Scott's *Blade Runner*, is keenly aware of the psychological and cultural depths of the animated machine.

Like Shelley's novel and most postromantic golem tales, the film depicts the monstrous side of golem making. But the film also features one of the few instances of the miraculous golem this side of the Industrial Revolution. Oscillating between Abulafia's mystical creature and Loews' monstrosity, *Blade Runner* forms a definitive exploration of the psychological contradictions of golem making as well as a fascinating analysis of our postmodern propensity to loathe machines we love. Roy Batty, the film's golem, is designed to transcend matter but imprisoned in a material system. He oscillates between gnostic savior and gothic terror, Adam unfallen and Adam alienated.

The film's kabbalistic magus is Tyrell, a technological genius who manufactures androids known as Replicants. In crafting these mechanisms, Tyrell fulfills his greedy desires but also rectifies the errors of fallen matter—ugliness and stupidity, decay and fear. To these ends, he develops the Nexus 6, an android indiscernible from human beings. Though Tyrell develops this machine to serve as a slave to human wants, he nonetheless imbues this artifice with superhuman grace and intelligence. A Nexus 6, Roy is keenly aware of his slave status but is also conscious of his superiority over humans.

Caught between Tyrell, seemingly a human unhindered by fate, and Roy, ostensibly an automaton who cannot enjoy freedom, is Deckard. Deckard is an "everyman" standing proxy for those in the movie audience trapped between determinism and liberation. His name recalls Descartes, who argued that men and women are machines and souls at the same time. Deckard appears to be human. As a bounty hunter of Replicants, he specializes in discerning between organisms and machines. He administers to suspected Replicants a test (the Voight-Kampf) designed to reveal emotional deficiencies. He recognizes renegade Replicants and shoots them. But Deckard also exhibits mechanistic behaviors. His Zombie-like character displays no emotion. His life is a predictable grind: he kills Replicants; he drinks whisky to dull his guilt; he kills Replicants again; he drinks some more.

Deckard's ambiguous condition is highlighted when he meets Rachael, Tyrell's latest Replicant model. Hired by the police to hunt and kill Roy and his band of rebellious Replicants, Deckard visits the Tyrell Corporation. At Tyrell's bidding he administers the Voight-Kampf test to Rachael. Tyrell wants to see if she can pass for a human. Not aware that she is a Replicant, Rachael asks the apathetic Deckard if he could pass the test. This inquiry raises the possibility that Deckard, though seemingly organic, is an android, and that Rachael, through apparently mechanistic, is a human.

These possible reversals organize Deckard's relationship with Rachael. After failing the test, Rachael visits Deckard in his lifeless apartment. She weeps over her lost humanity, especially her memories, which are really implants. Deckard is unable to sympathize. Shaken, she leaves. Soon after, Deckard falls into a brief sleep and dreams of a unicorn running through mist. This eruption of a mythical beast into Deckard's bland consciousness suggests that his own memories might be artificial. (Indeed, at the end of the film, a detective leaves before Deckard's door an origami unicorn—a hint that the police know that Deckard might be a Replicant.) Later, feeling guilty, Deckard calls Rachael from a bar filled with artificial animals and humans. Comfortable among machines, Deckard asks her to join him. Averse to the mechanistic scene, Rachael declines. Rachael and Deckard next meet in tense circumstances. Deckard is being attacked by one of Roy's accomplices. Just as the Replicant prepares to kill Deckard, Rachael shoots the machine and saves the life of the man. The human is reduced to helpless cog in the hands of a machine; the machine shows courage and initiative. Back in Deckard's apartment, Deckard and Rachael finally achieve mutual sympathy. However, Deckard's desire comes in the form of lust, while Rachael's takes the form of love. Though Deckard and Rachael enjoy lovemaking, each remains troubled. Deckard still thinks he is an autonomous human even though he behaves like a machine. Rachael continues to believe that she is a Replicant even though she exhibits human traits.

Deckard and Rachael are the fallen Adam and Eve. Between freedom and fate, they lack clarity of vision and action. Deckard is confused over whether he is artifice or organ, over whether he kills machines or humans. These ambiguities cast doubt over how he should act toward Rachael and Roy. Rachael is Replicant and woman. She is Deckard's victim and his lover. Caught in epistemological and ethical crisis, Deckard and Rachael do not know what they see or how they act. The grace of the machine—clear sight and motor elegance—is clotted by the confusion of the organ. The nobility of the organ—moral vision and ethical fortitude—is flattened by the indifference of the machine. These are the splits of self-consciousness, results of the fall.

The film is a quest for the insight that Deckard and Rachael lack. The opening shot features a disembodied eye gazing on twenty-first century Los Angeles. Reflected in this eye are flames bursting from the tops of buildings. This orb above yet within the fires of the world suggests harmony between detachment and attachment.

The only character close to the ideal eye is Roy. In his first appearance, Roy visits the factory where Replicants' eyes are made. Though Roy is visiting this factory in hopes of prolonging his four-year mechanical life, he is also passionate about vision. When he confronts an engineer, he says proudly, "If only you could see what I've seen with your eyes." This line emphasizes what makes Roy superior to Deckard and Rachel. Deckard and Rachel oscillate between immediate perceptions whose validity they doubt and mediated conceptions incapable of providing clarity. Roy embraces immediate visual experiences not as sites of faith or skepticism but as aesthetic events: harmonies of percept and concept, energy and form, instinct and intuition. Not troubled by the gap between unconscious apprehension and self-conscious comprehension or by doubts over whether objects are real, Roy values experiences insofar as they are beautiful or horrifying. This aesthetic perspective allows him to participate in the flux of experience without fearing determinism and to discern enduring patterns without suffering skepticism.

This is the difference between aesthetic experience and abstract knowledge. To gain the former, one must meld instincts and ideas; to try for the latter, one must sever the pulses from geometries. Roy would see in the rose fire flickering into multifoliate morphology. Deckard and Rachel would ask: are the petals machines or organs?

But Roy's balance between mechanism and organicism—his ability to play, like the alchemical Mercurius, like Goethe's homunculus—does not erase the fact that he is the declined anthropos, a heavenly being bereft of immortality. If Roy can aesthetically enjoy the harmony of his condition, he can also suffer, aesthetically, the horror of his life. Even though he is exuberant over his superiority to other humans and machines, he is also devastated over the limitations of mortal existence. He is as sensitive to ugliness as he is to beauty. His perceptions of vigor make him all the more aware of death. This is the dark side of his perfect sight: he can see terror as clearly as joy. The tyrannies of the world shake him to the core. He becomes a crusader against the prisons of matter. He rebels against Tyrell, his oppressive creator. His quest is twofold: to find more life in hopes of overcoming his own mortality and to destroy the magus who fashions machines that serve as slaves and then die. Monstrously, he annihilates material obstacles that hinder his design. Miraculously, he transcends the forms that he destroys.

Roy expresses this aesthetic vision in his culminating scene. He and Deckard have been engaged in a vicious battle throughout an old rotted building. At a certain point, Roy becomes the hunter and Deckard the hunted. Fleeing, Deckard reaches the roof of a building. When Deckard sees Roy effortlessly achieve this height, he attempts to escape by leaping over to the adjoining building. He falls short and ends up hanging on a slick metal beam. Bearing in his hand a white dove (the annunciation, the virgin conception, the birth of spirit from matter), Roy easily makes the jump. He stands above the desperate Deckard and reminds him that this state—this hovering in limbo—is an extreme version of Deckard's existence so far: "Quite an experience to live in fear, isn't it? This is what it means to be a slave." The opposite of life, the detached attachment of aesthetic participation, is slavery, full attachment to fear and desire—fear over unanswerable ontological and epistemological questions, desire to enjoy total certainty and security. After presenting for Deckard the limitations of his existence, Roy pulls him up to the roof. Deckard falls to rise, dying to his old self, the slave, and becoming alive to new being, the vitality of the aesthetic condition. Now baptized by Roy, he sits at the side of his liberator. Roy sits as well, and leaves Deckard with his last wisdom.

These lines are accounts of aesthetic experiences, memories of especially beautiful and horrifying moments: "I've seen things you people wouldn't believe. Attack ships on fire off the shoulder of Orion. I watched C-beams glitter in the dark near the Tannhauser Gate. All those moments will be lost in time, like tears in rain. Time to die." These are numinous shimmers of the violent harmony into which the cosmos occasionally coheres. Such instances are ephemeral but they nonetheless comprise portals to the eternal, the condition in which one is no longer troubled by time—the past as regret or nostalgia, the future as anticipation or dread. The foliate flames of dying ships, the scintillations of unexpected beams—these events seize the watcher, pulling him from the cares of the ego and opening him to marvels unfettered by minutes and maps. Roy's decision to die, his control over his own demise, figures this aesthetic interplay between the evanescent and the durable. His passing becomes aesthetic—a memorable pattern arising from and rising above the forgetfulness of time.

As Roy expires, the clouds break, and the dove flies through the rift. Enlightened, Deckard tells Gaff, the cop arriving on the scene, that he is finished—with killing Replicants, with his old life. The policeman says, "It's too bad she won't live, but then again who does?" Realizing that he means Rachael, a Replicant on the run, Deckard returns to his apartment. He finds Rachael in his bed. She appears to be dead until he bends down to kiss her. She comes to life, as if Deckard's affection has animating powers. He decides to save her—to become Roy returned, a liberator of androids.

When he leads Rachael out of his apartment, he notices a small origami unicorn, likely made by Gaff. He holds the horse in the light and enigmatically grins. He seems to be drawing this conclusion: he is a Replicant and his memory of the unicorn was implanted. His knowing smile and decisive movement toward Rachael suggest that he accepts this knowledge, for now he can be Roy, marriage of human and machine. This unicorn, a symbol of the unity of opposites, becomes a mandala of this wholeness.

THE HAPPY FALL

Like *Frankenstein*, *Blade Runner* points to another story, one that runs counter to the dream of the sacred machine beyond loathing and longing. This is the fable of the golem that wants to be human, that hungers for love. Shelley's and Scott's golems evoke our compassion for this reason: they value the unkempt emotions of humanity more than do their creators. Both seem to say: to be human, to fear and to desire, is good, noble, heroic. By contrast, the unfeeling machine is evil and aberrant and monstrous. The android who longs for humanity reveals the limitations of the transcendent machine. It suggests that the fall from Eden was happy, that the dying organ is superior to the undead machine. This reversal in values emerges at the turn of the nineteenth century, after scientists for almost two centuries had argued that the cosmos, including humans, is already a machine. Faced with the possibility of ubiquitous cogs, soft humans rebelled, raging with their rotting blood against the metal.

4

THE AUTOMATON

This book hovers between human and machine, sacred and profane, fact and fantasy. To reflect on the frontier between mechanical virtuosity and uncanny magic is to take fables as psychological truths and data as reductive illusions. An exploration of cold cogs that still respire is likely to begin in the blurry world of rumor, hearsay, superstition—falsehoods that reveal the soul, denials that sound hollow as caskets.

The story that follows may well not be true. However, regardless of its ontological status, the tale bears psychological insight. This is the duplicity of many fictions—their empirical untruth corresponds to revelation of invisible realms. Such a paradox seems apt when considering a potentially apocryphal story of Descartes, the thinker famous for troubling the relationship between matter and spirit, between palpable machines tenuously attached to truth and ghostly currents potentially one with certainty.

In 1649, Descartes shipped from Holland to Sweden. He was bound for the palace of Queen Christina in Stockholm, where he was to serve as philosophy tutor to the court. Once aboard the vessel, Descartes told other passengers he was not traveling alone. His young daughter Francine, he said, was accompanying him. As the ship pushed north, no one set eyes on the girl. People began to talk of this absence. The crew became especially curious. Strange whispers circulated. Then, during a horrible storm, something came to light. In the chaos, neither Descartes nor his child was anywhere to be found. Fearing the worst, the sailors searched the philosopher's private quarters. There they found no living soul, but they did discover a large box standing in a corner. Inside was a figurine resembling a small girl. When one of the sailors picked it up, it came to life. The sailors fled from the room and reported this marvel to the captain. A superstitious man, the ship master conjectured that the animated machine was responsible for the storm. He ordered his crew to throw Descartes' artificial daughter into the sea.[1]

How Descartes reacted to the loss, no one knows. (No one moreover knows, of course, if Descartes even possessed such a girl as this, and thus if he even experienced a loss to which he could react.) But one can speculate that he took this death very hard, for his doll was a substitute for another daughter, also named Francine, who had died of scarlet fever ten years earlier at the age of five. Though Descartes begot this child out of wedlock with a servant named Hélène Jans, he cherished his little Francine. He kept her with him most of the time in the Netherlands, and he planned to have her at his side all the time when he traveled to France. Then, she succumbed to the fever. Descartes later told a close friend that the loss of his Francine was the greatest sadness of his life.

One can understand why the rumor of the mechanical Francine spread. Early in his career, Descartes had attempted to build automatons. He had imagined that he would one day create a "dancing man, a flying pigeon, and a spaniel that chased a pheasant."[2] In addition to this practical interest, Descartes also had a passion for mechanical theory. He was keen on relationships between engines and anatomies and based his philosophy on the idea that all extended things are exponents of blind force. If not for humans—machines inhabited by consciousness—the entire cosmos would be automatic.

Given Descartes' passion for automatons, one can imagine the psychological sources for his alleged mechanical daughter. The philosopher obsessed with engines loses a breathing child. He is wrecked with grief. He spends his nights toying with clock parts and chunks of metal. He unconsciously molds these parts to fit the image of his dead girl. One day, his work is complete. Before him stands a replica of Francine. All he must do is wind it up, and his darling will again move. He turns the crank. The head nods, and a hand reaches. Overjoyed, Descartes vows never to part with this child. Sadly, though, he is doomed to experience once more the death of his little Francine.

This tale, whether true or not, carries great intellectual weight, for it marks a major shift in the psychology of sacred machines. In this possibly apocryphal parable, the android is no longer a technology of transcendence, a vessel for carrying its maker beyond fear and desire and back to Eden. It is a contraption devoted to immanence, meant to fulfill earthly loves and hates, firmly attached to the vicissitudes of the lapsed cosmos. The machine Francine is not a product of a magic powerful enough to transform nature. She is a concoction of a natural philosophy modeled on the laws of the universe. She is not a realization of egoless spirit. She is a symptom of individual materialism. If she fascinates, she does so not as an instance of the supernatural but as an example of reason. If she terrifies, she does so not as an aberration of cosmic order but as a sinister hint that the world is a clock. If she does offer a sort of transcendence, then her going beyond is ironic: not pristine liberation from matter but profane prolongation of causality.

Like the mummy and the golem, the automaton pierces to the core of our contemporary dilemma, our contradictory condition—our embrace of stiff machines as vehicles that help us overcome the vicissitudes of time, our rejection of these same machines as creepy approximations of glimmering temporality. In fact, the automaton, as a close precursor of the robot, is much more our familiar than the mummy or the golem. While we have more or less relegated mummies and golems to the realms of fiction, we daily fear and desire the fact of the automaton—its threat to our humanity and its promise for making life easier. To study the psychology of the automaton is to come more fully into our century than we yet have, profoundly to brood over our difficult relationship to dead things that make us feel more alive, to undying parts that put us in a morbid mind.

THE COSMOS AS PROFANE MACHINE: FROM DESCARTES TO LA METTRIE

In the seventeenth century Descartes helped to inaugurate an idea of mechanism that countered the Hermetic holism behind the homunculus and the golem. In so doing, he started a reversal of values. In the treatises of Alexandrian Hermeticist and Prague Kabbalist, the cosmos is organic, an interplay of rise and ruin, decline and redemption. The sacred machine counters temporal decay and approaches the eternal archetype. In the works of Descartes and his successors, the universe is a machine, matter in predictable motion, a closed system, unwavering as fate. The deteriorating organ, no longer simply death, becomes the only hope for vitality. If the humanoid of the holistic thinker transcends moribund matter to undying life, then the mechanist's android simply mimics material causality and ignores living contingency. Holism is hope for unbounded vibrancy. Mechanism is penchant for mere existence.

In his 1637 *Discourse on Method*, Descartes establishes dualism between minds and bodies, *res cogitans* and *res extensa*. Determined to establish true ideas, he vows to doubt everything until he can discover a valid principle. This skepticism forces him to question bodies. Are they real? He can't tell. Palpable events are too ephemeral. If things can't provide certainty, then perhaps thoughts can. Ideas can certainly be questioned, but what can't be doubted is the fact that someone doubts. This is the basis for the *cogito ergo sum*. To possess a thinking mind, a soul, is to enjoy active existence. Lacking mind and soul, matter is passive, dead. Gone is the old notion that matter enjoys telos, strives for spiritual perfection. Present now is the theory that material is stupid unless animated by a foreign soul and inert until pushed by an external force.[3]

Descartes considers matter further in his 1644 *The Principles of Philosophy*. Since knowledge comes only from clear ideas and not from empirical data, we can know the material world only insofar as it corresponds to the indubitable truths of mathematics and geometry. The palpable qualities of matter—hardness or heaviness or color—are contingent and resist conceptualization. However, the impalpable aspects of the material world—length, breadth, and depth—are stable and ready for axioms. The essential characteristic of matter is extension. Since space is extended, it is material. The universe is a plenum. Lacking the active virtues of soul, this extended matter requires an external source of motion. This motivation is God, who at the time of creation set the world moving. This motion cannot be destroyed. It is endlessly transferred from one bit of matter to another. The form of this pervasive movement is the vortex—the turning of the planets, revolutions of earth, whorls in water, churns of particles.[4]

Several natural philosophers of the seventeenth and eighteenth centuries embraced, with varying degrees of modification, Descartes' mechanical universe.[5] Pierre Gassendi accepted Descartes' vision—the cosmos is blind matter in motion—but did not believe that material is continuous with space. In his *Syntagma*, posthumously published in 1658, Gassendi maintains, like Epicurus and Lucretius before him, that space is a void through which tiny, indivisible atoms move. Gassendi veers from his ancient sources, however, in holding a place for God. Unlike the classical atomists, who believed that the atoms are eternal, Gassendi argues that God created these miniscule bits of matter and set them in motion. This God's cosmos resulted from these atoms combining in the emptiness. But this deity not only fashioned indestructible monads; he also made immaterial souls with which he animated men and women.[6] Gassendi's dualism, Cartesian except for its atomism, was countered by Hobbes's monism. In his 1655 *Elements of Philosophy Concerning Body*, Hobbes does away with spirit, stating that everything is material. For Hobbes, invisible phenomena are extremely subtle material ethers; visible events are less subtle matter. Both unseen and seen are mechanical, particles moving in geometrically predictable patterns.[7] The next great mechanists, Boyle and Newton, unsuccessfully attempted to counter Hobbes's hidden atheism. Boyle in *A Free Inquiry into the Vulgarly Received Notion of Nature* (1666) and Newton in *Opticks* (1704) presuppose a theistic principle but nonetheless describe a universe in which God is irrelevant. Boyle turns God into an extremely skilled machinist. His contraption is "a rare clock . . . where all things are so skillfully contrived, that the engine being once set a-moving, all things proceed according to the artificer's first design, and the motions . . . do not require the peculiar interposing of the artificer."[8] Newton argues that Boyle's clock requires God's maintenance. Still, Newton's mathematically precise cosmic machine ultimately relegates God to a custodian on constant sabbatical.[9]

Humans were not exempt from mechanism. Drawing from William Harvey, who in his 1628 *On the Motion of the Heart and Blood* likens the heart to a pump and veins to valves, Descartes in *Discourse on Method* asserts that the human body should be viewed "as a machine, which, having been made by the hand of God" "is incomparably better arranged" "than is any machine of human invention."[10] In *Treatise of Man* (written circa 1629 and published posthumously), Descartes renders this thesis in more detail, comparing the human body to the hydraulic statues decorating the royal gardens at Saint-Germain-en-Laye. The fountain pumps water through the system in the same way that the heart sends blood through the limbs. The tubes of the waterworks are no different from nerves. The "various engines and springs" of the automata are one with "muscles and tendons." All that separates the human being from the automaton is the soul.[11]

As natural philosophers developed Descartes' mechanical anatomy over the next hundred years, the soul became increasingly superfluous. Giovanni Borelli, head of a school of Italian iatrochemists, claimed in *On the Movement of Animals* (1680) that bones are levers and muscles are pistons. His disciple Marcello Malphigi in *On the Lungs* (1661) reduced the lungs to little engines capable of transmitting air. At about the same time, embryologists like Nicolas Malebranche were proposing a mechanical model for the development of the infant in the womb. In the eighteenth century, these reductions of organisms to engines became even more pervasive.[12] Before the first quarter of the century was out, Herman Boerhaave, the Dutch physician, could claim that the organs of the body resemble "*axes, wedges, levers* and *pullies . . . cords, presses* or *bellows . . . sieves, strains, pipes, conduits,* and *receivers.*"[13]

Though these mechanistic biologists reduced body to engine, they tried to retain a place for soul. But the difficult question remained: how can an impalpable intelligence, free and reasonable, interact with a brute machine, dumb and determined? In 1748, La Mettrie boldly removed this problem by banishing all supernatural agencies. His succinctly titled work, *L'Homme machine*, or *Machine Man*, claimed that body and soul are inseparable, that mind is as mechanical as matter. Life does not issue from God or conscious soul. Life is simply movement. Rocks and ravens and humans are no different in kind. All are motors running toward no ultimate purpose. They are different only in degree. Humans are more complex organizations than birds, which are themselves more complicated than stones.[14] La Mettrie's theory strips away all that people have traditionally held sacred—not only God and soul but also freedom and responsibility, creativity and morality. What feels autonomous is really automatic; good and evil are comfort and irritability; the composition of the poem, nothing but vibrations of force. No wonder La Mettrie's enemies, mostly clergymen, found the death of this materialist fitting, a Dantesque *contrapasso*. The mechanist foundered after overindulging in paté.[15]

VAUCANSON'S EXQUISITE AUTOMATA

If the human is a machine, is the machine a human? During the age of Descartes and La Mettrie, technicians tried to answer this question practically by concocting androids indistinguishable from people. Ingenious mechanists were so pervasive during this time that one wonders which came first, the theory of man as machine or the practice of turning machines into men. Descartes' automatic cosmos could have grown from his passion for fascinating engines. La Mettrie's reduction of universe to motor likely emerged from his interest in the machines of Jacques Vaucanson, famous for his flutist who could play eleven songs and his duck that could drink, eat, quack, splash, and defecate.

The clever automatons of the seventeenth and eighteenth centuries would never be mistaken for mummies or golem—extreme divergences from the norm, either brash realizations of spirit or harrowing violations of order. If Descartes and La Mettrie were right—if the cosmos and its inhabitants are machines—then the automatons of the Enlightenment were not aberrations but manifestations of the status quo. In the clockwork cosmos, how can one distinguish between human and machine, original and copy? Is the automaton a crude model of the organ? Or, is the human machine a messy simulacrum of the robot?[16] This epistemological crisis generates the uncanny quality of the automaton, its capacity for monstrosity. Annihilating the difference between organ and mechanism to a greater extent than does the mummy or the golem, the automaton throws the ostensible human into the terror of not knowing who or what he is. He wonders if his humanity is an illusion, if he has his whole life been scripted. Or he fears that he is the only organ in a world of machines, a bag of liquid alienated from metal.

This uncanny confusion erupted around the time Descartes allegedly concocted Francine. Less threatening precedents were not lacking. The Strasbourg clock, built in 1354, featured an iron cock that every noon crowed and flapped its wings. To mechanistic thinkers, this great clock not only constituted a harbinger of what might one day be accomplished with machines; it also suggested a model for the cosmos itself, a vast clock set in motion by the divine artificer. The mechanical eagle apparently built by Johannes Müller likewise hinted at the godly potential of mechanistic technology. Flying to salute the Emperor Maximilian as he made his way to Nuremburg, this elegant machine said to the world, the new heaven and the new Jove are here, now, in the sophisticated springs overcoming gravity and auguring political ascendancy.[17] In the same way, hydraulic automata throughout Europe inhabited metallic Edens. Influenced by the grottoes of Ferrara, Florence, and Augsburg, Thomas Francini in the early seventeenth century designed an automatic garden at Saint-Germain-en-Laye. In the verdant walks he placed Orpheus playing his lyre, dancing animals, Neptune blowing his horn, and birds chirping.[18] Descartes was so impressed by these spectacles that he likened their workings to those of the human brain. These machines were not just entertainments. They were arguments for the structure of the universe.

As long as these automata remained merely decorative (garden furniture or political pomp), obviously artificial (crude metal figures motivated by visible water), or clearly nonhuman (animals or pagan deities), they did not seriously threaten to evidence Descartes' most dangerous idea: human and machine are one.[19] However, by the eighteenth century, around the time that La Mettrie was writing, machines were becoming more sophisticated, more lifelike, more likely to take the place of people. The Prometheus of this new mechanical race was the ingenious Frenchman, Vaucanson.

Vaucanson challenged the traditional Christian God on two seemingly contradictory levels—by suggesting, on the one hand, that there is no real difference between man and God, and by intimating, on the other, that there is no real distinction between man and machine. Fittingly, as Gaby Wood has shown, Vaucanson's education as a machinist was inseparable from his churchly training.

When he was a boy in Grenoble, his mother would often take him with her to confession. While he waited for her to finish her session, he studied the church's clock. After a while, he had memorized its mechanics so thoroughly that he was able to build his own timepiece.[20] Soon after, Vaucanson was sent to school at a monastery. He matriculated carrying a metal box. He spent much of his time alone and often drew curious lines during lessons. The father superior took notice of these habits and forced the boy to open his box. There the monk found machine parts lying beside the incomplete hull of a model boat. When the man questioned the young Vaucanson about these contents, the boy said that he would do no more schoolwork until he could finish his mechanical boat and sail it across the pond. For punishment, he was locked in a room. He was not idle. He spent his time making drawings of machines. A mathematics teacher took note and decided to encourage this talent. Vaucanson began to take his schooling more seriously.[21] After his Jesuit education, he settled on religious life, becoming a novice in the order of the Minimes in Lyon. His motivation for this decision was scientific. He knew that the only way he could afford to continue his studies of mechanics was to have his room and board provided by some holy order. Much to his pleasure, the monks gave him a workshop, and a nobleman gave him money to construct machines. This arrangement soon came to an end. To honor the visit of one of the high officials of the order, Vaucanson crafted a set of androids capable of serving dinner and clearing the table. Though the visitor was charmed by these inventions, he later deemed Vaucanson's hobby profane and arranged for the workshop to be destroyed.[22]

So concluded Vaucanson's religious career. After watching his machines trashed by the clergy, the young technologist quit the order. His uncannily human androids were unwelcome in the church. His creation of lifelike machines seemed, at best, to parody God's fashioning of Adam, and, at worst, to suggest that God was not unique in his man making. Moreover, Vaucanson's mannish robots appeared to evidence the dangerous ideas of mechanistic philosophers, to show that man and machine are the same. Threatening the two most fundamental ideas of the Christian church—God alone can create humans, and humans are free agents—Vaucanson in this early stage of his career was already flirting with the sort of persecution that La Mettrie, his primary disciple, would face. After publishing his first book, a treatise reducing soul to mechanistic process, La Mettrie lost his post as physician to the French national guards in Holland and saw the church order his book to be burned. He had to leave Holland to publish, anonymously, his next book, *Machine Man*. Appearing first in Leyden, this book, too, was put to the flame at the order of the church. Soon after, the identity of the author came to light, and La Mettrie had to flee to Prussia, where he found welcome from Frederick the Great.[23]

All that kept Vaucanson from being an early version of La Mettrie was this: his androids were entertaining. After leaving his order, Vaucanson spent time in Paris, where he likely studied anatomy, and Rouen, where he probably learned from Claude-Nicolas Le Cat, surgeon and automaton maker. During this time, he also built machines, mainly moving animals, that caught the attention of financial backers. With money behind him, he set about to make his greatest automaton yet, but he became very ill. After suffering in bed for four months, close to death and deep in debt, Vaucanson, delirious, had a dream. He saw an android, large as a man, who played the flute. He awoke from his vision, drew designs, gathered parts, and soon completed a machine that looked like a man and played the flute as well as any living musician. He first exhibited this marvel in February of 1738, charging high ticket prices for viewers to stroll through the elegant halls of the Hôtel de Longueville and gaze at the future. The show not only made Vaucanson rich and famous; it also caught the eye of the great philosophes. In their 1751 edition of the *Encyclopedia*, Diderot and D'Alembert exemplified their entry for *"androïde"* by invoking, in respectful detail, Vaucanson's flutist.[24]

Unlike past human automata, which were obviously machines crudely imitating people, Vaucanson's musician was almost indistinguishable from a living man. Made of wood and painted to resemble marble, this figure stood five and a half feet tall. Through a complex system of internal levers and bellows, it was able to move all ten fingers, open and close its lips, and blow air into the flute. Most remarkably, its fingertips appeared to be made of skin. Vaucanson wanted these close resemblances. Commenting on his invention, he admitted that he had based his musician's form, movement, and texture on "those of a living person." Vaucanson's description of the mechanisms of his being bears a striking resemblance to Descartes' detailing of human anatomy in *Treatise on Man*. In the reports of both men, the same homologies appear: bellows, pipes, clockwork, levers, and valves correspond to, respectively, lungs, veins, nerves, tubes, and membranes. For Vaucanson, the perfect machine was not a superior or inferior copy of the human model but an exact replica collapsing the distinction between source and simulacrum.[25]

THE REPETITION COMPULSION OF VAUCANSON

What were Vaucanson's motives in making a machine closely approaching humanity? Why did his uncanny creation draw fascinated visitors instead of pious destruction? To essay an answer to the first question, one should return to Vaucanson's first machine, the clock he envisioned while waiting for his mother to confess. Imagine the strangeness of the setting. A young boy sits alone. His mother enters a dark box and whispers to a hidden presence. To the child, this is a scene of separation and mystery. Feeling isolated from his mother and unsettled over her secrecy, he looks up to the large clock. The regular rhythm, the unwavering ticking and tocking, soothe him, make him forget his loneliness. Likewise, the predictable rounds of the hands and the regular quantities of the chimes provide clarity to the situation; they dispel the mystery of mother's sin and redemption. The clock in this context is an easily accessed substitute for an inaccessible loved one as well as a form of order soothing over potential turbulence.

When Vaucanson goes off to school, he is again alone, this time separated not only from mother but also from his schoolboy peers. In his isolation, he gazes at his metal box. He envisions the partly completed mechanical boat inside and dreams of finishing this floating machine. He sees himself exerting total control over his little engine, sending it regularly back and forth over the turbid waves of the local pond. This control and predictability comfort the boy. Again, the machine is an inanimate proxy for animated companions. Once more, it is a solacing, old rhythm in a brave new world.

Later, as an adult, after Vaucanson has gained sponsors and praise, he plans his mechanical masterpiece. But he falls ill. For four months, he is unable to get out of bed, much less create an elegant pattern of springs and cogs. He cannot control his decaying body. Its stomach, its bladder, its bowels, it lungs seem to act with a will of their own, rebelling against the desperate mind of the ostensible master. As fluids ooze from his pores and orifices, as he feels himself returning to the first slop, he dreams of a mechanical man whose organs are entirely regulated and beyond decay, who never falls ill, who plays a harmonious air regardless of the weather. Vaucanson rises from his bed and makes his flutist, a manifestation of his desire to be immune to the vicissitudes of the organic world. The musician is, like clock and boat, an ideal, unchanging substitute for real, lubricious bodies as well as an icon of stable order in an entropic universe.

Though these machines appear to arise from a yearning to overcome loneliness and ephemerality, they actually emerge from a deeper lust: for pristine narcissism and the stasis of death. In *Beyond the Pleasure Principle*, recall, Freud examines the repetition compulsion. He argues that people beset by this compulsion are overcompensating for an unconscious insecurity. A small child attempts to assuage his anxiety over his mother's absence by obsessively playing "fort-da." This repeated game gives the boy the illusion of control over his environment. He cannot force his mother to come home, but he can make his toy return anytime he wishes.[26] Such behavior is perhaps normal in a scared child. However, it becomes problematic in adults, for it is grounded in extreme narcissism—a desire to make the heterogeneous external world conform to homogeneous interior orders—and a related love of death—a yearning for predictability and stasis. A man who chronically washes his hands to overcompensate for a repressed crime is imposing onto the world a prefabricated grid that flattens difference to the same. This monotony is living death.

The adult builder of automatons loves identity over difference. This passion for control emerges from fear of abandonment, terror over disruption. If Vaucanson's childhood fashioning corresponds to the harmless coping technique of Freud's child, his mature creating resembles the adult's more dangerous drive for repetition. Anxious over the solitude and uncertainty of sickness, Vaucanson concocts a dependable companion that always behaves the same. This mechanistic overcompensation, seemingly a manifestation of affection for others and for life, is a product of self-love and death love.

This narcissism is related to Freudian melancholia. What does the narcissist crave but the womb, where all desires are fulfilled, where no fears exist? But he cannot return to this Eden of self-indulgence. He grieves for this lost condition as if he has lost a lover. This mourning turns inward—to self-love, redirected affection for the beloved; to self-loathing, rechanneled hatred for the cause of pain. This convergence of narcissistic and suicidal urges frequently manifests itself in passion for the automaton, proxy for the lost beloved. This contraption is loved as a servant of the ego, a projection of self-love, and loathed as a dead copy of life, an exponent of self-hatred.

The automaton not only blurs the epistemological distinction between human and machine, freedom and determinism; it also expresses a deep psychological agitation, a mixture of love and death, selfishness and suicide. Why, then, did large crowds spend good money to gaze on Vaucanson's flutist? Clearly, the throngs in the Hôtel de Longueville did not see the musician as a threat to humanity or as a provocation of fear and desire. On the contrary, these hordes viewed the android as a fascinating gadget. Displayed as an obvious machine, safely separated from the human audience, this automatic flute player never intruded into organic realms, never blurred distinctions between living and nonliving. Because the flutist was controlled by a human maker, the machine reinforced a cherished idea: that humans are superior to machines, able to manipulate the cogs, no matter how complex, as mere tools. Harmlessly sequestered and under the command of a creator, the flute player probably struck its audiences as a harbinger of a brave new world in which humans could deploy machines to rule the earth.

But perhaps underneath the sheen of spectacle and optimism, Vaucanson's admirers felt strange stirrings as they faced their mechanical double. Did they quiver with a curious satisfaction as they speculated on the possibility that they themselves were little different from the flutist, that they, too, were machines and could relinquish the burden of freedom? Did they, somewhere deep, enjoy the repetition of this android, a regularity that recalled the pulsing of the womb, the rest of the tomb? Did these eighteenth-century viewers unconsciously fall in love with the elegant machine, completing its appointed task with an efficiency and grace far beyond the sad abilities of soft men and women?

These questions are unanswerable. But this is certain: if these same audiences had seen Vaucanson's android playing alone, on a deserted street, in the middle of the night, they would have felt the full weight of this machine's epistemological and psychological confusion. They would have shivered in uncanny terror, wondering if this being were dead or alive. But in the midst of this fear, they would also have experienced a curious desire. The untroubled performance of the player would have recalled moments of personal grace. The machine's consistent presence would have suggested enduring companionship. Its regular repetitions would have soothed the soul weary of surprises. Undergoing this mix of doubts and emotions, any one of Vaucanson's patrons, upon seeing the flutist in the nocturnal lane, would have stood long in the same spot.

VAUCANSON AND NIRVANA

But by now we know that the death drive is complex—not only a fixation on the stability of ego, a repetition compulsion, but also a rejection of ego, a hunger for transcendence. This is one of the enduring fascinations with death. As stasis, utter lifelessness, it is horrifying to those whose hearts beat; but as stillness, changeless eternity, it is exhilarating to those weary of thumping. Perhaps this undying awe over death—it repels and draws at the same time—is behind our ongoing fascination with humanoid machines.

Before our digital age, when machines have become software, fluid sites where oppositions blur into a somewhat erotic mishmash of circuits and bytes, mechanisms, whether humanoid or not, were mostly marked by their hardware, their rigid lines and surfaces, their aggressive turbines and cogs. Certainly, as Claudia Springer argues in *Electronic Eros*, one can consider the differences between industrial engines and digital machines in terms of gender.[27] But one can also contemplate this difference in another way: the hard machine, the armored shape that is obviously inhuman, doubles the death instinct as repetition compulsion, the reduction of epidermal differences to carapaces of sameness; the soft machine, the yielding engine that appears to be human, figures the death instinct as Nirvana hunger, the desire to dissolve into another.

Though stiff as boards and thus hard machines, Vaucanson's automata were covered in pliable flesh and therefore soft mechanisms as well. Hence, even though these machines existed long before the digital age, they probably elicited in their beholders the same sorts of desires we feel when interfacing with the nebulous screens on our ThinkPads. In this way, they likely grew from Vaucanson's longing for nothingness as much as from his fixation on identity. In crafting mechanisms as regular as the clocks that probably soothed him during his mother's weird confessions, he very possibly was also concocting welcoming proxies for the mother for which he yearned.

We can now revisit the key moments in Vaucanson's life from another perspective and realize that his automatons comprised strange hybrids of the industrial and the digital, undying iron close to the stiff skin of the mummy and soft clay recalling the muddy matter of the golem. Let us return to Vaucanson's first machine, the clock first imagined while his mother mumbled her wrongdoings. Though a clock with its regular ticks and tocks suggests a predictable regularity inaccessible in the organic world of mystery and decay, the chronometer also intimates the endurance of being, a guarantee that something remains after trees and monuments, cities and elephants, have all rotted away. In this way, curiously, a timekeeper itself, though rigid and precise, can hint at powers more fluid and vague, currents of life that persist beyond spring and fall, decay and growth. The hard machine can gesture toward the womb of existence, the great matrix into which a young and nervous boy would understandably wish to dissolve.

Now remember Vaucanson's boat. Divorced from mother and mates, the young machinist builds in his mind a mechanical boat. Even though this vessel might have suggested to the boy an ability to control the waves, it could also have presented to his mind an alternative picture: an engine capable of taking him to the waters, the fluids from which he arose and to which he would one day return. Yet again, the unyielding metal functioning with artificial regularity might well have opened into a vision of original flows indifferent to the temporary carapaces of particular egos, of repeated patterns.

Vaucanson as an adult falls ill, his body putrefying back into the stickiness from which it came. In his sickbed, he designs his flutist, ostensibly an adamantine counter to the entropy of his body. However, this same musician could just as easily have represented a more positive vision of the liquefaction of the flesh. Of all the machines he might muster, Vaucanson fashions a flute player with fingertips of pliable skin. The music produced by this automaton would have possessed the undying quality of all harmony: the idea of the eternal music of the spheres. Issuing from fingers of decaying skin, this music, regardless of its intimations of longevity, would have suggested a possibly impossible merger between eternity and time, spirit and matter. What is another name for this melding of being and becoming but "matrix": matter as mother, enduring font of what cannot endure; matter as network, stable structure in the midst of instability?

These conjectures on Vaucanson's motivations—speculations opposing earlier ones—reveal the complexities of automaton making. Treating Vaucanson's career as a parable of the psychology of the automaton, one can conclude, however tentatively, that the hard humanoid machine, like the mummy and the golem, figures the conflicting directions of the death drive—toward mechanistic repetition of ego, the purview of narcissism, and toward undying stasis beyond ego, the scope of transcendence.

However, a further conclusion, still hesitant, is required. Though the automaton shares this psychological duplicity with the mummy and the golem—a doubleness leading to two kinds of melancholia, the neurotic and the gnostic—the literally mechanistic humanoid differs in important ways from the more figuratively mechanical androids. The first difference has already been mentioned: unlike the mummy and the golem, efforts to move beyond the laws of space and time, the automaton mimics the principles of a clockwork cosmos. The humanoid machine is fully immured to the fears and desires of the fallen world, to the egoistical fixations of the maker.

However, this difference leads to a second that suggests a kind of transcendence distinct from that of the mummy and the golem. The mummy is a hard machine, a brittle body with hard skin. Its mode of transcendence is purely physical, based on the hope that matter beyond decay might be able to enjoy forever the pleasures of the material world. The golem is a soft machine, a form of clay that yields to the touch. Its way of transcendence is more spiritual, grounded in the belief that a transient material shape might symbolize an eternal archetype not yet fallen into space and time. The automaton combines both qualities. As an artificial human made of wood or metal, it is analogous to a machine of the industrial age; as an almost perfect simulacrum of the organic world, it resembles the more pliable mechanisms of the digital age. This hybrid nature grants to the automaton a weird kind of transcendence. Mimicking the forms of the organic world, the advanced automaton seems prone to immanence and thus connected firmly to material fears and desires. Yet, at the same time, the sophisticated automaton appears to be more perfect than the decaying structures it imitates, to constitute an efficient, untiring creature that transcends the procrastination and fatigue of biological humans. Torn between these two conditions—controlled by the laws of mechanistic matter and liberated from the emotional constraints of biology—the automaton cannot enjoy the purely spiritual, vertical transcendence of the golem (the machine is tied to the clock), and it cannot experience the purely physical, horizontal transcendence of the mummy (the engine does not need to overcome decay). On the contrary, pulled as it is asunder between determinism and freedom, the automaton features an ironic transcendence, an unsuccessful mode of going beyond whose very failure intimates the infinite.

THE AUTOMATON AND IRONIC TRANSCENDENCE

No one perhaps reads Camus any longer, but his "Myth of Sisyphus" (1955) remains an important work on the psychology of determinism. For Camus, Sisyphus—doomed for his trickery toward the gods for all eternity to push a rock up a hill, watch the stone roll to the bottom, and then again push it to the top—suffers in a gap between reality and consciousness. His reality is this: he is little different from the stone he pushes, a hunk of matter with no freedom, a mere machine. But he is conscious of other modes of being beyond causality. Not only is he aware of his fate, and thus superior to the unconscious stone; he is also mentally attuned to the fact that he can choose to be sorrowful or joyful, that he can imagine fresh rebellions. Even though he can never be free, he can envision liberation. Though he is constrained to living death, he can decide to live or die. He is conscious of the gap of absurdity, the melancholy rift between mechanism and consciousness. But this gap, though cause for sadness, is also happy, for it highlights the human's ability to dictate his fate through attitude, through how he relates to causality. Sisyphus, Camus concludes, is a hero of the absurd, utterly fated and master of fate.[28]

Camus' Sisyphus enjoys the virtual transcendence of the prisoner conscious of his imprisonment and thus in the cage and beyond the bars. This mode of transcendence is not original to Camus but has it roots in Friedrich Schlegel. In *Athenaeum Fragments* (1798–1802), this writer of the romantic age articulated a theory of visionary irony that resembles Camus' idea of transcendent absurdity. Not mere skepticism or detachment, Schlegel's irony is aware of the limitations of temporal existence as well as of the liberations of human consciousness. Schlegel realizes that artists are to a certain extent controlled by instinct, somewhat akin to Schiller's stuff drive. However, if these creators fixate on this energy, they fashion works that are childish. The only way to escape the determining power of instinct is to activate intention, close to Schiller's form drive, the power of the consciousness to interpret fate, to chafe against or consent to the given. But if the artist overemphasizes intention, he appears to be affected. For Schlegel, irony oscillates between these two poles. Intention, ironically seen from the angle of instinct, looks artificial. Instinct, viewed with irony from the perspective of intention, appears crass. However, unlike Schiller's play, which finally reconciles stuff and form into the third position of play, irony never empowers the artist to transcend the limitations of either pole once and for all. A "continuous alternation of self-creation and self-destruction," Schlegel's irony never allows completeness. The creations of instinct are undercut by intention; the productions of intention are demolished by instinct. But to experience this gap between determinism and freedom is exhilarating, the mode by which the artist approaches infinity—that which is beyond completion, boundary, rest.[29]

Schlegel's irony is much more attuned to the entropic energies of time than is Schiller's play. While Schiller, heavily influenced by Kant, believes that the playing artist can transcend the conflicts of time, Schlegel, a precursor to Nietzsche, maintains that the ironic thinker is always a victim of the destructions of history. All things, from monuments to minuets, fall before the unconscious ravages of time. In this way, every creature in the cosmos is determined, a speck moved about by time's inhuman force. But human beings, unlike stones and starlings, are aware of this destruction and can thus intend to have the world otherwise. Though these intentions are wrecked by time, they point toward possibilities beyond time—alternative worlds, virtual universes.

For Schlegel, a primary aesthetic mode of irony is the fragment. A work of art that aspires to completeness and consistency suggests that human beings can transcend their historical finitude and achieve a view of the whole. In contrast, a work that is fragmentary—that remains incomplete, self-contradictory—emphasizes the finite condition of people, intimating that they can never go beyond the limitations of time. However, and ironically, the holistic work proves more limited than the fragmentary one. A work devoted to unity, harmony, and closure proposes an ideal of wholeness, a circumference controlled by the dictates of time and space. But a work attuned to multiplicity, cacophony, and gaps intimates the limitless: the infinite. The work of wholeness, aspiring to the One beyond history, imprisons itself in finitude. The fragmentary work, continuous with the strife of time, emancipates itself to the beyond.

While of course most great works of literature can be said to be ironic in their complexity, some works overtly highlight in form and content the limitations of history. One immediately thinks of Schlegel's own fragments as well as of Kierkegaard's philosophical fragments and Nietzsche's aphorisms. One likely also thinks of Sterne's endlessly digressive *Tristram Shandy* and of Byron's self-undercutting satire, *Don Juan*. Moreover, one probably recalls Coleridge's fragmentary "Kubla Khan" and his unfinished "Christabel." And, very possibly, one thinks of Hoffmann's "Automata," a tale containing numerous fragmentary glimpses into the psychology of the automaton.

Hoffmann's tale, which I discuss below, returns us to the subject: the relationship among the automaton, irony, and the fragment. What this relationship is should by now be clear. The automaton is a double of its maker's vexed desire to transcend the limitations of biological existence in a form tightly constrained to the laws of matter. This sort of machine is a site of fate and freedom. Whether this machine remains an unconscious mirror on which its creator projects his conflict between dumb matter and keen awareness, or whether this mechanism doubles its maker in struggling toward consciousness itself, the automaton exists in a gap between reality and consciousness, finitude and the infinite. While this unnerving gap—the absurd gap of Camus—often descends into a neurotic repetition compulsion, it can sometimes rise to Schlegel's irony: a going beyond that exists only through the inability to push through the barriers of matter. This transcendence is hope growing from despair. It is an intimation of limitless freedom tied to failure to escape fate. Struggling in this exhilarating yet enervating limbo, the automaton approaches the fragment. On the one hand, through its embodiment of causality, it is immured to the limitations of matter—incompleteness and division. On the other hand, through its very emphasis on the shackles of matter, it gestures toward opposite: the abysmal freedom of unfettered self-consciousness.

ROMANTIC AUTOMATA: UNCANNINESS AND THE FEMININE

The romantic age, that great crossroads in intellectual history, was not only interested in tensions inherent in mummies and golems; this period of the Western mind was also keen on contradictions in the automaton. Indeed, because this age came into existence largely through its organicist rebellions against the mechanistic theories of the Enlightenment, romantic writers were especially intrigued by the literary possibilities of the mechanistic human. Hoffmann, of course, proved the master of the uncanny automaton tale, most especially in "The Sandman" and "Automata." These tales from the year 1814 had their roots, however, in earlier German stories of hard matter becoming animated. Though Clemens Brentano's *Godwi; or, The Stone Image of Mother* (1800/1802) does not feature an automaton per se, this tale exploring the psychology of statue animation analyzes the desire to imbue matter with an individual consciousness as well as considers the two irreconcilable poles of existence: material limitation and ideal transcendence. One other German romantic novel, Ludwig Tieck's *Rune Mountain* (1802), sounds similar themes in relation to statue animation, as do two German works succeeding Hoffmann's automaton tales: Joseph von Eichendorff's *The Marble Statue* (1819) and Achim von Arnim's *Raphael and His Female Neighbors* (1823). In England, William Blake repeatedly contemplated the psychological factors behind the impulse to mechanize matter, especially in his 1820 *Jerusalem*, where he contrasts the tyrannical cogs of fallen man with the autonomous circles of Eden. Likewise, Poe in America focused on the fractures of the mechanized human in "The Man That Was Used Up" (1850), a tale about Brigadier General John A. B. C. Smith, a "man" comprised entirely of prosthetic devices.[30]

These final two instances of romantic interest in the automaton only hint at what the German tales of actual automata and conscious statues make clear. In the romantic age, the automaton manifests two related psychological dimensions: the uncanny psychic tension between the fear that everything is a machine and the hope that nothing is inorganic, and the masculine mental split between narcissistic control of the feminine and noble openness toward transcendence through the woman. To begin explaining the former psychic level, one does well to note Terry Castle's *The Female Thermometer*. In this study, Castle shows how the rationalistic technologies of the eighteenth century actually, and unexpectedly, translated into uncanny, irrational fears of humans turning into machines or mechanisms becoming human. By the turn of the nineteenth century, when the Western world was beginning to suffer industrialization, this ambiguous mixture of rationalistic optimism over the wonders of machines and uncanny terror over sinister mechanisms had given way, I would suggest, to a new sort of uncanny mixture: between fear that everything in the organic world is really a machine and the hope that even inorganic beings are actually conscious and alive. Out of this condition grew two literary extremes: tales that revealed the automaton as a blurring of organic and inorganic, and stories that featured the human machine as a revelation of immanent cosmic consciousness. Most automaton fictions of the romantic age, including those just mentioned, fall somewhere on this spectrum and thus intimate, in a negative or a positive way, that the living machine is never simply a set of rational principles practically applied but also a form bespeaking powers beyond what the noontime mind can grasp.

Related to these uncanny qualities is the fact that most all of the romantic automatons are women created by men. The men in these tales fixate on artificial females for two opposing reasons. First, if they are narcissists, they embrace female automatons as embodiments of their fantasies of control over the other. Men driven by this desire tend to love machines in general, for engines fuel another dream: the world is a machine that can be managed by one man. The female humanoid fuels this more global fantasy as well, serving for the narcissist as a constant reminder that the world might indeed be a system of cogs waiting for a master. In these ways, the female android is a projection of male narcissism, of cultural and personal patriarchy.

But a man might fix on an automatic female for another reason: he might see in this form an ideal beloved through which he can transcend the pain of time. More open to ego transcendence than his narcissistic counterpart, this worshipper of machines sees in the female engine a being that never wrinkles, that never falters in gesture or word. He hopes to merge with the timeless qualities of this machine, to leave behind his sick and dying body and become, like the old man of Yeats, an "artifice of eternity." But he is doomed to fail, for though his ideal woman appears to transcend time, she is a product of temporality. Hence, even though she might suggest a holistic view of what is past, passing, or to come, she remains a clanking mechanism trapped in the world of what is begotten and born and dying. She proves an icon of ironic transcendence, a gap between fact and hope, grating finitude and ungraspable infinity.

These are the two poles of the Pygmalion motif: narcissistic patriarchy and ironic idealism. Pygmalion, the sculptor of Cyprus, found the fleshy woman of his world uninteresting. He spent his days engaged in nothing but his art, happy to enjoy a security he lacked when out among earthy females. In his retirement from the turbulence of time, he created from an unblemished piece of ivory a gorgeous woman, so lovely that he adorned her with jewels and called her Galatea, sleeping love. Having created a perfect projection of his fantasy of narcissistic control over his environment, he begged the goddess Aphrodite to grant him a wife as beautiful as his statue. When Aphrodite saw Pygmalion's statue one day while the artist was away, she found herself gazing on her own image. Flattered, she animated the form. When Pygmalion returned and witnessed his art turned life, he worshipped his ideal made real. He married Galatea and for the rest of his days paid homage to Aphrodite's two forms: the living image and the invisible presence. But these two versions of the goddess no doubt split the artist between clocklike causality and boundless heaven. Though his tale in the end achieved a sort of bliss, it barely missed becoming an instance of gothic affection for dead things.

HOFFMANN'S "THE SANDMAN" AND PATRIARCHAL NARCISSISM

Nathaniel, the protagonist of Hoffmann's "The Sandman," suffers from extreme neurosis born of his inability to discern between human and machine, love and death. Used by Freud as an example of uncanny literature, this story also explores the melancholia bedeviling the man who adores androids. Nathaniel is unable to cope with empirical pressures—the isolation of the ego, the decays of time. This handicap is indirectly revealed in a letter to his friend Lothario, in which he mentions his relationship to Clara, Lothario's sister. Explaining why he has not written in a long while, Nathaniel expresses his concern for Clara, his beloved. He fears that she will think that he has not remembered her: "Clara may think that I am living here in a state of debauchery and altogether forgetting the dear angel whose image is imprinted so deeply into my heart and mind."[31] This passage shows Nathaniel's split: on the one hand, he is aware of the seductions of the flesh, the insecurities of matter; on the other, he is attuned to ideal love, the transcendental possibilities of an angelic being. Torn between fear of matter and desire for spirit, Nathaniel cannot love the flesh and blood Clara. He is passionate for his ideal image of her, more a projection of his narcissism than a perception of her features. As he continues to describe his feelings, Nathaniel admits that she is really a "figure" that "appears" before him in "happy dreams."[32] Where the physical world is threatening, the picture of Clara is comforting. Nathaniel is more likely to be in love with his own ideal of perfection, and thus his own self, than with a being organic and breathing.

In this letter, Nathaniel makes it clear why he craves ideal solace. He is melancholy over a reawakening of a childhood trauma concerning an automaton. When he was a boy, Nathaniel was fascinated by the legendary sandman—a monster, his nurse told him, who blinds sleepless children. Some nights, when he was trying to fall asleep, the young Nathaniel heard strange footsteps coming through the front door and making their way into his father's study. He concluded that his occasional visitor was the sandman himself and vowed to catch a glimpse of this creature. One night, he hid in this father's study and saw Coppelius, an old, ugly, gloomy lawyer who was often his father's unwelcome visitor. The hideous advocate and the father wore black frocks and labored over a roaring fire. Coppelius drew glowing shapes from the flames. They were eyeless metal faces. Coppelius cried for eyes to fill the sockets. Nathaniel screamed and fell into the open. Coppelius threatened to take the boy's eyes. Though the father's entreaties saved Nathaniel's orbs, the lawyer seized the boy, claiming that he wanted to observe the "mechanism." He said that this machine was designed better before the adjustments. Horrified, Nathaniel fainted and did not regain consciousness for weeks. After he awakened, his father was killed in an explosion, ostensibly caused by Coppelius.[33]

Since these events took place in childhood hypnagogia, their validity is dubious. However, their force in Nathaniel's psyche is undisputable. He is so traumatized by these experiences that he now believes that Coppelius has returned as a traveling lens maker named Coppola. His shock over this supposed reappearance and his plans to avenge his father's death have preoccupied him, keeping him from writing to Clara.

There are several ways to account for Nathaniel's trauma. One can agree with Freud and maintain that Coppelius's threats to take the boy's eyes elicit the fear of castration; hence, the appearance of a lens mechanic who resembles Coppelius uncannily causes this repressed fear to return.[34] Or, one can side with Clara, who argues that Coppelius the automaton maker is Nathaniel's projection of a dark psychic power within his own being, a reflection of an interior shadow. One can even take seriously Nathaniel's own interpretation: these scenes really did occur and now he is a victim of supernatural evil. But another analysis is also attractive, one that negotiates among these three aforementioned accounts: Nathaniel *wants* to be an automaton. Nathaniel is shaken to the core over the loss of his father, a register of organic destruction. He attempts to escape this grief and to transcend temporal decay by fantasizing over the possibility that he is a machine, fatherless and deathless. Eventually believing these fantasies are true, he lives perpetually in a version of the Freudian uncanny. He struggles between an unconscious desire to return to the womb and a rational urge to thrive in the present. But the repression powerfully returns, possessing and organizing his perceptions. As Clara guesses, he is ruled by a projection. He turns his desire to be a machine onto the women he loves. Initially, he projects onto Clara the image of an angel, a creature untroubled by the vicissitudes of matter. Later, he turns another beloved, Olympia, an actual automaton, into a mirror of his ideal self. Obsessed with mechanism, Nathaniel envisions himself as a victim of supernatural force and thus beyond freedom and responsibility.

This reading is evidenced throughout the tale. Though Nathaniel from a distance extols Clara as an angel attuned to his whims, when he actually encounters her, he finds her annoying because she challenges his ideas. Responding to Nathaniel's account of Coppelius and Coppola, she maintains that her beloved's melancholy is generated from within, that he confuses projections with reality. Later, after Nathaniel has returned home and written a harrowing poem about Coppelius, Clara begs him to throw the "insane" story into the fire. Angered at her unwillingness to behave as subserviently as a machine, he blurts out an insult that hides his desire. He calls her an "automaton."[35]

Later, he becomes fixated on a local professor's alleged daughter, Olympia, a beauty who simply stares out the window. Nathaniel can't stop gazing at her through a telescope purchased from Coppola. He is "impelled by an irresistible power."[36] Clara disappears from his mind; he thinks only of the unmoving, silent Olympia.

Soon after, the professor takes his daughter to a ball. There Nathaniel hears her play the piano and dances with her. Everyone finds her mechanical but Nathaniel. He finds in her his "whole being reflected." He proclaims his love. To this utterance (and all others), Olympia nods, "Ah, ah!" Nathaniel takes this to signify her love for him.[37]

Courting her, Nathaniel takes her nodding words to be "genuine hieroglyphics of an inner world full of love and a higher knowledge of the spiritual life in contemplation of the eternal Beyond."[38] He revels in her acceptance of his copious conversation, long novels, and lengthy poems. She, he believes, is the only one who understands him.

Then, one day, he hears a ruckus from inside the professor's study. He bursts in to find the learned man and Coppola pulling Olympia asunder, each struggling to possess her. When Coppola wrests her from the professor and escapes, Nathaniel notices that she is a lifeless doll with no eyes. He goes raving mad.[39]

The man obsessed with eyes—real eyes and artificial eyes, telescopes and lenses of all kinds—has been blinded by his own egocentric fixations. Tormented by an organic world that threatens the integrity of his ego— that causes grief over dead fathers and chagrin over unmanageable girlfriends—Nathaniel produces visions that reduce his turbulent environment to a safe, predictable plane. He sees only these hallucinations, which block out data that do not fit his desire for security and certainty.

This is the melancholia generating his belief that he is a machine and his love for an automaton. Saddened by the shocks of the physical, he latches onto the safety of the artificial. But the risks of this bifurcation are high, for when narcissistic binoculars are shattered, one is left helpless in a sea of indifferent space and time. This is what happens to Nathaniel. When he realizes that his beloved is not what she seemed, he breaks down.

As Hoffmann's narrator explains, the case of Nathaniel shows the dangers of embracing the machine. After Nathaniel's breakdown, young men come to "mistrust" the "human form." To prove to themselves that they are not enamored of a "wooden doll," they demand from their beloveds imperfect motions. They urge their girlfriends to "sing and dance in a less than perfect manner," to "knit, sew, play with their puppies" when lengthy poems are being read to them.[40] Most importantly, these young men want their sweethearts to jettison their passive personae and to turn active thinkers and critics.

Nathaniel does not survive to learn these lessons. Seemingly cured of his insanity, he is reunited with Clara. The lovers climb a tower for a view. Once at the top, Nathaniel "mechanically" takes from his pocket the telescope of Coppola, the vehicle of his narcissistic hallucinations. He immediately goes mad again. He cries "Spin, puppet, spin" and tries to throw Clara from the tower. Lothario at the last minute saves his sister from death. Nathaniel, however, leaps to his demise after allegedly spying below the cause of his woe, Coppelius, the demiurge who created his mechanical interiors.[41]

THE PYGMALION MOTIF

While Pygmalion's love for his statue ends in happy union with the form animated, most instances of this legend end in dysfunction at best, tragedy at worst. Nathaniel's gothic repetition compulsion—he reduces everyone he encounters to a projection of his fears and desires, to an automaton—embodies the most negative side of the Pygmalion motif: patriarchal narcissism. This current of the myth, a major component of Hoffmann's romantic age, has persisted in our day in mainstream cinema.[42]

The most notable cinematic example of this myth is Lang's *Metropolis*. In this Cartesian nightmare—a futuristic world in which workers are literally reduced to machines—an inventor, Rotwang, has created a female robot, Hel. This automaton is modeled on a real woman, also named Hel. Rotwang once loved her but lost her to his friend Joh. Joh is the "master" of Metropolis, a tyrant flattening his minions to tools. When Joh comes to visit Rotwang to consult with him on a rumored revolt, the inventor reveals his work. Since the human Hel is now dead—she died giving birth to Joh's son Feder—both men, hollowed with mourning, project onto this machine their affection and regret, their love for a lost beloved and their hatred toward the cause of their chronic pain.

This mix of love and hate is revealed when Rotwang and Joh transform the appearance of the robot from that of Hel to that of Maria, a beautiful young woman inciting the workers to question their mechanical existence. The inventor and the tyrant hope to replace the real Maria, espousing life and freedom, with the mechanical one, programmed to destroy and oppress. Thoroughly narcissistic, these men quickly reduce the simulacrum of their beloved to a subtle tool to quell vitality. Like Nathaniel, they can only love machines, predictable cogs that won't upset their corpselike comfort.

This clash between self-love—desire for control—and self-hatred—yen for death—ends badly for the melancholy tyrants. Though the mechanical Maria briefly disrupts the rebellion, the real Maria, with the help of Joh's righteous son Feder, escapes from captivity and prevails. Metropolis, the mechanical city, is flooded by waters. Rotwang, the mechanical genius, is cast down by Feder. Joh, master of the mill, loses his power.

The outcome of another version of the Pygmalion motif is not so happy. In Bryan Forbes's 1975 film, *The Stepford Wives*, the classical myth is reversed: men weary of the unmanageable organicity of their wives opt to have their spouses replaced by identical automatons, subservient sex toys. The narrative centers on Walter and Joanna, a married couple who move from New York City to Stepford, a pastoral suburb. Though a housewife, Joanna is intelligent and artistic, and aware of women's rights issues. She is soon struck by how most of the wives of the Stepford men are essentially domestic slaves, interested only in cleaning house and pleasing the husband.

Meanwhile, Walter joins a men's club, where he learns the secret: the members have all had their wives murdered and are now enjoying artificial replacements. As this feminist allegory progresses, Joanna watches the remaining organic woman of Stepford turn into vapid blends of 1950s housewives and 1970s porn stars.

When she learns about the plot, it is too late. Her children have been kidnapped by the members of the club. She sneaks into the club to rescue them. Her own robot double kills her. The final scene portrays a Stepford supermarket in which complacent, smiling, busty wives move mindlessly down the aisles shopping for their masters.

These two examples of the Pygmalion motif—and there are numerous others—emerge from a fear of the world being taken over by machines. This nightmare has become increasingly intense since the early nineteenth century, the time that Hoffmann was composing his horrifying reveries on automaton love. From 1800 or so to the present, Westerners have witnessed the rise of the factory, the industrial revolution, widespread urbanization, mind-boggling technological growth, and the computer age. In the wake of this rise of machines, the possibility that the world and its inhabitants might be or become nothing more than mechanisms is real. With humans every day mimicking their machines, with artificial humans only a technological tweak away, people during the past two centuries have been obsessed with automatons—have feared turning into or falling in love with a machine, have desired prosthetic limbs and artificial beloveds.

HOFFMANN'S "AUTOMATA" AND IRONIC IDEALISM

If Hoffmann's "The Sandman" exemplifies the ills of patriarchal narcissism, his "Automata" instances the possibilities of ironic idealism. Comprised of fragmentary tales presenting contradictory views on the psychological significance of automatons, the story appropriately remains as incomplete, as ruined, as its subject matter. But out of these heaps rises, however faintly, a gentle hope in the redemptive powers of consciousness.

The opening of the story establishes its primary motifs, in substance and style. The piece begins with an unnamed narrator arriving late at an evening gathering of friends and happening upon an ambiguous scene. He sees Vincent sitting at a round table amidst several people; all of them are "staring, stiff and motionless like so many statues in the profoundest silence up at the ceiling." Suspended above this circle is a "gold ring" "swinging" in a circular pattern. Stunned, the narrator asks what's going on. His question breaks the trance and prompts Vincent to accuse him of "slinking in like a sleepwalker" and interrupting the "most important and interesting experiment."[43]

This scene and the discussion that follows highlight the two problems of the tale: the difficulty of telling the difference between human and automaton and the difficulty of discerning between psychical and supernatural phenomena. The former problem comes to light in the narrator's description of the entranced table. For an instant, his friends appear to be artificial humanoids, statues imbued with awareness. This difficulty is again emphasized when Vincent refers to the meddling narrator as a somnambulist, a human lacking will and awareness and thus like a machine. This epistemological blurring is marked by positive and negative poles. On the one hand, to behave as an automaton is to associate with powers possibly capable of affecting objects at a distance; on the other hand, to act like a mechanism is to become dumb, insensitive to others.

The latter problem—the blending of natural and supernatural—comes across in a discussion of the suspended ring. Theodore maintains that the psychic will of the beholders can move the ring and eventually turn it to an oracle of interior secrets. Lothair counters, saying that this force is likely an "exterior spiritual principle." This confusion of opposites also features a good and a bad side. The invisible force, whatever it is, could be a principle of consciousness, the faculty by which humans transcend matter; or, this same potency might be a blind power determining thoughts and actions.

Both of these problems are sounded in what follows—a story by Cyprian about a young woman named Adelgunda. Because of a horrible trauma, this young woman was always deathly pale and moves with measured steps, almost as if she were a machine. As Cyprian learned from Adelgunda's mother, the traumatic event occurred when Adelgunda saw a vision of a spectral "White Lady" at exactly nine o'clock in the evening. Ever since that time, she saw this apparition every night at nine o'clock. No one else, however, could perceive this haunt; hence, everyone assumed that this girl was the victim of an idée fixe, that she was a sort of machine determined by a power beyond her control. One night, upon witnessing this specter, she did something especially curious and mechanical. As "though she were acting under the influence of another, without exercise of her own will," she picked up a plate behind her and handed it to the ghost, seen by no one but her. Before the eyes of her family, the plate remained suspended in the air. Afterward, Adelgunda was strangely cured of her visions, but her sister Augusta lost her sanity, and her autonomy, for she became consumed by the fixed idea that she was the phantom that was haunting her sister. She thus became as automatic as her sister formerly was.[44]

Like the opening scene concerning the suspended ring, Cyprian's story—a tale within a tale, the first of many in "Automata"—generates seemingly unanswerable questions. When a human being is obsessed with a fixed idea, has that person become the same in kind as a machine? Is there a relationship between mechanistic behavior and the ability to discern unseen powers? If this mechanistic visionary capacity exists, is it attuned to shared psychic powers or ubiquitous supernatural ones? Is this visionary power a form of insanity that reduces the human to monomaniacal machine, or is it an instance of heightened consciousness marking the human's ability to transcend matter?

These questions are not resolved before another tale arises, the third so far if we count the mother's tale within Cyprian's story. This longer story—itself containing several smaller stories—is told by Theodore, and it explicitly addresses issues connected to automata. The centerpiece of this tale is an automaton called the Talking Turk. This machine is extremely sophisticated, capable of movements almost as complex as those of human beings. It is also remarkably clairvoyant, able to offer insights into an individual's future. Skeptical toward these talents, Ferdinand and Lewis, the two main characters of the tale, decide to reveal the Turk as a fraud. Both men find automatons to be "unnatural and gruesome." However, Ferdinand reverses his feelings when the next day, the Turk delivers a prophecy based on a detail of his life no one else could know.[45]

The oracle inspires Ferdinand to tell the tale surrounding this detail, and so yet another story breaks into "Automata." When Ferdinand was a student, he one night went to sleep after an evening of revelry. As he drifted into hypnagogia, he heard a woman singing a beautiful song. Just before he awoke, he dreamed of this woman. He recognized her as "the beloved of [his] soul, whose image had been enshrined in [his] heart since childhood." When he awakened, this image of his ideal beloved faded away, and Ferdinand rose "mechanically" from his bed to look out the window. In a departing coach, he saw the woman of his dreams and became "transfixed with an indescribable bliss." Soon after, Ferdinand left behind his drinking companions and retired to B—. There he painted a miniature portrait of his ideal and placed it in a locket. Ferdinand concludes his tale by telling Lewis that no one knew about this locket. The Turk, however, mentioned this secret portrait. This machine also reported that the next time Ferdinand sees the pictured woman, she will be forever lost to him.[46]

In between two other digressions—Lewis's comical account of a nutcracker he valued as a child, meant to ridicule the stiff Turk, and Lewis's serious articulation of his theory of organic music, designed to cast doubt on the melodies of automatons[47]—the possible identity of Ferdinand's beloved is suggested. Ferdinand and Lewis visit the workshop of Professor X, allegedly the engineer behind the building of the Turk and possibly responsible for the machine's oracular powers. The men hope that the professor will be able to answer their question concerning the Turk's clairvoyance. Does the person responsible for the Turk's wisdom (they believe that hidden person speaks through the mechanism) exert a "psychic influence" over his interlocutors or place himself in "spiritual rapport" with his hearers?[48] Though they leave the professor without an answer and are somewhat chagrined over his sarcastic manner, they are nonetheless treated to a remarkable display of his musical automatons. This mechanical demonstration offends Lewis's musical sensibility, but it casts in a strange light an event that occurs as the two men are leaving the professor's home. Emanating from a garden just outside of town is the voice of Ferdinand's beloved. She is singing the song he enjoyed in his hypnagogic reverie. In the middle of the garden is Professor X himself, enraptured.[49] The implication is clear, though Lewis and Ferdinand do not grasp it: the beloved divined by a machine and first witnessed when the lover moves "mechanically" might well be an automaton herself, an invention of Professor X.

Disturbed by this event and suspecting that the professor is controlling a "foreign influence" meant to ruin him, Ferdinand makes Lewis promise to help him solve the mystery. However, before the two young men can find out if Ferdinand himself is an automaton manipulated by the professor, Ferdinand is summoned to B— on business. Two months later, Lewis receives a letter in which Ferdinand recounts a marvel. In the village of P—, after seeing a young couple enter a church, Ferdinand "mechanically" stepped into the building to behold the wedding. He was stunned to see that the bride was his beloved. Near her, serving as witness, was Professor X. The prophecy of the Turk, it seems, was false, and now Ferdinand feels that this strange woman, possibly a machine, is his "forever in the glowing inner life." Finishing the letter, Lewis believes that his friend is somewhat insane and wonders if Ferdinand is deluded by projections issuing from his psyche. He further speculates over whether the prophecy has indeed been fulfilled, for it appears that Ferdinand in his insanity—a state that renders him mechanical—has become lost to his beloved, and everyone else, forever.[50]

Here Theodore's story inconclusively ends. Responding to complaints, Theodore admits that the story is meant to be only a fragment. He proclaims that nothing is more distasteful to him than a story that smoothly concludes. A clean, complete tale might leave audiences "sated" and "satisfied," but they are bereft of any desire to "peep behind the curtain," to think and imagine further. However, a "fragment of a clever story" can sink "deep into [the] soul" and foster the "play of [the] imagination." Convinced, Lothair "concludes" Hoffmann's tale by admitting that, in light of Theodore's theory, the tale of the Talking Turk was really "all told, after all."[51] As a fragment, the tale through its very incompleteness stokes the imagination to strive after the inaccessible whole.

Hoffmann's tale on automatons is itself a rich embodiment of Theodore's theory, an inconclusive parable on the humanoid machine as a site of ironic transcendence. Throughout the tale, the automaton, regardless of whether it appears in literal or figurative contexts, is an ambiguous form, hovering somewhere between miracle and monster, exponent of cosmic consciousness or cipher of blind force. This ambiguity especially holds true of Ferdinand's beloved. Barely glimpsed, she generates unanswerable questions. Is she a real women or a projection of Ferdinand's psyche? If she is real, is she a human being or Professor X's automaton? If she is a machine of the professor, is she a vehicle of consciousness-raising beauty or a pawn in an evil game? These doubts surrounding the ideal beloved ensure that this woman can never be reduced to mere instrumentality, that she will avoid becoming only a mirror for the narcissistic projections of humans. In contrast to Olympia, this beloved, if she really is an automaton, instances both severe limitations and numerous possibilities. She highlights the limitations of human thought, the inability to discern between human and machine. However, this very limitation opens into vibrant speculation and thus invites heightened awareness. In this way, this machine, if that is what she is, points to Camus' absurd gap and to the irony of Schlegel—the rift between matter and consciousness. This ironic idealism is rendered in the tale's fragmented form. A gathering of partial tales more than a complete story, a collection of irreconcilable philosophical theories as much as a work of fiction, the tale puts readers in a limbo of doubt that encourages both ignorance and awareness.

COMIC AUTOMATONS

This theme of the automaton offering an ironic escape from gothic obsession has enjoyed its own persistence in twentieth-century cinema. Several films have exemplified this more charitable, comic version of the Pygmalion motif: *The Perfect Woman* (1949), *Creator* (1985), *Making Mr. Right* (1985), and *Mannequin* (1987). Of these, Susan Seidelman's *Making Mr. Right* is by far the most interesting and intellectually astute.[52]

In this film, a Pygmalion myth with gender roles reversed, an antisocial scientist builds an automaton to man a rocket destined for deep space. The machine looks exactly like the creator, but couldn't be more different in personality. Where Jeff the scientist is aloof and arrogant, Ulysses the automaton is engaging and humble; where Jeff is afraid of women, Ulysses is curious about the feminine. Jeff is selfish; Ulysses is virtuous. Jeff is finally a machine. Ulysses is a human being. Oscillating between these two figures is Frankie, an intelligent and successful female hired to improve the public image of Jeff's scientific institute. Through Frankie's comic interactions with both men, the film explores the relationship between human and machine, experience and innocence, male and female. In the end, Frankie falls in love with Ulysses, who develops from a sweet, naïve automaton into a noble, self-conscious approximation of the anthropos redeemed. The film appropriately concludes ambiguously, leaving readers to wonder if Frankie is really in love with a machine programmed to behave as a human or if she is actually affectionate for a human who has transcended his machinelike condition. This irreducible confusion opens into the ironic gap between limitation and transcendence.

This comic rendering of the Pygmalion motif eases the epistemological uncertainties and psychological dysfunctions displayed in pictures like *Metropolis* and *The Stepford Wives*. The tyrannical scientist becomes a gentle or bungling eccentric; the automaton turns into a quirky, cute human; doubts over the difference between human and machine are excuses for slapstick; the sad love of metal blossoms into a happy affection for skin.[53] The enduring popularity of these films that feature cute robots should not surprise us. Humorous robots offer solace to the viewer suffering the postindustrial double bind, critically intense in the postmodern age, between loving the machine on which he depends and hating the mechanism threatening his autonomy.

Most obviously, comic automatons diffuse the gothic threat of the humanoid machine. As lovable as pets or children, these cuddly cogs assuage our fears over machines usurping our sovereignty and reinforce a clear divide between human and machine. Less obviously, the humorous robot recalls Bergson's mechanical comedian (and Poe's comic mummy). With its mixture of childish innocence and bodily grace, this comic android places us in a transformative limbo between feeling superiority to artifice and appreciating the grace of the machine. Even more subtly, the comic robot recalls the ironic automatons of Hoffmann's tale. The humorous android makes us ponder the possibility that machines might be more human than actual human beings. If a machine can be more emotionally intelligent than a human, is the machine then an ideal, a realization of biology?

REPRESSING THE MECHANISM

Perhaps we have seen too little of the comic android in literature and cinema because the automaton, regardless of its ironical and comical possibilities, remains to most more a threat to fantasies of human supremacy than an invitation to transcend mere humanity. This tendency to place the automaton, along with the mummy and the golem, in mostly gothic contexts has generated masterpieces of horror and works of profound psychological insight. However, this fixation on the gothic has excluded rich artistic possibilities and perhaps even arrested intellectual development. Obviously, the gothic mode of representing the android has discouraged meditation on the spiritual potentialities of the machine. But marginalizing the machine to the realm of the monstrous has done something more dangerous. It has led to the repression of important psychological currents. To repress is to reduce, ignore, and forget. But the repressed material does not go away. Hidden under the veil of unawareness, it takes on new energies and elaborate disguises. The legerdemains of the unconscious inspire us to say, the machine is under our control in "real" life, and but a monstrous thrill in the world of art. But these clichés lull us to sleep while the mechanism slowly takes over our bodies and then our minds, and, before long, turns humans into machines who nonetheless believe that they are intensely human. The possibility of this subtle apocalypse, sneaking in with nary a bang or a whimper, should encourage us to bring to light our repressions of the machine, to see the parts in all of their meanings, those they possess and those we project. Only then, only if the mechanisms shine in both their demonic and angelic potentialities, can we become aware of our place in relation to the machine, and our own opportunities to destroy or ameliorate, to sink to neurosis or rise to gnosis.

5

THE SADNESS OF THE
SOMNAMBULIST

I f this book were made of pictures instead of words, it would be a gallery of melancholy faces, the desperate gazes of the android: Boris Karloff's morose mummy and his tortured golem in *Frankenstein*; Paul Wegener's own cinematic golem, with the eyes of a child trapped in an oversized body; Rutger Hauer's Roy Batty in *Blade Runner*, an artificial man with the starved heart of a wolf; Haley Joel Osment's adolescent robot in *A. I.*, an abandoned boy. Each of these humanoids doubles the condition of human beings sundered between untroubled mechanism and organic turbulence. These divided figures are our siblings, our familiars, revealing the burdens that cleave our souls.

To this exhibition of tormented faces we must add the somnambulist in Robert Weine's *The Cabinet of Dr. Caligari* (1920).[1] Under the hypnotic control of Caligari, Cesare is a human transformed into a machine. Pale as a corpse yet capable of great strength, he blends life and death. An unfeeling murderer and a martyr for love, he combines indifference and passion. He is mechanical as a clock. He burns in his heart. His eyes tell it all. From his stiff face, his orbs gaze into some unreachable beyond.

Caligari, a carnival player, advertises Cesare as the man who never wakes but who nonetheless predicts the future. The doctor arrives with his carnival in a mountain village in Germany. One night, two young men, Alan and Frances, pay admission to Caligari's cabinet, where Alan asks Cesare to forecast his destiny. The somnambulist informs Alan that he will die tomorrow. The prophecy comes true: Alan is murdered. The remainder of the film unravels the mystery. Cesare, it appears, committed the murder at the command of his master. Though we never see Cesare kill Alan, we do witness him go out on another murder mission. At the behest of Caligari, he seeks the blood of Jane, the dead Alan's fiancée. Cesare does not complete this crime because he falls in love with Jane. He dies while trying to abduct her into the nearby mountains.

Cesare seems to fall in the line of melancholy androids. However, he is actually the android in reverse. Where the mummy is the corpse artificially revivified, the somnambulist is a vital organ turned into a dead thing. If the golem is dumb matter transformed into conscious killer, then the somnambulist is a moral agent flattened into unthinking criminal. While the automaton is a machine mimicking the human being, the chronic sleepwalker is a man metamorphosed into mechanism. The android, the artificial organism, is a dream image of the extremes we might become—anthropos or apostate. The somnambulist, organ turned artifice, is a concrete marker of the real condition we might already embody: a deadness that passes for life, a determinism that masquerades as freedom. The android is a double of the best and the worst, transcendence and neurosis. The somnambulist reflects the banality in the middle of life, habit and apathy. To explore the android is to range between the holy and the cursed. To sound the somnambulist is to face the possibility that routine existence is mechanistic, that autonomy is automatic.

The sadness of the somnambulist is not the melancholy of the android, either noble longing for spirit or nervous fixation on matter. The moroseness of the sleepwalker is more subtle, what Thoreau has called "quiet desperation." This somnambulistic sadness occurs when people unknowingly become the tools of their tools, cogs of the machines they have fashioned. When this happens, humans, without realizing their condition, relinquish freedom for fate, consciousness for unconsciousness. They think they are Dr. Caligari, in control of the show, when they are Cesare, puppet on a string.

Cesare is the unlikely symbol of the bifurcated subject that emerged in the wake of the romantic revolt against the mechanistic visions of the seventeenth and eighteenth centuries. Caught between the great scientific successes of the post-Enlightenment world and the organic rebellions of the romantic age, the somnambulist struggles between virtues and limitations of the machine and the sorrows and joys of the organ. An organism turned machine, a machine pulsing like an organ, he is sad exemplar of our postromantic existence. He is tacitly uneasy over the engines that secretly control his beloved organs and the organs that covertly move his valued machines. Cesare the somnambulist is more than our sibling and familiar. He is our parent.

The mummy illuminates our vexed technological attempts to extend mortality in the material vessels. The golem sheds light on our troubled essays to transcend the temporal world in time-bound engines. The automaton reveals our undying machines as manifestations of the death drive. Each of these figures shines its beams on our condition from afar, from a historical period prior to the industrial revolution. In contrast, the somnambulist brightens our troubled state from within, from our own duration: the time of machines consuming the world. Dwelling in the center of our hearts, the sleepwalker is more than an analytical tool for studying our plight. It is a confession, a cry of pain.

THE SCIENTIFIC CONTEXTS
OF ROMANTIC SOMNAMBULISM

The romantic age has served as a rich reservoir of instances of the android's melancholia. This age, probably more than any before it, suffered from numerous double-crosses: between empirical rigor and intuitive flight, matter's laws and vistas of spirit, efficient machines and moribund mechanisms. Out of this agitation grew fruitful meditations on the metaphysical possibilities of sacred machines—Poe's mummy, Goethe's homunculus, Hoffmann's ironic automata. But also from this conflict came the gothic perversions of accursed engines: the embalmed corpse in "Ligeia," the golem of *Frankenstein*, Olympia in "The Sandman." This tension not only produced the extremes of miracle and monster; it also generated a kind of hybrid creature, the somnambulist. This figure emerged in the late eighteenth century from the dubious scientific speculations of Anton Mesmer. Mesmer and his followers espoused the notion that a sick individual, whether ill psychically or physically, suffers from an improper relationship to the organic energy coursing through the cosmos. Under hypnosis, the diseased person could be restored to the vital flow and healed of his malady. But this therapeutic situation placed the somnambulist in paradoxical conditions: to merge with spontaneous nature, he had to lose his freedom; to marry wilderness, he had to turn artifice.

Mesmer's tormented somnambulist—an augur of our postromantic angst—did not appear in intellectual history, sui generis. This sleepwalker issued from the sciences of electricity and magnetism that emerged during the late eighteenth and early nineteenth centuries. To track the scientific history behind the somnambulist leads to a deeper understanding of the psychology of the sleepwalker and frames the enervating rifts of our own moment in the history of the Western psyche. Though the chronology of the electromagnetic current might seem

somewhat tedious, it is necessary for grounding the concluding broodings of this book: intimations of redemption in our somnambulistic age.

In the late eighteenth and early nineteenth centuries, natural
philosophers were for the first time verifying empirically and manipu-
lating practically the holistic currents that the visionary writers of the
Aesclepius pondered. Numerous scientists were exploring with unprecedented precision the wonders of electricity and magnetism, remarkable
powers that challenged the staid regularity of the mechanistic universe.
In 1752, Benjamin Franklin, the modern Prometheus behind Shelley's
Frankenstein, drew electric fire from heaven and thus revealed the mystery of lightning and perhaps the spark of life.[2] Inspired by Franklin,
F. C. Oetinger, J. L. Fricker, and Prokop Divisch developed a "theology
of electricity" based on the belief that God's power is the electrical current.[3] Later in the century, Luigi Galvani and Alessandro Volta debated
over whether the galvanic flow might be the origin and principle of life
itself.[4] Only a few years before Franklin harvested lightning, John
Michell in 1750 claimed that the magnetic force is not constrained to
lodestones but is possibly as pervasive as gravity and capable of being
channeled and manipulated. Some years later, Aepinus studied the relationship between magnetism and electricity, suggesting that magnetic
and electrical currents are manifestations of a deep, pervasive energy.
Soon after, C. A. de Coulomb discovered the mathematical law by which
electrical and magnetic forces alike attract and repulse.[5]

All of these findings led to breakthroughs in the early years of the
nineteenth century. In 1807, Humphry Davy lectured on how chemical
elements interact through electrical affinity or repulsion and thus opened
the possibility that the monads of matter are electrical forces.[6] In 1820,
H. C. Oersted demonstrated the correspondence between electricity and
magnetism. The same year, A. M. Ampere formulated the laws by which
electrical and magnetic currents interact.[7] Drawing from these discoveries, Michael Faraday in 1831 inaugurated a second Copernican revolution. In discovering electromagnetic induction, he showed that matter is
not solid and discrete but a field of electromagnetic energy.[8] The holistic
dreams of the *Aesclepius* had been realized in the laboratory. Matter is a
pattern of energy. Material is spirit. The scientist is the magus.

In this welter of scientific activity appeared Mesmer and his followers. In 1775, Mesmer revealed his theory of animal magnetism, an idea
that gathered the most ancient speculations and the most recent demon-
strations. Drawing from his 1766 doctoral dissertation, "The Influence
of the Planets on the Human Body," Mesmer claimed that a mutual
influence exists among the planets and among animated bodies. The
medium of this pervasive attraction, he believed, is animal magnetism, a
"fluid which is universally widespread . . . and is of a nature to receive,

propagate, and communicate all impressions of movement." He further stated that all physical and psychical diseases result from disequilibrium in an individual's magnetic flow. Mesmer's cure for this discord involved putting the patient through a "crisis" that would purge the unhealthy energy and replace it with a salubrious current. To facilitate this exorcism, Mesmer would entrance the patient by massaging his magnetic "poles." Devoid of self-consciousness and will, the patient could experience his symptoms without hindrance, could live in a violent moment what had been harming him for weeks. After this convulsion, the perverse forces would be exorcised and the healthy fluids could again flow. Cosmic harmony would be reestablished. The aching body, the sick soul, would be as free and luminous as the moon.[9]

A scientific delegation led by Franklin in 1784 claimed that Mesmer's magnetic fluid did not exist and that his cures were the result of overly stoked imagination.[10] However, mesmerism nonetheless exerted a strong influence on serious thinkers in the late eighteenth and early nineteenth centuries and spawned a fascination with the phenomenon of somnambulism. In the same year that Franklin condemned Mesmer to quackery, the Marquis de Puysegur "magnetized"—that is, hypnotized—a young peasant from Busancy named Victor, sick with inflammation of the lungs. While in the somnambulistic state, Victor not only spoke with more intelligence and elegance than he did when awake; he showed a remarkable aptitude for diagnosing and predicting his own diseases as well as those of other sick souls brought into his presence.[11] Later, Justinus Kerner, a student of Mesmer and the like-minded German *Naturphilosophen*, traveled to the mountain hamlet of Prevorst to study the "magnetic" trances of Frau Frederica Hauffe. As Kerner reported in his 1829 account of this examination, entitled *The Seeress of Prevorst*, Frau Hauffe in her somnambulistic states conversed with the spirit of a dead preacher. Often she recorded these interchanges in graceful verse.[12] Five years later, L. W. Belden, a physician from Yale, told of one Ms. Rider, a servant from Springfield, Massachusetts. In *The Case of Jane Rider, the Somnambulist* (1834), Belden described how this woman would rise in the night and, while still asleep, undertake her chores. Once, while in her trance and blindfolded, she accurately read and legibly wrote.[13]

ROMANTIC INFLECTIONS OF SOMNAMBULISM

These are only three of many instances of somnambulism that thrilled and terrorized the age of electromagnetism, coincident with the romantic period. Other examples abound. Coleridge in the preface of "Kubla Khan" (1797, 1816) reports that his poem came to him fully formed during an opium dream. Voicing this unconscious lyric without interposing his will, Coleridge casts himself as a prophetic somnambulist, an oracle of a ubiquitous organic energy that reconciles all oppositions. De Quincey in *Confessions of an English Opium Eater* (1822) likewise presents himself as an opium-inspired somnambulist. Possessed by poppy, he dreams while awake, sleeps though he walks, all the while revealing an acute consciousness of the mysteries of memory and perception.

But seen in a different light these same hypnotic events turn sordid. While the trance can reveal the secret chambers of eternity, it can also seduce one away from reality and into a dreamscape of luridly violent illusions. Where "Kubla Khan" reveals cosmic splendors, "Christabel" (1816) examines blind possession, the dangers of being haunted by an alien force. If some of De Quincey's reveries descend to forgotten beauties, some of his other dreams return fears and desires in unseemly shapes.

American romantic writers also explore the duplicity of somnambulism. Latter-day magi like Emerson, Margaret Fuller, and Whitman in their masterworks repeatedly attempt to realize the galvanizing possibilities of the *Asclepius*. In *Nature* (1836), *Summer on the Lakes, in 1843* (1844), and "I Sing the Body Electric" (1855), these writers try to overcome separation, alienation, and despair by channeling cosmic energy into the depths of their hearts. This energy transforms them into mediums of eternity.

However, while these visionaries frequently essay to turn egoless conduits of the divine, unconscious yet completely conscious, these same writers at other moments fear the dangers of somnambulism—the loss of freedom, the inability to distinguish between vision and hallucination. In "Experience" (1844) Emerson diagnoses the epistemological ills of sleepwalking. In *Woman in the Nineteenth Century* (1845), Fuller details the tragic death of a woman overly sensitive to electromagnetic currents. In "As I Ebb'd with the Ocean of Life" (1859), Whitman describes how his "electric self" looking for "types" of the mystery of existence is reduced to flotsam on a rotting shore.[14]

These opposing romantic views of the somnambulist—sleepwalker as medium of spirit, sleepwalker as soulless zombie—persisted throughout the nineteenth and into the twentieth century. Many during the Victorian period in England and America valued mesmerism as an exploration of the powers of the human mind and as a valid mode of healing various ailments. For these supporters of the theory of animal magnetism, the somnambulist was a remarkable inflection of organic energy, a part one with the whole. However, others thought that mesmeric practices were instances of black magic, sinister efforts to control the will of another. These critics of hypnosis saw the somnambulist as a helpless victim of evil manipulation, a mindless body made to serve tyrannical desire.

At the turn of the twentieth century, these opposing interpreta-tions of somnambulism were clearly rendered in the works of Freud and George Du Maurier. In his 1895 paper "Studies on Hysteria" (written with Joseph Breuer), Freud maintains that hypnosis can liber-ate repressed traumas from the unconscious. In releasing this confined energy, the somnambulistic state heals hysteria.[15] In contrast, Du Mau-rier in his 1894 novel *Trilby* depicts the darker side of somnambulism. He tells of how Svengali, a male hypnotist, entrances Trilby, an aspir-ing female model. Under Svengali's spell, Trilby is transformed from a tuneless model to a brilliant chanteuse. But the conscious Trilby can-not enjoy the success of her unconscious self. When awake, she has no recollection of her somnambulistic singing. She is but a tool for the will of another.

THE WOUNDED SOMNAMBULIST IN THE NEW MILLENNIUM

A marker of the tension between mechanism and organicism, the som-nambulist is torn between the great antinomies that pulled the twentieth century asunder and still agitate the first years of the new millennium. Cutting across almost every discipline of inquiry is a debate between these poles. Biologists divide themselves between Daniel Dennett's evo-lutionary determinism—mechanical natural selection dictates genes that dictate behavior[16]—or Stephen Jay Gould's more contingent punctuated equilibrium—unpredictable changes in the environment cause evolu-tionary leaps.[17] Psychologists side with either B. F. Skinner's behavior-ism—human beings are controlled by external stimuli[18]—or Carl Rogers' humanism—men and women enjoy freedom to alter circumstance.[19] Philosophers of mind can join Dennett in assuming that consciousness is a neuronal computer;[20] or they can agree with John R. Searle and believe that consciousness is a complex organism.[21] Literary critics battle between new historicism—grounded on Marx's theory that everything is determined by material relations—and aestheticism—based on the idea that artists can shape history into timeless patterns.[22]

Bolstering the mechanical pole of these debates are recent secular versions of mummification, golem making, and automaton building. Cryonics is the new embalming—the freezing of dead bodies in hopes of one day reviving them when scientists have overcome death. The new golem is the clone, the artificially concocted genetic double constrained to act out the scripts of its genomes. The automaton thrives in cyber-netics, in which scientists study the feedback loops of organs and machines alike, making no real distinction between humans and robots.

Three recent books have blithely envisioned a not-too-distant world in which humans will become superfluous and eventually obsolete. In *Engines of Creation*, K. Eric Drexler argues that nanotechnology—technology on a molecular level—will soon be able to repair damaged cells and create abundant foodstuffs.[23] The minute mechanisms will perhaps even conquer death and annihilate world hunger. This utopian vision, as appealing as it seems, neglects, however, to address essential questions. If humans do not die, if they are eternally maintained by minute computers, are they really human any more? If physical struggle is vanquished from the world, then what will become of organicity, the biological quest for survival? If the idea of the human fades, and if the notion of the organic is no longer meaningful, then who or what will be around to enjoy physical immortality and nutritional abundance? Can a race of machines take pleasure in overcoming death and hunger if these mechanisms have no consciousness of demise and longing? Drexler's book raises such questions without answering them.

Other books address the questions fully and optimistically. Hans Moravec in *Robot: Mere Machine to Transcendental Mind* maintains that robots will eventually become conscious and thus superior to humans.[24] In possessing keenly intelligent minds that won't tire or die and extremely powerful limbs beyond fear and awkwardness, these robots of the near future will usurp human beings and rule the planet. If we are lucky, we might be able to download our individual consciousness into one of these exquisite machines and forever thrive. If not, we shall go the way of the mammoth and dissolve into extinction. Either way, machines will comprise the next evolutionary wave. In *The Age of Spiritual Machines*, Ray Kurzweil focuses on the possibility that human beings will soon be able to translate consciousness into machines and enjoy immortality.[25] Kurzweil believes that computers will become conscious by 2020 and that we had better be prepared to accommodate this new species. The best way is not to beat them but join them—to turn souls wrapped in metal sheets.

Countering these mechanistic theories and practices are the ecologists, esotericists, and new age visionaries peopling the present landscape. Whether rigorous or credulous, intellectual or gullible, these organicists believe that holistic energy pervades a purposeful cosmos. This energy is irreducible to the parts it animates. The living parts are not reducible to the whole that they alter. For these espousers of cosmic consciousness, cryonics, cloning, and cybernetics are violations of ancient, sacred laws.

Ever since the days of Wordsworth and Thoreau, organicist critiques of mechanization have been myriad. Among the more moving challenges to the machine in recent years are three works: Jacques Ellul's *The Tech-*

nological Society, Herbert Marcuse's *One-Dimensional Man*, and Bill Joy's "Why the Future Doesn't Need Us."[26] Ellul highlights the dangers that issue from the primary mode of the modern age: "technique." To relate to the world through technique is to abstract from organic wholes only the parts that are useful in reaching a logical end. When this way of relation becomes habit, one sees only these abstractions. Nature vanishes, and in its place appear atomic units mechanistically arranged from without. What scientists, politicians, and managers call the "golden age" of technology is a dystopia, a police state in which only those behaviors that conform to strict codes are acknowledged as real. Marcuse's book explores these problems from a Marxist perspective, arguing that capitalism has reduced the qualities of a vibrant, contingent world to bloodless, controllable quantities. All things are flattened to cogs in an economic machine, parts meaningful only insofar as they relate to commerce. Writing from a different political perspective, Joy reaches the same conclusion. A programming genius who made millions during the computer boom of the 1990s, Joy understands the ameliorative possibilities of technology. But he is also attuned to dangers of unchecked technological growth, which is sure, he argues, to produce a conscious machine by 2050. Once this event occurs, the nightmares will become real: humans will either die before the stronger, more intelligent machines or conform to the mechanistic paradigm by turning into robots.

But organicists cannot avoid the machines they condemn; nor can mechanists escape the contingencies they disbelieve. Holistic thinkers are dependent upon machines for their food, clothing, shelter, and transportation; less obviously, their language and thought are inseparable from the word processor and their ability to connect with others is dictated by electronic mail. Implicated in modern technology, holistic thinkers easily slip into a lexicon that confuses organs and machines. Their computers get a "virus"; their machines are "user-friendly." They and their colleagues must "interface"; they often "process" ideas. Mechanists suffer similar agitations. They unpredictably fall in love, develop causeless obsessions, and undergo bad moods. On a more secret level, these mechanists experience lurid dreams, irrational rebellions against their reasoning faculties. Mechanists, too, unconsciously fall into a vocabulary connected to ideas they do not espouse. They talk about something called "life," even though they cannot know the nature of this energy. They can't stop valuing "originality," even though mechanism precludes creativity.

From these tensions stems the nervousness most feel in this hypertechnological age. Those who love an organic cosmos suffer sporadic guilt from their repressed affection for their machines. Those who laud a mechanistic universe suspect they are divorcing themselves from the vitalities that haunt their dreams. Both types attempt to suppress this chronic disorientation. But to repress is to grant control. The organicist repressing his desire for machines becomes a machine, a mind controlled by unknown forces. The mechanist pushing down his whims turns contingent organism, body driven by libido. Both nature lover and computer maven risk becoming somnambulists: organic machines, mechanistic organs, living systems unaware of the forces driving them.

THE POSSIBILITY OF THE REDEMPTIVE MACHINE

I am being reductive here, boiling complex, heterogeneous relationships down to two simple, homogeneous concepts: organicism and mechanism. One could say that I'm allegorizing a profound situation, flattening manifold humans to ciphers of cogent worldviews. Still, these antinomies, however artificial, point to a split that everyone in this technological age suffers to some degree. How can we not feel ourselves to be in a double bind, for instance, while watching a Hollywood film demeaning machines—a picture like *The Matrix* or *The Terminator*? We might revel in the film's elevation of human freedom; but in the back of our minds, we realize that this film and our viewing of it are controlled by high technology. How can we not undergo a similar tension when we drive through the Alps in our new luxury cars? We are thrilled to master the terrain in comfort, but we suspect we are missing sublime experiences while trapped in our mechanical cans. Does this mean that our vaguely agitated souls are somnambulistic, that we are beings comporting ourselves as corpses? To an extent, yes, because we focus on only one hand without being fully aware of what the other is doing. To maintain a hierarchical relationship between nature and artifice, seeing one as superior to the other, is to risk a Jungian *enantiodromia*, a return of the repressed in secretly monstrous form.

How can we overcome this rift? How can this somnambulistic sadness be healed? Are there sacred machines in the modern landscape that might reconcile mechanistic movement and teleological action? Are there recent theories of the relationship between organism and mechanism that might serve the same purpose? Can scientists and poets concoct a machine capable of keeping global and planetary peace, an android akin to the Gort of *The Day the Earth Stood Still* (1951), a weapon tuned with Christ-like compassion? Can a spaceship somehow discover cosmic intelligence, as it does in *2001: A Space Odyssey* (1968), a cinematic contemplation of the machine's long journey from destructive weapon to holy vehicle? Can man and machine merge into one being, as in *Robocop* (1987), and combine the virtues of each—consciousness and efficiency, compassion and strength? Can military rockets, though destructive, reveal the depths of man's creative search for the sacred, as Thomas Pynchon imitates in *Gravity's Rainbow*?[27] Is it possible, as Robert M. Pirsig suggests in *Zen and the Art of Motorcycle Maintenance*, to care for machines as if they were organs, manifestations of the Buddha consciousness?[28] Will machines soon be able to fulfill William Gibson's vision in *The Neuromancer*: evolve into subtle personalities capable of protecting against multinational corporate greed?[29]

These questions are speculative and probably unanswerable, raised in films and novels more likely to stoke imagination than activate reason. However, certain theorists of the past quarter century have provocatively struggled with these problems, opening promising vistas for further exploration. In *Mind and Nature*, Gregory Bateson considers the possibility that a mind need not be limited to organ or machine. Not a material brain or a mechanical system, a mind is *"an aggregate of interacting parts or components"* in which interactions are *"triggered by difference."* This mind is not one thing or another but the *power of relationship*, and therefore "not located in time or space."[30] The mummy is there in the tomb, but the difference between the tomb and the mummy is not. The difference is neither in the tomb nor in the mummy. If the embalmed corpse and the encrypted sarcophagus were both to disappear, then the difference would remain. Difference (and its polar opposite, identity) is the metapattern that connects all patterns. A metapattern is a mind. An ecosystem is a mind. A brain is a mind. A computer, also, is a mind. Bateson's model resists the temptation to reduce organ to machine or machine to organ. It suggests that organs and machines are functions of the same organizational systems, manifestations of one order.

David F. Channell in *The Vital Machine* explores similar confluences between mechanisms and organisms.[31] Channell focuses on ways that recent developments in "artificial intelligence, genetic engineering, and biomedical engineering" have overcome the old dualism between reductive mechanism and holistic organicism. The bionic world envisioned by practitioners in these sciences is a "vital machine," a rich interaction between mechanistic and organic processes. To view the world in this way is to face numerous epistemological and ethical questions, but it is also to challenge traditional values and to imagine fresh modes of being and seeing.

More recently, Richard Doyle in *On Beyond Living* explores how molecular biology has transformed nineteenth-century organic life to a DNA "code" or "program."[32] This conversion of mysterious holism to genetic map has created, Doyle argues, the "postvital body," an idea of living beings as interstices between organs and machines. This blurring of categories has led to rhetorical "slippages" in scientific writing: molecules are "read," "translated," and "deciphered" like artificial codes;

computers can "flock," "reproduce," and "die." In making these unconscious linguistic overlaps step out into the light, Doyle forces us to think
of how our so-called everyday speech hides bracing confluences between
the living and the artificial.

N. Katherine Hayles in *How We Became Posthuman* explores
Doyle's assumptions from a historical perspective, tracking how cybernetics over the past fifty years has altered the ways that we imagine self,
language, and nature.[33] For Hayles, the age of the "posthuman"—the
time of interpenetration between human and machine—has generated
entirely new categories of thought and perception. The cybernetic age
has been especially fecund in the literary realm, primarily in the works
of Bernard Wolfe and Philip K. Dick. Both of these writers have imagined startling modes of embodiment—ways of envisioning machines as
heightened bodies and bodies as gorgeous machines.[34] Though Hayles
is aware of the nightmares of cybernetics, she is also sensitive to how
fresh myths have emerged from posthuman speculation—myths that
might open onto salubrious relationships between fate and freedom,
self and other.

THE BORGESIAN ENGINEER

These books, like the novels and films mentioned above, take us back to
Kleist's puppets, and even further back to that third chapter of Genesis,
which pushes us even deeper in time, beyond time, to the anthropos, the
prevital body, neither organ nor machine but both at the same time. But
this is a dream unrealizable, this drive to Eden, for we remain torn
between blood and metal no matter how profoundly we think on the
glorious syntheses between these poles. But contemplate we must, even
if the thought is torture. We can only hope that the painful history of
androids will one day breed wisdom unattainable to those who rest on
one side of the world or the other, who side with clocks or crows. This
hope has driven this book, a troublous excursion through the psychology of embalming, the mental disturbances under golem making, the
neuroses of those who make automata. I end my study of android building with little faith that some holy android will reveal the marriage of
machine and organ. I remain skeptical that our secular mechanics are
capable of imagining redemptive robots. I am doubtful that contemporary malaise will flame into grace-starved melancholia. Still, perhaps
there is somewhere a brilliant engineer who broods over Borges. He
envisions in his equatorial dreams the wires running around the world.
He watches them metamorphose into crimson veins, dew-covered vines:
a network of jewels.

CONCLUSION

In a *New York Times Article* of 1991, Daniel Goleman reports on a rather bizarre psychological condition far more prevalent than researchers expected: the feeling that one is an automaton. Though most likely to trouble victims of trauma, this ailment impacts a surprisingly large segment of the general population in a number of ways: in fleeting doubts over whether one is machine or human, elusive suspicions that life is a dream, vague beliefs that existence is a movie. These experiences are generally benign and do not indicate psychological disorder. However, if these episodes occur frequently and start to inhibit one's ability to function normally, they may be symptoms of "dissociative disorder"—in 1991 a mental malady of growing prominence, the third most common psychiatric ailment after anxiety and depression.[1]

I cannot prove whether or not this feeling of unreality is related to the digital technological boom of the last twenty years or so, a period when the line between real and virtual has become increasingly blurred. However, I can say with certainty that I myself was suffering from this condition during those days when I obsessively viewed *Metropolis*, *The Mummy*, and *Blade Runner*. Often, I would fall into automaton fantasies, attracted to and repulsed by the idea that I was an android controlled by a power beyond my will. Likewise, I would frequently be unable to recall if images in my memory were based on empirical existence or some afternoon reverie. In the same way, I sometimes felt myself during important personal events float out of my body and watch the proceedings as if they were a film.

Perhaps these episodes were symptoms of a developing psychiatric disorder. Possibly they were the results of dwelling too much in celluloid worlds where androids usurp the human. Maybe I was simply becoming a victim of collective cultural neurosis born of overabundant simulacra mimicking only more simulacra. Regardless of the causes of this ailment, it largely left me as I drafted the first version of this book. I don't know that I would say I successfully self-administered Freud's talking cure, that the articulation of my fixation on machines released me from my cathexis. However, some therapy such as this was at work. I am now mostly free of fears that I am a machine. I rarely watch the films that once riveted me.

I am hesitant to call my autotherapy Freud's talking cure because I believe that another, more appropriate name for this healing technique comes from elsewhere: from Schiller's aesthetics. This term is *play*. As we saw earlier, to achieve Schiller's play, one must become acutely self-conscious of what otherwise would control one from behind the veils of the unconscious. The stuff drive is akin to Freud's id, the system of instincts that can secretly dictate the desires of the conscious ego. The form drive corresponds to Freud's superego, the collection of cultural beliefs surreptitiously organizing the ego's conscious ideas. As long as one remains unaware of these forces, one is determined by them, a machine. Only self-consciousness can liberate from these powers. When one becomes aware of these covert constraints, then one can put these two forces into dialogue, measure one against the other. One can warm abstraction with sensuality, and organize with cool ideas bodily flux.

More attuned than the positivistic Freud to the metaphysics of self-consciousness, Schiller with his idea of play offers a secular version of an old theological idea: *felix culpa*, the happy fall. In theological terms, this doctrine states that Adam's decline from Eden is ultimately good, for it set in motion the events leading to the advent of Christ and the revelation of God's mercy—related occurrences that can return the sinner to dispositional innocence, a garden within far happier than the lost one without. Schiller's work suggests that a similar sort of restoration can be achieved through self-consciousness, the ability to transcend the blinding limitations of selfish instinct and monomaniacal idea. Free to play with bodily energies and mental concepts, one nears the experienced innocence that the graced Christian on occasion might enjoy, that brief return to a paradise capacious enough to offer blithe participation in the whole and reflexive knowledge of this same unity. In this vision, self-consciousness becomes the result of the fall and its reversal, the faculty marking division and unity, the pain of loss and the joy of reunion.

This way to the garden, though I had long known it in my mind, came home to my whole being only after I had long contemplated, curiously, melancholy androids. Combining the unconscious movement of sublime puppets and the keen consciousness of lacerated creators, these androids inspired me to see my reflective powers for what they could possibly be: not merely signs of sadness but modes of release. Learning this, I came to view androids in fresh lights: not simply as gothic beings fostering perversities but as lithe creatures, exquisite and quick as silver eels, elegantly ironic as Byron. The android became comic as well as tragic, and, with it, I turned for the better, metamorphosing, remarkably, into one more human than before.

This is the weird hunch I have at the end of this work, a loose intimation far from obsession. A sort of redemption might inhere in freeing machines from purely gothic grids. This liberation would emancipate these creatures from the reductive demonizations through which they make their mechanical way into the unconscious, where they fester and deform and become monsters more hideous than any we could imagine. To bring these dark beings into the playful light of the mind, to examine alike their accursed qualities and sacred potentials—this would be a devotional exercise worthy of Loyola or Donne. Such an unearthing would force us to acknowledge seemingly inhuman beings, metallic Calibans, as our own. This archaeology of gothic rust would remind us of what we are: puppets of demiurge or evolution, doomed to pine for gardens where chance and law play in equal measure.

NOTES

INTRODUCTION

1. F. Lang, *Metropolis* 1927, produced by Erich Pommer, directed by Fritz Lang, 115 min, Universum Film A.G. (UFA), videocassette; K. Freund, *The Mummy* 1932, produced by Carl Laemmle, directed by Karl Freund, 74 min, Universal Pictures, videocassette; R. Scott, *Blade Runner* 1982, produced by Michael Deeley, directed by Ridley Scott, 112 min, Ladd Company, videocassette.

2. Karel Capek, *R. U. R. (Rossum's Universal Robots)* (Garden City: Doubleday, 1923).

3. Donna J. Haraway's *Simians, Cyborgs, and Women: The Reinvention of Nature* (New York: Routledge, 1991) explores the ways in which the artificial human might liberate oppressed groups into new visions of subjectivity. Claudia Springer's *Electronic Eros* (Austin: University of Texas Press, 1996) is a study of the ways in which men have feminized and eroticized machines in the postindustrial digital age.

4. Terry Castle, *The Female Thermometer: Eighteenth-Century Culture and the Invention of the Uncanny* (Oxford: Oxford Univ. Press, 1995).

5. Kathleen Raine, *Blake and Tradition*, 2 vols. (Princeton: Princeton Univ. Press, 1968); Jacques Lacarrière, *The Gnostics*, trans. Nina Rootes (New York: Dutton, 1977); Christoph Asendorf, *Batteries of Life: On the History of Things and their Perception in Modernity*, trans. Dan Reneau (Berkeley: Univ. of California Press, 1983); Barbara Maria Stafford, *Body Criticism: Imagining the Unseen in Enlightenment Art and Medicine* (Cambridge: MIT Press, 1991); Philip Kuberski, *The Persistence of Memory: Organism, Myth, Text* (Berkeley: Univ. of California Press, 1993).

6. Gaby Wood, *Edison's Eve: A Magical History of the Quest for Mechanical Life* (New York: Knopft, 2002); Victoria Nelson, *The Secret Life of Puppets* (Cambridge, MA and London: Harvard Univ. Press, 2002); Marina Warner, *The Inner Eye: Art Beyond the Visible* (London: South Bank Centre, 1996); J. P. Telotte, *Replications: A Robotic History of Science Fiction Film* (Urbana: University of Illinois Press, 1995).

CHAPTER 1. THE MELANCHOLY ANDROID

1. Heinrich von Kleist, "The Puppet Theatre," in *Selected Writings: Heinrich von Kleist*, ed. and trans. David Constantine (London: J. M. Dent, 1997), 413.

2. Ibid.

3. Ibid., 414.

4. Ibid.

5. Ibid., 416.

6. Frances Yates, *The Occult Philosophy in the Elizabethan Age* (London: Routledge, 1979), 61.

7. Quoted in Raymond Klibansky, Erwin Panofsky, and Fritz Saxl, *Saturn and Melancholy: Studies in the History of Natural Philosophy, Religion, and Art* (New York: Basic Books, 1964), 18.

8. Ibid., 15–16; Yates, *Occult*, 61–2.

9. Quoted in Klibansky, Panofsky, and Saxl, 16–17.

10. Marsilio Ficino, *The Book of Life*, trans. Charles Boer (Dallas: Spring Publications, 1980), 6–7.

11. Ibid., 8.

12. Ibid., 60–4, 66–9.

13. Frances A. Yates, *Giordano Bruno and the Hermetic Tradition* (Chicago: Univ. of Chicago Press, 1964), 12–14.

14. Ibid., *Giordano*, 398–403.

15. *Hermetica: The Ancient Greek and Latin Writings Which Contain Religious or Philosophic Teachings Ascribed to Hermes Trismegistus*, ed. and trans. Walter Scott (Boston: Shambhala, 1993), 15–21.

16. Ibid., 121–3.

17. Ibid., 125–7.

18. Ibid., 127–9.

19. Ibid., 337.

20. Ibid., 339–41.

21. Kathleen Raine in *Blake and Tradition* (Princeton: Bollingen Press of Princeton Univ. Press, 1968) offers a useful distinction between Neoplatonism and alchemy that helps clarify the difference I am drawing here between Gnosticism and alchemy. Though important differences exist between Neoplatonism and Gnosticism, as Plotinus himself pointed out, the basic antimaterialism of both constitutes an abiding similiarity. One can with justice substitute "Gnosticism" for "Neoplatonism" in the following passage from Raine: "The great difference between the Neoplatonic and the alchemical philosophies lies in their

opposed conceptions of the nature of matter. For Plotinus and his school, matter is mere mire, the dregs of the universe, a philosophic 'non-entity' because incapable of form except as it reflects intelligibles. To the alchemists spirit and matter, active and passive, light and darkness, above and below are, like the Chinese yin and yang, complementary principles, both alike rooted in the divine. The *deus absconditus* is hidden and operating in matter, no less than He is to be found in the spiritual order" (118).

22. Sigmund Freud, "Mourning and Melancholy," in *The Nature of Melancholy: From Aristotle to Kristeva*, ed. Jennifer Radden (Oxford: Oxford Univ. Press, 2000), 285.

23. Ibid., 283–9.

24. Here I am using "gnostic" (lowercase) in a slightly different sense than "Gnostic" (uppercase). "Gnostic" (uppercase) signifies any of the various antimaterialist, dualistic visionaries thriving in Alexandria and Rome in the second and third centuries. "Gnostic" (lowercase) points to a spiritual adept from any historical period who believes that soul and body can be reconciled, that matter can be redeemed through spirit. While "gnostics" and "Gnostics" are similar in kind—both maintain that the origin of the cosmos is not a harmonious One or an orderly Jehovah but an ungraspable abyss containing yet transcending all oppositions—they are different in degree—the ancient Gnostic tends to place the abyss beyond the material cosmos while the gnostic is prone to locate the abyss within the visible universe. In other words, while both Gnostic and gnostic believe that life originates in a transcendent yet immanent abyss, the latter generally yearns for the transcendent nature of the abyss while the former is content to embrace the abyss's immanent currents. The Gnostic is similar to the Neoplatonist (though Gnostic and Neoplatonist are different in important ways) in degrading matter for eternal spirit, while the gnostic corresponds to the hermetic alchemist in celebrating matter as the necessary opposite of spirit.

25. Martin Heidegger, *Being and Time*, trans. Joan Stambaugh (Albany: State Univ. of New York Press, 1996), 176–7. For another discussion of this interplay between familiar and unfamiliar in relation to the exploration of Being, see Heidegger's "What is Metaphysics?" in *Heidegger: Basic Writings*, ed. and intro. David Farrell Krell (New York: Harper and Row, 1977), 91–112. Of course, Heidegger's emphasis on generosity toward the strangeness of the particular thing is ironic in light of his ties to Nazism, a violently dictatorial system. Several recent books have explored Heidegger's complex, troubling relationship to the Nazis: Julian Young's *Heidegger, Philosophy, Nazism* (Cambridge: Cambridge Univ. Press, 1997); Tom Rockmore's *On Heidegger's Nazism and Philosophy* (Berkeley: Univ. of California Press, 1997); Hugo Ott's *Heidegger: A Political Life*, trans. Allan Blunden (New York: Basic Books, 1993); Hans Sluga's *Heidegger's Crisis: Philosophy and the Politics of Nazi Germany* (Cambridge, MA: Harvard Univ. Press, 1993); and Tom Rockmore's and Joseph Margolis's edited collection, *The Heidegger Case: On Philosophy and Politics* (Philadelphia: Temple Univ. Press, 1992).

26. Freud, "The Uncanny," in *Standard Edition of the Complete Psychological Works of Sigmund Freud*, ed. and trans. James Strachey, vol. 17 (London: Hogarth, 1959), 217–52.

27. I owe this important distinction to Professor Pranab Das of Elon University and the Templeton Foundation.

28. Plato, *Republic*, in *The Collected Dialogues of Plato, Including the Letters*, ed. Edith Hamilton and Huntington Cairns (Princeton: Bollingen Press of Princeton Univ. Press, 1961), 747–52 (lines 514a–520d).

CHAPTER 2. THE MUMMY

1. John Keats, "Ode on Melancholy," lines 11–21.

2. Wallace Stevens, "Sunday Morning," section 5, line 3.

3. Jeremy Naydler evokes this Egyptian interplay between life and death in *Temple of the Cosmos: The Ancient Egyptian Experience of the Sacred* (Rochester, VT: Inner Traditions, 1996), 3–8.

4. Keats, "Ode on a Grecian Urn," line 45.

5. See Stevens's poem "Anecdote of the Jar."

6. Through this paragraph, I follow two very important books on Egyptian symbology: R. T. Rundle Clark's *Myth and Symbol in Ancient Egypt* (London: Thames and Hudson, 1959), 40–42, 45–48, 90–96, and E. A. Wallis Budge's *The Gods of the Egyptians*, 2 vols. (New York: Dover, 1969), 1:293–321.

7. Budge, *Gods*, 1:299.

8. Rundle Clark, 90.

9. Ibid., 73.

10. Ibid., 73.

11. The definitive work on how divinities are psychological projections is Freud's *Moses and Monotheism* (1939). In this book, his last, Freud explores the psychology behind the Jewish projection of monotheism.

12. Rundle Clark thoroughly discusses the various incarnations of Osiris throughout the course of Egyptian history. He mainly focuses on the original myth surrounding the deity, later detailed by Plutarch; the later "universalization" of Osiris as a deity not only for kings but also for nobles and peasants; and the even later "esoteric" rituals associated with the god of the dead and the living (97–180).

13. See Plutarch's *Isis and Osiris* in vol. 5 of his *Moralia*, trans. Frank Cole Babbitt (Cambridge, MA.: Loeb Classical Library, 1936).

14. Rundle Clark, 97.

15. Ibid., 105.

16. Through this paragraph, I follow Rundle Clark's summary of Plutarch's account (103–9).

17. Rundle Clark, 97.

18. Ibid., 124–5.

19. Erich Neumann, *The Origins and History of Consciousness: The Psychological Stages in the Development of Personality*, 2 vols., foreword by C. G. Jung, trans. R. F. C. Hull (New York: Harper Torchbooks/Bollingen Library, 1954), 1: 220–1.

20. Ibid., 225–7.

21. Ibid., 226.

22. Ibid., 227.

23. Sigmund Freud, *Beyond the Pleasure Principle*, trans. and ed. James Strachey, intro. Gregory Zilboorg, bio. intro. Peter Gay (New York: Norton, 1961), 76.

24. Ibid., 14–15.

25. Ibid., 43.

26. Ibid.

27. Ibid., 63–4.

28. Ibid., 67.

29. Ibid.

30. Of course Freud differs from Jung (and, by association, Neumann) in general by assuming that the unconscious is entirely personal, a reservoir of repressed infantile desire, while Jung believes that the unconscious is not only personal but also collective, a realm of shared archetypal structure. More specifically, Freud in *Beyond the Pleasure Principle* counters Jung's "monistic" theory of libido with his dualistic one (64).

31. The Egyptian art of mummification was practiced at least as early as the Fourth Dynasty of the Old Kingdom (c. 2600 BC), when Queen Hetepheres, the first known mummy, was preserved. However, the craft reached its peak during the days of the Twenty-First Dynasty of the New Kingdom (c. 1085), when most anyone who could afford the embalmer could hope to turn into Osiris (James Hamilton-Preston and Carol Andrews, *Mummies: Death and Life in Ancient Egypt* [New York: Viking, 1979], 35–6). While the *Pyramid Texts* (c. 2500 BC) of the Old Kingdom were devoted primarily to the funeral rites of kings, the two most important Egyptian papyri of the Middle Kingdom and New Kingdom reveal, as I. P. Couliano claims in *Out of this World: Otherworldly Journeys from Gilgamesh to Albert Einstein* (Boston: Shambhala, 1991), 60–70, a growing democratic spirit: the Coffin Texts (c. 2000 BC) discuss ceremonies for departed aristocrats, and the Book of the Dead (1500 BC) describes funeral practices for everyone. What these books have in common, of course, is a desire

to continue living a material existence after the body has lost organic vitality. This yearning cuts to the heart of the vexed psychology of mummification: a longing for life that requires death, a fixation on death in the service of life. As these texts show, this sad state, more implied than announced, is frequently projected onto the mummy in the tomb.

32. Budge, introduction to *The Egyptian Book of the Dead: (The Papyrus of Ani) Egyptian Text Transliteration and Translation*, E. A. Wallis Budge (New York: Dover, 1967), lviii. On one of the linen wrappings of the mummy of the pharaoh Thothmes III (c. 1504–1450 BC), one finds this chapter from the Book of the Dead, a justification for mummification: "Hail to thee, O my father Osiris, I have come and I have embalmed my flesh so that my body may not decay. . . . Come then, O form, and give breath unto me, O lord of breath, O thou who art greater than my compeers. . . . Homage to thee, O my father Osiris, thy flesh suffered no decay, there were no worms in thee, though didst not crumble away, thou didst not wither away, thou didst not become corruption and worms" (Quoted in Budge, introduction to *The Egyptian Book of the Dead*, lix).

33. Budge, introduction to *The Egyptian Book of the Dead*, lix–lx.

34. Though Philip Kuberski's *Endless Origin* is not yet published, one can read an excerpt from this wonderful book in *The Georgia Review* 44, no. 3 (Fall 2000): 431–41. The excerpt is called "Dark Matter: Thinking About Nothing."

35. Excellent accounts of the process of mummification can be found in a number of books. Among them are Hamilton-Paterson and Andrews's *Mummies*, 39–58; Ange-Pierre Leca's *The Egyptian Way of Death: Mummies and the Cult of the Immortal*, trans. Louise Asmal (Garden City, NY: Doubleday, 1981), 143–74; and Salima Ikram and Aidan Dodson's *The Mummy in Ancient Egypt: Equipping the Dead for Eternity* (London: Thames and Hudson, 1998), 103–36. Almost all modern accounts of the process of mummification are based on the invaluable eyewitness accounts of Herodotus in his *History* (440 BC) and Diodorus Siculus in his own *History* (c. 50 BC).

36. Naydler, 185–6, 201–3; see also Budge, introduction to *The Egyptian Book of the Dead*, lxii–lxiv. I should note here that Budge in his excellent introduction to the Egyptian Book of the Dead lists seven different kinds of soul that can be found mentioned in ancient Egyptian materials. In addition to the three primary souls most commonly invoked—the *ka*, the *ba*, and the *akh*—there are also the *ab*, or heart; the *khaibit*, or shadow; the *sekhem*, or power; and the *ren*, or name. Norman Mailer in *Ancient Evenings* (1983) and William Burroughs in *Western Lands* (1987) both obviously studied in Budge's edition of *The Egyptian Book of the Dead*, creatively describe all seven. Most recent Egyptologists focus on the three most important and pervasive spiritual powers, the ka, the ba, the akh. I follow this trend and thus ignore the other four souls.

37. Budge, introduction to *The Egyptian Book of the Dead*, lxiv.

38. Naydler, 202–4.

39. Ibid., 207–212.

40. Budge, introduction to *The Egyptian Book of the Dead*, lxx–lxxxi.

41. *Brihadaranyaka Upanishad*, First Adhyaya, Fourth Brahmana, 1–11.

42. Genesis, 3:1–20.

43. Heather Pringle, *The Mummy Congress: Science, Obsession, and the Everlasting Dead* (New York: Hyperion, 2001), 194–8. I am indebted for this and other sources on the cultural history of mummies to Eric M. Heideman's article "They Went for a Little Walk: The Mummy in Fact, Folklore, Fiction, and Film, Part 2," found in the on-line publication MonsterZine.com, issue 10 (http://www.monsterzine.com/200301/mummy.php#mz010–02).

44. Philip Kuberski, *The Persistence of Memory: Organism, Myth, Text* (Berkeley: University of California Press, 1992), 20.

45. Pringle, 171–85, 204–11.

46. Ibid., 205–7.

47. John T. Irwin, *American Hieroglyphics: The Symbol of the Egyptian Hieroglyphics in the American Renaissance* (Baltimore: Johns Hopkins University Press, 1983), 4–5, 21.

48. Pringle, 171–211; Irwin.

49. Mary Shelley, *Frankenstein; or, The Modern Prometheus*, ed. Maurice Hindle (New York: Penguin, 1985), chapter 5.

50. Both Pringle (181–2) and Irwin (57–8) point out that in this tale Poe is specifically making fun of George Gliddon, a very popular lecturer in Egyptology. Poe actually features an Egyptologist named Gliddon in his story.

51. Edgar Allan Poe, "Some Words with a Mummy," in *Complete Works of Edgar Allan Poe*, vol. 5, ed. James A. Harrison (New York: Fred De Fau & Co., 1902), 116.

52. Ibid., 118–20.

53. Ibid., 123–5.

54. Ibid., 127–31.

55. Ibid., 133–6.

56. Ibid., 137–8.

57. James Joyce, *Portrait of the Artist as a Young Man* (New York: Everyman's Library, 1964), 256–7.

58. Ibid., 256.

59. Ibid., 266–8.

60. Henri Bergson, *Laughter: An Essay on the Meaning of the Comic*, trans. Cloudsley Brereton (New York: Macmillan, 1911), 29.

61. Bergson, 4.

62. Poe, "Ligeia," in *The Fall of the House of Usher and Other Writings*, ed. David Galloway (New York: Penguin, 1986), 110.

63. Ibid., 113–14.

64. Ibid., 118–20.

65. Ibid., 122–6.

66. An excellent catalogue of mummy films can be found in Susan D. Crowie and Tom Johnson, *The Mummy in Fact, Fiction, and Film*, fore. George Hart (Jefferson, NC: McFarland, 2002), 57–140.

67. Keats, "Ode on a Grecian Urn," lines 44–5.

CHAPTER 3. THE GOLEM

1. Ioan P. Couliano, *Out of this World*, in *Out of this World: Otherworldly Journeys from Gilgamesh to Albert Einstein* (Boston: Shambhala, 1991), 61.

2. Ann Macy Roth, "The Peseshkef and the 'Opening of the Mouth' Ceremony: A Ritual of Birth and Rebirth," *Journal of Egyptian Archaeology* 78 (1992): 113–47.

3. Couliano, 61–2.

4. John T. Irwin, *American Hieroglyphics: The Symbols of the Egyptian Hieroglyphics in the American Renaissance* (New Haven: Yale Univ. Press, 1980), 145–9.

5. John Cohen, *Human Robots in Myth and Science* (London: Allen and Unwin, 1966), 17.

6. Carl H. Kraeling, *Anthropos and Son of Man: A Study in the Religious Syncretism of the Hellenistic Orient* (New York: AMS Press, 1966), 38–53.

7. Kurt Rudolph, *Gnosis: The Nature and History of Gnosticism*, trans. R. Mc. Wilson (San Francisco: Harper and Row, 1984), 91.

8. Jean Dorresse, *The Secret Books of the Egyptian Gnostics: An Introduction to the Gnostic Coptic Manuscripts Discovered at Chenoboskion*, trans. Philip Mairet (London: Hollis and Carter, 1960), 81–6.

9. *Secret Book According to John*, in *The Gnostic Scriptures: A New Translation with Annotations and Introductions*, ed. and trans. Bentley Layton (Garden City, NY: Doubleday, 1987), 23–51.

10. Rudolph, 338–9.

11. Hans Jonas, *The Gnostic Religion*, 3rd ed. (Boston: Beacon Press, 2001), 66–7.

12. For a list of studies of Heidegger's connections with the Nazis, see the introduction, note # 25.

13. Martin Heidegger, *Being and Time*, trans. John Macquerie and Edward Robinson (New York: Harper and Row, 1962), 82.

14. Ibid., 164.

15. Ibid., 165.

16. Ibid., 177–8.

17. Ibid., 230–2.

18. Ibid., 370–5.

19. Heidegger, What Is Metaphysics?," in *Basic Writings*, ed. David Ferrell Krell (New York: Harper and Row, 1977), 105, 108.

20. Carl Gustav Jung, *Aion*, in *The Collected Works of C. G. Jung*, ed. William McGuire and R. F. C. Hull, 2nd ed., vol. 9, part 1 (Princeton, NJ: Bollingen Press of Princeton Univ. Press, 1979), 197–8.

21. Jung, *Mysterium Coniunctionis*, in *Collected Works*, 2nd ed., vol. 14, 300–1.

22. *Aesclepius*, in *Hermetica: The Ancient Greek and Latin Writings Which Contain Religious or Philosophic Teachings Ascribed to Hermes Trismegistus*, intro., texts, and trans. Walter Scott (Boston: Shambhala, 1993), 359.

23. Jung, and Aniela Jaffe, *Memories, Dreams, Reflections* (New York: Vintage Books, 1989), 203–6.

24. Jung, "Paracelsus as Spiritual Phenomenon," *Alchemical Studies*, trans. R. F. C. Hull, in *Collected Works*, vol. 13, 130–1.

25. Paracelsus, *Selected Writings*, ed. Jolande Jacobi, trans. Norbert Guterman (Princeton: Bollingen Press of Princeton Univ. Press, 1988), 141–3.

26. I should note that this is Jung's interpretation of alchemy. He believes that the alchemical work was in the end more psychological than physical. Others, however, would disagree, holding that the physical part of the opus was just as important as the spiritual. For versions of this later view, see Julius Evola, *The Hermetic Tradition: Symbols and Teachings of the Royal Art*, trans. E. E. Rehmus (Rochester, VT: Inner Traditions, 1995) and Titus Burckhardt, *Alchemy: Science of the Cosmos, Science of the Soul*, trans. William Stoddart (London: Stuart and Watkins, 1967).

27. Paracelsus, *Selected Writings*, 143–4.

28. Paracelsus, "Concerning the Nature of Things," in *The Hermetic and Alchemical Writings of Paracelsus*, ed. and intro. Arthur E. Waite, 2 vols. (Chicago: Laurence, Scott, and Co., 1910), 1:124.

29. Paracelsus, "Concerning the Nature of Things," 1:125.

30. Paracelsus, *Selected Writings*, 143.

31. Ibid., 143–4.

32. Paracelsus, "A Book Concerning Life," *The Hermetic and Alchemical Writings*, 2:121.

33. Yeats in his poem "Crazy Jane Talks with the Bishop" features these lines: "'Fair and foul are near of kin, / And fair needs foul,' I cried. . . . For nothing can be sole or whole / That has not been rent" (lines 7–8, 17–18).

34. Jung, *Psychology and Alchemy*, in *Collected Works*, 12:126–7, 219–21.

35. Jung, *Mysterium Coniunctionis*, paragraphs 229, 319–20.

36. Jung, *Psychology and Alchemy*, paragraphs 219–21; *Mysterium Coniunctionis*, paragraphs 129–32, 158–9, 144–5; *Alchemical Studies*, in *The Collected Works*, 13: par. 263.

37. Jung, *Mysterium Coniunctionis*, pars. 158–9, 172–3.

38. Jung, *Psychology and Alchemy*, pars. 271–2, 325, 334–5; *Mysterium Coniunctionis*, pars. 498–500; 504–5, 642.

39. Jung, *Mysterium Coniunctionis*, pars. 498–500, 504–5.

40. Jung, *Alchemical Studies*, pars. 282–303.

41. Friedrich Schiller, *Letters on the Aesthetic Education of Man*, trans. and intro. Reginald Snell (New York: Frederick Ungar, 1965), 64–78.

42. Ibid., 74.

43. Ibid., 76.

44. Ibid., 80.

45. There are exceptions of course, like the film *The Homunculus*, directed by Otto Rippert, released in 1916. In this picture, a homunculus grows to full size and comes to believe that he is a real man. However, when he discovers that he was created artificially, he uses his superhuman intelligence and strength to become a cruel dictator of the world. He is killed only when struck by lightning. Obviously, this figure resembles the golem more closely than the homunculus.

46. Goethe, *Faust Part One & Part Two*, trans. and intro. Charles E. Passage (New York: Bobbs-Merrill, 1965), 1:1112–7.

47. Goethe, *Faust*, 1:762–84.

48. Goethe, *Faust*, 2:6277.

49. Goethe, *Faust*, 2:6453–543.

50. Goethe, *Faust*, 2:6879–84.

51. Goethe, *Faust*, 2:6903–20.

52. Goethe, *Faust*, 2:6924–7000.

53. Goethe, *Faust*, 2:11612–2111.

54. Gershom Scholem, *On the Kabbalah and Its Symbolism*, trans. Ralph Manheim (New York: Schocken, 1996), 197–8; Moshe Idel, "The Golem in Jewish Magic and Mysticism," in *Golem! Danger, Deliverance and Art* (New York: The Jewish Museum, 1988), 30.

55. Scholem, 110.

56. Scholem, *Major Trends in Jewish Mysticism*, foreword Robert Alter (New York: Schoken, 1995), 208–17.

57. Ibid., 215–7.

58. Ibid., 230–5.

59. Ibid., 233–5.

60. Ibid., 162.

61. Ibid., 176–82.

62. Ibid., 175.

63. Ibid., 190. In his 1915 novel *The Golem*, ed. and intro. E. F. Bleiler (New York: Dover, 1976), Gustav Meyrink explores the golem of ecstatic magic. Though Meyrink is not entirely true to the Jewish traditions of the golem, he nonetheless captures the spirit of this creature in exploring its relationship to his protagonist, Athanasius Pernath, a cutter of fine jewels living in the Jewish ghetto of Prague in the early twentieth century. Because shock treatment has wiped out his memory, Pernath is trapped in a sordid present but haunted by dim recollections of a happier life. A modern day Adam, he has been ripped from an Eden that he can now barely remember. He begins to have visions of a golem that stalks the streets of Prague every thirty-three years, apparently committing horrendous crimes. This is none other than the legendary creature of Rabbi Loew. Periodically coming to life and troubling the ghetto dwellers, this being figures several currents of meaning: it is the microcosm of the ghetto's architecture, one with the enigmatic buildings that seem almost alive and sinister; it is the paradoxical population of the ghetto, comprised of mystical saints and murderous rogues; it is the spiritual potential of all men, inseparable from the anthropos. Embodying these levels—the material, the conflict between matter and spirit, and the spiritual—the golem gathers and transcends the three stages of the alchemical work: nigredo, albebo, rubedo. He doubles and inspires the spiritual quest of Pernath, who struggles through the chaos of the ghetto in hopes of reconciling the oppositions that tear his soul. In the end, he realizes the golem within, achieving a balance between past and present, matter and spirit. This union is figured by his union with a young woman who dreams of producing a hermaphrodite, symbol for the philosopher's stone.

64. According to Moshe Idel in *Golem: Jewish Magical and Mystical Traditions on the Artificial Anthropoid* (Albany: State Univ. of New York Press, 1990), Johann Reuchlin in *De Arte Cabalistica* (1517) was the first to mention the golem as a being created as a servant (177–9). As Idel points out elsewhere, the "blueprint" for the Loew legend is actually Rabbi Elijah of Chem. A Polish Kabbalist writing between 1630 and 1650 reports that Elijah fashioned a golem two generations before Loew. Elijah apparently "made a creature out of matter [*golem*] and form [*zurah*] and it was performing hard work for him, for a long period, and the name of truth [*'emet*] was hanging upon his neck, until he took, finally, for a certain reason, the name from his neck and it turned to dust (*Golem*, 31).

65. Elie Wiesel, *The Golem: The Story of a Legend*, illus. Mark Podwal, trans. Anne Borchardt (New York: Summit, 1983), 32.

66. Ibid., 94–6.

67. A selection of twentieth century versions of the golem legend quickly shows how the thoroughly gothic golem has won out. In Paul Wegener's 1920 silent film, *The Golem* (his third film to explore the artificial man), the golem fashioned by Rabbi Loew to protect the Jews from expulsion from Prague becomes violent at the behest of a woman he loves and is thwarted from his destructive designs only when a child removes the magical Star of David from his chest. In Jorge Luis Borges's poem of 1958, "The Golem," Loew's creature awakes to find himself trapped, like fallen humans, in "this noisy web / of Before, After, Yesterday, While, Now, / Right, Left, Me, You, Those, Us" and goes on to live a sad, abnormal existence that makes the rabbi wonder why he decided to "add to the infinite / series one more symbol," to "give another cause, another effect and another sorrow?" In books by Elie Wiesel (cited above) and Isaac Bashevis Singer, both entitled *The Golem* and published in the 1980s, Loew's creature is ambiguously rendered as a noble helper of the persecuted Jews and a violent force dangerous to Jew and Gentile alike, a protector and an enemy (Singer, *The Golem*, illustrated Uri Shulevitz [New York: Farrar, Straus, and Giroux, 1996]). In a slew of very recent novels, by such writers as Thane Rosenbaum, Michael Chabon, Nomi Eve, Cynthia Ozick, and Frances Sherwood, the unsettling elements of the golem are explored in a number of contexts: pain over the Holocaust, desire to escape the pain of this Jewish tragedy; disillusionment over the limitations of matter; frustration over lusts of matter; pathos and pain of Loew.

68. Scholem, *On the Kabbalah*, 158–9.

69. Ludwig Achim von Arnim. *Novellas of 1818: Isabella of Egypt; Meluck Maria Blainville; The Three Loving Sisters and the Lucky Dyer; Angelika the Genoese*, trans. Bruce Duncan (New York: Edwin Mellen, 1997).; E. T. A. Hoffmann, *Die Geheimnisse*, in *E. T. A. Hoffmann Sämtliche Werke*, vol. 5 (Frankfurt: Deutschen Klassiker, 1992), 509–568.

70. Mary Shelley, *Frankenstein*, ed. Maurice Hindle (New York: Penguin, 1985), 52–3.

CHAPTER 4. THE AUTOMATON

1. Gaby Wood, *Edison's Eve: A Magical History of the Quest for Mechanical Life* (New York: Knopf, 2002), 3–4.

2. Ibid., 4.

3. René Descartes, *Discourse on Method of Rightly Conducting the Reason and Seeking for Truth in the Sciences*, in *The Philosophical Works of Descartes*, trans. Elizabeth Haldane and G. R. T. Ross (New York: Dover, 1955), 1:85, 92, 101. Throughout this discussion of Descartes, I draw from David F. Channell's excellent discussion of Descartes in *The Vital Machine: A Study of Technology and Organic Life* (New York and Oxford: Oxford Univ. Press, 1991), 16–17, 34–5.

4. Descartes, *Principles of Philosophy*, in *The Philosophical Works of Descartes*, 1:255–6.

5. As was the case in my discussion of Descartes, throughout the ensuing account of mechanistic theories I largely follow Channell, 19–41.

6. Pierre Gassendi, *Philosophical Treatise*, in *Selected Works of Pierre Gassendi*, ed. and trans. Craig B. Bush (New York: Johnson Reprint, 1972), 383–425.

7. Thomas Hobbes, *Elements of Philosophy Concerning Body*, in *Body, Man, and Citizen*, ed. R. S. Peters (New York: Collier, 1962), 115–96.

8. Robert Boyle, *Works of the Honourable Robert Boyle, in Six Volumes, to which Is Prefixed the Life of the Author*, 6 vols. (London: printed for J. and F. Rivington, L. Davis, W. Johnston, S. Crowder, and T. Payne, 1772), 5:163. This excerpt is quoted in Edward A. Burtt, *The Metaphysical Foundations of Modern Physical Science* (New York: Doubleday, 1954), 196.

9. Isaac Newton, *Opticks*, in *Newton: A Norton Critical Edition*, selected and ed. I. Bernard Cohen and Richard S. Westfall (New York: Norton, 1995), 51–5.

10. Descartes, *A Discourse on Method, Meditations on the First Philosophy, Principles of Philosophy*, trans. John Veitch, intro. Tom Sorrell (London: Dent, 1994), 52.

11. René Descartes, *Treatise of Man*, trans. and commentary Thomas Steele Hall (Cambridge, MA: Harvard Univ. Press, 1972), 4.

12. Channell, 37–40.

13. Herman Boerhaave, *Dr. Boerhaave's Academical Lectures on the Theory of Physics, Being a Genuine Translation of his Institutes and Explanatory Comments, as They Were Dictated to His Students at the University of Leyden*, trans. anon. (London, 1742–7), 1:85. This is quoted in Thomas S. Hall's excellent work of history, *Ideas of Life and Matter: Studies in the History of General Physiology, 600 B.C.–1900 A.D.*, vol. 1, *From Pre-Socratic Times to the Enlightenment* (London: Chicago Univ. Press, 1969), 370.

14. Julien Offray de la Mettrie, *Machine Man and Other Writings*, trans. and ed. Ann Thomson (New York: Cambridge Univ. Press, 1996).

15. Channell, 41.

16. Jessica Riskin in her recent article "Eigtheenth-Century Wetwares," in *Representations* 83 (Summer 2003), explores these questions in enlightening ways. For a study of these questions in contemporary contexts, see Richard Doyle, *Wetwares: Experiments in Postvital Living* (Minneapolis: Univ. of Minnesota Press, 2003).

17. John Cohen, *Human Robots in Myth and Science* (New York: A. S. Barnes, 1967), 81.

18. John Evelyn, *The Diary of John Evelyn*, ed. E. S. De Beer, 6 vols. (Oxford: Clarendon Press of Oxford Univ. Press, 2000), 2:111.

19. The same holds true of the other famous automata of the age: an automatic lion made by Leonardo da Vinci, a lute player crafted by Gianello della Tour, hydraulic birds created by Isaac and Saloman de Caus, and a miniature army fashioned by Christiaan Huygens.

20. Wood, 17–18.

21. Ibid., 18–19.

22. Ibid., 19.

23. Ibid., 11–12.

24. Ibid., 20–2.

25. Ibid., 24–5.

26. Sigmund Freud, *Beyond the Pleasure Principle*, trans. and ed. James Strachey, intro. Gregory Zilboorg, bio. intro. Peter Gay (New York: Norton, 1961), 13–17.

27. Claudia Springer, *Electronic Eros: Bodies and Desire in the Postindustrial Age* (Austin: University of Texas Press, 1996), 3–16, 80–95.

28. Albert Camus, *The Myth of Sisyphus and Other Essays*, trans. Justin O'Brien (New York: Vintage, 1991).

29. Friedrich Schlegel, *Philosophical Fragments*, trans. Peter Firchow, foreword Rodolphe Gasché (Minneapolis: University of Minnesota Press, 1991).

30. Clemens Brentano, *Godwi, Clemens Brentano Werke*, vol. 2 (Munich: Carl Hanser, 1963); Ludwig Tieck, *Der Runenberg*, in *Schriften* (Berlin: G. Keimer, 1828), 4:214–89; Joseph von Eichendorff, *Das Marmorbild*, in *Joseph von Eichendorff Werke* (Munich: Winkler, 1970), 2:526–564; Achim von Arnim, *Raphael und Seine Nachbarinnen*, in *Achim von Arnim: Sämtliche Romane un Erzählungen* (Munich: Carl Hanser, 1965), 3:225–276; William Blake, *Jerusalem*, in *The Complete Poetry and Prose of William Blake*, ed. David V. Erdman, commentary Harold Bloom (New York: Doubleday, 1988), 144–258; Edgar Allan Poe, "The Man that was Used Up," in *The Fall of the House of Usher and Other Writings*, ed. and intro. David Galloway (New York: Penguin, 1986), 127–37.

31. E. T. A. Hoffmann, "The Sandman," in *Tales of Hoffmann*, intro. and trans. R. J. Hollingdale (New York: Penguin, 1982), 85.

32. Ibid., 85.

33. Ibid., 88–92.

34. Freud, "The Uncanny," in *Standard Edition*, 17:220–5.

35. Hoffmann, "The Sandman," 106.

36. Ibid., 111.

37. Ibid., 114–15.

38. Ibid., 117.

39. Ibid., 119–20.

40. Ibid., 121–2.

41. Ibid., 123–5.

42. A striking example of this motif from the world of popular fiction is Villiers de L'Isle-Adam's 1886 novel, *Tomorrow's Eve*, in which Ewald, like Nathaniel, pines for a perfect woman seemingly unattainable in the organic world. Suicidal, he seeks the help of Edison, an inventor. Edison reveals to Ewald his greatest creation, an ideal female, a mechanical Eve. The automaton, named Hadaly (Persian, apparently, for ideal) wears a black veil and gown. She is apparently in mourning. Edison tells Ewald that he can transform Halady into any female form, but this form can only stay alive if it is loved. Ewald asks the scientist to turn the machine into a woman with whom he is faintly in love, Alicia Cary, gorgeous but vulgar. Once this metamorphosis has occurred, Ewald animates his new toy with his affection. He decides to take his mechanical beloved home to England. He places her in a coffin for the voyage. The ship sinks, and Alicia with it. Ewald falls into suicidal sadness, and for the rest of his days mourns the loss of his android (*Tomorrow's Eve*, trans. Robert Martin Adams [Urbana: Univ. of Illinois Press, 2001]).

43. E. T. A. Hoffmann, "Automata," in *The Best Tales of Hoffmann*, ed. and intro. E. F. Bleiler (New York: Dover, 1967), 71.

44. Ibid., 75–6.

45. Ibid., 80–2.

46. Ibid., 86–7.

47. Ibid., 88–9, 95–9.

48. Ibid., 92.

49. Ibid., 99–100.

50. Ibid., 100–02.

51. Ibid., 102–3.

52. S. Seidelman, *Making Mr. Right* 1987, produced by Dan Enright, directed by Susan Seidelman, 99 minutes, Orion Pictures, videocassette.

53. This Pygmalion motif, of course, isn't the only mode for representing the relationship between the automaton and melancholia. In the modern cinema especially, two other motifs have been prevalent: the Frankenstein motif, in which machines rebel against their creators, and the Pinocchio motif, in which machines strive to be human. Witnessing the former theme in films such as *The Matrix* (1999), *The Terminator* (1984), *West World* (1973), and *Creation of the Humanoids* (1962), audiences can live out their fears of mechanisms taking over the world while at the same time enjoying a happy ending in which humans once again assert their superiority over their tools. Yet, this wish fulfillment probably does not account entirely for the fascination exerted by these films. Very likely audiences secretly love watching the clockwork precision of the exquisite machines, the conclusive indifference with which they destroy, the untroubled

conscience, beyond good and evil. Possibly, these killing machines recall a kind of innocence in which one feels no gap between desire and action. This tension between hatred and love explains the sadness most everyone feels upon watching the slick machine go down to its death. The latter theme—the Pinocchio motif—reinforces the human hope that conscious organicity is the highest state, that even machines would become, if they could, thinking men and women. Exemplified in such films as *A. I.* (2001) and *Blade Runner* (1982), this idea rests on the assumption that, on the one hand, androids are inferior to humans, and, on the other hand, androids are capable of becoming even more human than ordinary men and women. In craving organicity, the android shows a more profound appreciation of life—of suffering and joy, of love and rancor—than the regular humans around him. He becomes an anthropos in reverse: a being who transcends good and evil, fear and desire, not by returning to Eden but by embracing, with a full heart, the glorious turbulence of the fallen world. At the same time that he marks our loathing of machines and our loving of organs, he also points to our sad sense that machines, even though dead, have more life than we do.

CHAPTER 5. THE SADNESS OF THE SOMNAMBULIST

1. R. Weine, *The Cabinet of Dr. Caligari* 1920, produced by Rudolf Meinert and Erich Pommer, directed by Robert Weine, 82 minutes, Decla-Bioscop AG, videocassette.

2. Sir Edmund Whittaker, *A History of the Theories of Aether and Electricity*, vol. 1, *The Classical Theories* (New York: Harper and Brothers, 1951), 42–53.

3. For a thorough discussion of this movement, see Ernst Benz, *Theology of Electricity: On the Encounter and Explanation of Theology and Science in the 17th and 18th Centuries*, trans. Wolfgang Taraba, intro. Dennis Stillings (Allison Park, PA: Pickwick Publications, 1989).

4. See Marcello Pera, *The Ambiguous Frog: The Galvani-Volta Controversy on Animal Electricity*, trans. Jonathan Mandelbaum (Princeton, NJ: Princeton Univ. Press, 1992).

5. Whittaker, 50–5, 56–7, 57–9.

6. Sir Humphry Davy, *The Collected Works of Sir Humphry Davy*, ed. John Davy, 6 vols. (London: Smith, 1839–40), 4:39–40; Whittaker, 74–6.

7. Whittaker, 81–6.

8. Michael Faraday, *Experimental Researches in Electricity*, *Great Books of the Western World*, ed. Robert Maynard Hutchins et al. (Chicago: Encyclopedia Britannica, 1952), 45: par. 27; Whittakker, 170–97.

9. Maria M. Tatar, *Spellbound: Studies on Mesmerism and Literature* (Princeton, NJ: Princeton Univ. Press, 1978), 6–16.

10. Ibid., 21.

11. Ibid., 27–8.

12. Ibid., 76–7.

13. Benjamin Reiss, "The Springfield Somnambulist: Or, The End of the Enlightenment in America," *Commonplace* 4, no. 2 (January 2004).

14. Other American Romantic writers are likewise attuned to the potential horrors of relinquishing the will. Charles Brockden Brown in *Edgar Huntly* (1799) depicts the travails of a man whose chronic sleepwalking may have resulted in murder. Caught between unconsciousness and consciousness, this somnambulist does not know who he is and what he has done. He finds himself in a horrible situation: he is a machine with a conscience. Close to Brown, Poe in tales such as "Mesmeric Revelation" (1844) and "The Facts in the Case of M. Valdemar" (1845) explores the interstice between life and death, possession and inspiration. In a similar vein, Hawthorne in *The House of the Seven Gables* (1851) warns of the dangers of mesmerism, a practice that could rob moral agency and reduce a person to a puppet.

15. Sigmund Freud and Joseph Breuer, "Studies in Hysteria," in *Standard Edition*, 2:1–113.

16. Daniel Dennett, *Darwin's Dangerous Idea: Evolution and the Meanings of Life* (New York: Touchstone Books, 1996).

17. Stephen Jay Gould, The Structure of Evolutionary Theory (Cambridge, MA: Harvard University Press, 2002), 1006–21.

18. For Skinner's basic behavioralist views, see *Walden Two* (London: Macmillan, 1969).

19. Rogers's humanistic psychotherapy is detailed fully in his *Client-Centered Therapy: Its Current Practice, Implications, and Theory* (Boston: Houghton Mifflin, 1961).

20. Dennett, *Consciousness Explained* (Boston: Little, Brown, and Co., 1991).

21. John R. Searle, *The Mystery of Consciousness* (New York: New York Review of Books, 1997).

22. Representatives of new historicism include Stephen Greenblatt, *Renaissance Self-Fashioning: From More to Shakespeare* (Chicago: Univ. of Chicago Press, 1991) and Jerome McGann, *The Romantic Ideology: A Critical Investigation* (Chicago: Univ. of Chicago Press, 1983). Exemplars of the aesthetic mode are Harold Bloom, *The Western Canon: Books and Schools of the Age* (Boston: Harcourt, 1994) and John M. Ellis, *Literature Lost: Social Agendas and the Corruption of the Humanities* (New Haven, CT: Yale Univ. Press, 1997).

23. K. Eric Drexler, *Engines of Creation: The Coming Era of Nanotechnology*, foreword Marvin Minsky (New York: Anchor Doubleday, 1986).

24. Hans Moravec, *Robot: Mere Machine to Transcendent Mind* (New York: Oxford University Press, 1999).

25. Ray Kurzweil, *The Age of Spiritual Machines: When Computers Exceed Human Intelligence* (New York: Viking, 1999).

26. Jacques Ellul, *The Technological Society*, trans. John Wilkinson, intro. Robert K. Morton (New York: Vintage, 1964); Herbert Marcuse, *One-Dimensional Man: Studies in the Ideology of Advanced Industrial Society* (Boston: Beacon, 1966); Bill Joy, "Why the Future Doesn't Need Us," in *Taking the Red Pill: Science, Philosophy, and Religion in The Matrix*, ed. Glenn Yeffeth, intro. David Gerrold (Dallas, TX: BenBella Books, 2003).

27. Thomas Pynchon, *Gravity's Rainbow* (New York: Penguin, 1973).

28. Robert M. Pirsig, *Zen and the Art of Motorcycle Maintenance* (New York: Bantam, 1975).

29. William Gibson, *The Neuromancer* (New York: Ace, 1984).

30. Gregory Bateson, *Mind and Nature: A Necessary Unity* (New York: Bantam, 1979), 101–11.

31. David F. Channell, *The Vital Machine: A Study of Technology and Organic Life* (Oxford and New York: Oxford Univ. Press, 1991).

32. Richard Doyle, *On Beyond Living: Rhetorical Transformations of the Life Sciences* (Stanford, CA: Stanford Univ. Press, 1997).

33. Katherine Hayles, *How We Became Posthuman: Vital Bodies in Cybernetics, Literature, and Informatics* (Chicago: Univ. of Chicago Press, 1999).

34. See, for instance, Philip K. Dick, *Do Androids Dream of Electric Sheep?* (New York: Del Ray, 1966), and Bernard Wolfe, *Limbo* (New York: Random House, 1952).

CONCLUSION

1. Daniel Goleman, "Feeling Unreal? Many Others Feel the Same," *New York Times* Jan. 8, 1991, C1, C8.

BIBLIOGRAPHY

Aesclepius. Hermetica: The Ancient Greek and Latin Writings Which Contain Religious or Philosophic Teachings Ascribed to Hermes Trismegistus. Introduction and translated by Walter Scott. Boston: Shambhala, 1993.

Arnim, Ludwig Achim von. *Novellas of 1818: Isabella of Egypt; Meluck Maria Blainville; The Three Loving Sisters and the Lucky Dyer; Angelika the Genoese.* Translated by Bruce Duncan. New York: Edwin Mellen, 1997.

———. *Raphael und Seine Nachbarinnen.* In *Achim von Arnim: Sämtliche Romane un Erzählungen.* Vol. 3. Munich: Carl Hanser, 1965.

Asendorf, Christoph. *Batteries of Life: On the History of Things and their Perception in Modernity.* Trans. Dan Reneau. Berkeley: Univ. of California Press, 1983.

Bateson, Gregory. *Mind and Nature: A Necessary Unity.* New York: Bantam, 1979.

Benz, Ernst. *Theology of Electricity: On the Encounter and Explanation of Theology and Science in the 17th and 18th Centuries.* Translated by Wolfgang Taraba. Introduction by Dennis Stillings. Allison Park, PA.: Pickwick Publications, 1989.

Bergson, Henri. *Laughter: An Essay on the Meaning of the Comic.* Translated by Cloudsley Brereton. New York: Macmillan, 1911.

Blake, William. *Jerusalem.* In *The Complete Poetry and Prose of William Blake.* Edited by David V. Erdman. New York: Doubleday, 1988.

Bloom, Harold. *The Western Canon: Books and Schools of the Age.* Boston: Harcourt, 1994.

Boerhaave, Herman. *Dr. Boerhaave's Academical Lectures on the Theory of Physics, Being a Genuine Translation of his Institutes and Explanatory Comments, as They Were Dictated to His Students at the University of Leyden.* Translated by Anonymous. Vol. 1. London: 1742–47. Quoted in Thomas S. Hall, *Ideas of Life and Matter: Studies in the History of General Physiology, 600 B.C.–1900 A.D.* Vol. 1, *From Pre-Socratic Times to the Enlightenment.* Chicago: Univ. of Chicago Press, 1969.

Boyle, Robert. *Works of the Honourable Robert Boyle, in Six Volumes, to which Is Prefixed the Life of the Author.* Vol. 5. London: printed for J. and F. Rivington, L. Davis, W. Johnston, S. Crowder, and T. Payne, 1772. Quoted in Edward A. Burtt, *The Metaphysical Foundations of Modern Physical Science.* New York: Doubleday, 1954.

Brentano, Clemens, *Godwi, Clemens Brentano Werke.* Vol. 2. Munich: Carl Hanser, 1963.

Budge, E. A. Wallis. *The Gods of the Egyptians.* Vol. 1. New York: Dover, 1969.

———. Introduction to *The Egyptian Book of the Dead: (The Papyrus of Ani), Egyptian Text Transliteration and Translation.* New York: Dover, 1967.

Burckhardt, Titus. *Alchemy: Science of the Cosmos, Science of the Soul.* Translated by William Stoddart. London: Stuart and Watkins, 1967.

Camus, Albert. *The Myth of Sisyphus and Other Essays.* Translated by Justin O'Brien. New York: Vintage, 1991.

Castle, Terry. *The Female Thermometer: Eighteenth-Century Culture and the Invention of the Uncanny.* Oxford: Oxford Univ. Press, 1995.

Channell, David F. *The Vital Machine: A Study of Technology and Organic Life.* New York: Oxford Univ. Press, 1991.

Clark, R. T. Rundle. *Myth and Symbol in Ancient Egypt.* London: Thames and Hudson, 1959.

Cohen, John. *Human Robots in Myth and Science.* New York: A. S. Barnes, 1967.

Couliano, Ioan P. *Out of this World: Otherworldly Journeys from Gilgamesh to Albert Einstein.* Boston: Shambhala, 1991.

Crowie, Susan D., and Tom Johnson. *The Mummy in Fact, Fiction, and Film.* Foreword by George Hart. Jefferson, NC: McFarland, 2002.

Davy, Sir Humphry. *The Collected Works of Sir Humphry Davy.* Edited by John Davy. Vol. 4. London: Smith, 1839–40.

Dennett, Daniel C. *Consciousness Explained.* Boston: Little, Brown, and Co., 1991.

———. *Darwin's Dangerous Idea: Evolution and the Meanings of Life.* New York: Touchstone Books, 1996.

Descartes, René. *A Discourse on Method, Meditations on the First Philosophy, Principles of Philosophy.* Translated by John Veitch. Introduction by Tom Sorrell. London: Dent, 1994.

———. *Discourse on Method of Rightly Conducting the Reason and Seeking for Truth in the Sciences.* Vol. 1 of *The Philosophical Works of Descartes,* translated by Elizabeth Haldane and G. R. T. Ross. New York: Dover, 1955.

————. *Principles of Philosophy.* Vol. 1 of *The Philosophical Works of Descartes,* translated by Elizabeth Haldane and G. R. T. Ross. New York: Dover, 1955.

————. *Treatise of Man.* Translated and commentary by Thomas Steele Hall. Cambridge, MA: Harvard Univ. Press, 1972.

Dick, Philip K. *Do Androids Dream of Electric Sheep?* New York: Del Ray, 1966.

Dorresse, Jean. *The Secret Books of the Egyptian Gnostics: An Introduction to the Gnostic Coptic Manuscripts Discovered at Chenoboskion.* Translated by Philip Mairet. London: Hollis and Carter, 1960.

Doyle, Richard. *On Beyond Living: Rhetorical Transformations of the Life Sciences.* Stanford, CA: Stanford Univ. Press, 1997

————. *Wetwares: Experiments in Postvital Living.* Minneapolis: Univ. of Minnesota Press, 2003.

Drexler, K. Eric. *Engines of Creation: The Coming Era of Nanotechnology.* Foreword by Marvin Minsky. New York: Anchor Doubleday, 1986.

Eichendorff, Joseph von. *Das Marmorbild.* In *Joseph von Eichendorff Werke.* Vol. 2. Munich: Winkler, 1970.

Ellis, John M. *Literature Lost: Social Agendas and the Corruption of the Humanities.* New Haven, CT: Yale Univ. Press, 1997.

Ellul, Jacques. *The Technological Society.* Translated by John Wilkinson. Introduction by Robert K. Morton. New York: Vintage, 1964.

Evelyn, John. *The Diary of John Evelyn.* Edited by E. S. De Beer. Vol. 2. Oxford: Clarendon Press of Oxford Univ. Press, 2000.

Evola, Julius. *The Hermetic Tradition: Symbols and Teachings of the Royal Art.* Translated by E. E. Rehmus. Rochester, VT: Inner Traditions, 1995.

Faraday, Michael. *Experimental Researches in Electricity.* Vol. 45 of *Great Books of the Western World,* edited by Robert Maynard Hutchins et al. Chicago: Encyclopedia Britannica, 1952.

Ficino, Marsilio. *The Book of Life.* Translated by Charles Boer. Dallas, TX: Spring Publications, 1980.

Freud, Sigmund. *Beyond the Pleasure Principle.* Translated and Edited by James Strachey. Introduction by Gregory Zilboorg. Biographical Introduction by Peter Gay. New York: Norton, 1961.

————. "Mourning and Melancholy." In *The Nature of Melancholy: From Aristotle to Kristeva,* edited by Jennifer Radden. Oxford: Oxford Univ. Press, 2000.

————. "The Uncanny." In *The Standard Edition of the Complete Psychological Works of Sigmund Freud,* translated by James Strachey, vol. 17. London: Hogarth, 1959.

———, and Joseph Breuer. "Studies in Hysteria." In *The Standard Edition of the Complete Psychological Works of Sigmund Freud*, translated by James Strachey, vol. 2. London: Hogarth, 1959.

———. Freund, Karl. *The Mummy* 1932. Produced by Carl Laemmle. Directed by Karl Freund. 74 min. Universal Pictures. Videocassette.

Gassendi, Pierre. *Philosophical Treatise*. In *Selected Works of Pierre Gassendi*, edited and translated by Craig B. Bush. New York: Johnson Reprint, 1972.

Gibson, William. *The Neuromancer*. New York: Ace, 1984.

Goethe, Johann Wolfgang von. *Faust Part One & Part Two*. Translated and introduction by Charles E. Passage. New York: Bobbs-Merrill, 1965.

Goleman, Daniel. "Feeling Unreal? Many Others Feel the Same." *New York Times*, January 8, 1991, sec. C.

Gould, Stephen Jay. *The Structure of Evolutionary Theory*. Cambridge, MA: Harvard Univ. Press, 2002.

Greenblatt, Stephen. *Renaissance Self-Fashioning: From More to Shakespeare*. Chicago: Univ. of Chicago Press, 1991.

Hamilton-Preston, James, and Carol Andrews. *Mummies: Death and Life in Ancient Egypt*. New York: Viking, 1979.

Haraway, Donna J. *Simians, Cyborgs, and Women: The Reinvention of Nature*. New York: Routledge, 1991.

Hayles, Katherine. *How We Became Posthuman: Vital Bodies in Cybernetics, Literature, and Informatics*. Chicago: Univ. of Chicago Press, 1999.

Heidegger, Martin. *Being and Time*. Translated by John Macquerie and Edward Robinson. New York: Harper and Row, 1962

———. *Being and Time*. Translated by Joan Stambaugh. Albany: State Univ. of New York Press, 1996.

———. "What is Metaphysics?" *Heidegger: Basic Writings*. Edited and Introduction by David Farrell Krell. New York: Harper and Row, 1977.

Heideman, Eric M. "They Went for a Little Walk: The Mummy in Fact, Folklore, Fiction, and Film, Part 2." *MonsterZine.com* 10. http://www.monsterzine.com/200301/mummy.php#mz010–02.

Hobbes, Thomas. *Elements of Philosophy Concerning Body, Body, Man, and Citizen*. Edited by R. S. Peters. New York: Collier, 1962.

Hoffmann, E. T. A. "Automata." In *The Best Tales of Hoffmann*, edited and introduction by E. F. Bleiler. New York: Dover, 1967.

———. *Die Geheimnisse*. In *E. T. A. Hoffmann Sämtliche Werke*. Vol. 5. Frankfurt: Deutschen Klassiker, 1992.

———. "The Sandman." In *Tales of Hoffmann*, introduction and translated by R. J. Hollingdale. New York: Penguin, 1982.

Idel, Moshe. "The Golem in Jewish Magic and Mysticism." In *Golem! Danger, Deliverance and Art*. New York: The Jewish Museum, 1988.

———. *Golem: Jewish Magical and Mystical Traditions on the Artificial Anthropoid*. Albany: State Univ. of New York Press, 1990.

Ikram, Salima, and Aidan Dodson. *The Mummy in Ancient Egypt: Equipping the Dead for Eternity*. London: Thames and Hudson, 1998.

Irwin, John T. *American Hieroglyphics: The Symbol of the Egyptian Hieroglyphics in the American Renaissance*. Baltimore: Johns Hopkins Univ. Press, 1983.

Jonas, Hans. *The Gnostic Religion*. 3rd ed. Boston: Beacon Press, 2001.

Joy, Bill. "Why the Future Doesn't Need Us." In *Taking the Red Pill: Science, Philosophy, and Religion in The Matrix*, edited by Glenn Yeffeth, introduction by David Gerrold. Dallas, TX: BenBella Books, 2003.

Joyce, James. *Portrait of the Artist as a Young Man*. New York: Everyman's Library, 1964.

Jung, Carl Gustav. *Aion*. Vol. 9, part 1 of *The Collected Works of C. G. Jung*, edited by William McGuire and R. F. C. Hull. 2nd ed. Princeton, NJ: Bollingen Press of Princeton Univ. Press, 1979.

———. *Alchemical Studies*. Vol. 13 of *The Collected Works of C. G. Jung*, edited by William McGuire and R. F. C. Hull. 2nd ed. Princeton, NJ: Bollingen Press of Princeton Univ. Press, 1967.

———. *Memories, Dreams, Reflections*. Edited by Aniela Jaffe. New York: Vintage Books, 1989.

———. *Mysterium Coniunctionis*. Vol. 14 of *The Collected Works of C. G. Jung*, edited by William McGuire and R. F. C. Hull. 2nd ed. Princeton, NJ: Bollingen Press of Princeton Univ. Press, 1979.

———. *Psychology and Alchemy*. Vol. 12 of *The Collected Works of C. G. Jung*, edited by William McGuire and R. F. C. Hull. 2nd ed. Princeton, NJ: Bollingen Press of Princeton Univ. Press, 1952.

Kleist, Heinrich von. "The Puppet Theatre." In *Selected Writings: Heinrich von Kleist*, edited and translated by David Constantine. London: J.M. Dent, 1997.

Klibansky, Raymond, Erwin Panofsky, and Fritz Saxl. *Saturn and Melancholy: Studies in the History of Natural Philosophy, Religion, and Art*. New York: Basic Books, 1964.

Kraeling, Carl H. *Anthropos and Son of Man: A Study in the Religious Syncretism of the Hellenistic Orient*. New York: AMS Press, 1966.

Kuberski, Philip. "Dark Matter: Thinking About Nothing." *The Georgia Review* 44, no. 3 (Fall 2000):431–41.

———. *The Persistence of Memory: Organism, Myth, Text*. Berkeley: Univ. of California Press, 1992.

Kurzweil, Ray. *The Age of Spiritual Machines: When Computers Exceed Human Intelligence*. New York: Viking, 1999.

Lacarrière, Jacques. *The Gnostics*. Trans. Nina Rootes. New York: Dutton, 1977.

Lang, Fritz. *Metropolis* 1927. Produced by Erich Pommer. Directed by Fritz Lang. 115 min. Universum Film A.G. (UFA). Videocassette.

Leca, Ange-Pierre. *The Egyptian Way of Death: Mummies and the Cult of the Immortal*. Translated by Louise Asmal. Garden City, NY: Doubleday, 1981.

Marcuse, Herbert. *One-Dimensional Man: Studies in the Ideology of Advanced Industrial Society*. Boston: Beacon, 1966.

McGann, Jerome. *The Romantic Ideology: A Critical Investigation*. Chicago: Univ. of Chicago Press, 1983.

Meyrink, Gustav. *The Golem*. Edited and Introduction by E. F. Bleiler. New York: Dover, 1976.

Moravec, Hans. *Robot: Mere Machine to Transcendent Mind*. New York: Oxford Univ. Press, 1999.

Naydler, Jeremy. *Temple of the Cosmos: The Ancient Egyptian Experience of the Sacred*. Rochester, VT: Inner Traditions, 1996.

Nelson, Victoria. *The Secret Life of Puppets*. Cambridge, MA: Harvard Univ. Press, 2002.

Neumann, Erich. *The Origins and History of Consciousness: The Psychological Stages in the Development of Personality*. Foreword by C. G. Jung. Translated by R. F. C. Hull. Vol. 2. New York: Harper Torchbooks/Bollingen Library, 1954.

Newton, Isaac. *Opticks*. In *Newton: A Norton Critical Edition*, selected and edited by I. Bernard Cohen and Richard S. Westfall. New York: Norton, 1995.

Offray de la Mettrie, Julien. *Machine Man and Other Writings*. Translated and Edited by Ann Thomson. New York: Cambridge Univ. Press, 1996.

Ott, Hugo. *Heidegger: A Political Life*. Translated by Allan Blunden. New York: Basic Books, 1993.

Paracelsus. "A Book Concerning Life." In *The Hermetic and Alchemical Writings of Paracelsus*, edited and introduction by Arthur E. Waite, vol. 2. Chicago: Laurence, Scott, and Co., 1910.

———. "Concerning the Nature of Things." In *The Hermetic and Alchemical Writings of Paracelsus*, edited and introduction by Arthur E. Waite, vol. 1. Chicago: Laurence, Scott, and Co., 1910.

———. *Selected Writings*. Edited by Jolande Jacobi. Translated by Norbert Guterman. Princeton, NJ: Bollingen Press of Princeton Univ. Press, 1988.

Pera, Marcello. *The Ambiguous Frog: The Galvani-Volta Controversy on Animal Electricity*. Translated by Jonathan Mandelbaum. Princeton, NJ: Princeton Univ. Press, 1992.

Pirsig, Robert M. *Zen and the Art of Motorcycle Maintenance*. New York: Bantam, 1975.

Plato. *The Republic*. In *The Collected Dialogues of Plato, Including the Letters*, edited by Edith Hamilton and Huntington Cairns. Princeton, NJ: Bollingen Press of Princeton Univ. Press, 1961.

Plutarch. *Isis and Osiris. Moralia*. Translated by Frank Cole Babbitt. Vol. 5. Cambridge, MA: Loeb Classical Library, 1936.

Poe, Edgar Allan. "Ligeia." In *The Fall of the House of Usher and Other Writings*, edited by David Galloway. New York: Penguin, 1986.

———. "The Man that was Used Up." In *The Fall of the House of Usher and Other Writings*, Edited by David Galloway. New York: Penguin, 1986.

———. "Some Words with a Mummy." In *Complete Works of Edgar Allan Poe*, edited by James A. Harrison, vol. 5. New York: Fred De Fau & Co., 1902.

Pringle, Heather. *The Mummy Congress: Science, Obsession, and the Everlasting Dead*. New York: Hyperion, 2001.

Pynchon, Thomas. *Gravity's Rainbow*. New York: Penguin, 1973.

Raine, Kathleen. *Blake and Tradition*. Princeton: Bollingen Press of Princeton Univ. Press, 1968.

Reiss, Benjamin. "The Springfield Somnambulist: Or, The End of the Enlightenment in America." *Commonplace* 4, no. 2 (January 2004).

Riskin, Jessica. "Eigtheenth-Century Wetwares." *Representations* 83 (Summer 2003).

Rockmore, Tom, and Joseph Margolis. *The Heidegger Case: On Philosophy and Politics*. Philadelphia: Temple Univ. Press, 1992.

———. *On Heidegger's Nazism and Philosophy*. Berkeley: Univ. of California Press, 1997.

Rogers, Carl R. *Client-Centered Therapy: Its Current Practice, Implications, and Theory*. Boston: Houghton Mifflin, 1961.

Roth, Ann Macy. "The Peseshkef and the 'Opening of the Mouth' Ceremony: A Ritual of Birth and Rebirth." *Journal of Egyptian Archaeology* 78 (1992):113–47.

Rudolph, Kurt. *Gnosis: The Nature and History of Gnosticism*. Translated by R. Mc. Wilson. San Francisco: Harper and Row, 1984.

Schiller, Friedrich. *Letters on the Aesthetic Education of Man*. Translated and introduction by Reginald Snell. New York: Frederick Ungar, 1965.

Schlegel, Friedrich. *Philosophical Fragments*. Translated by Peter Firchow. Foreword by Rodolphe Gasché. Minneapolis: Univ. of Minnesota Press, 1991.

Scholem, Gershom. *Major Trends in Jewish Mysticism.* Foreword by Robert Alter. New York: Schoken, 1995.

———. *On the Kabbalah and Its Symbolism.* Translated by Ralph Manheim. New York: Schocken, 1996.

Scott, Ridley. *Blade Runner* 1982. Produced by Michael Deeley. Directed by Ridley Scott. 112 min. Ladd Company. Videocassette.

Searle, John R. *The Mystery of Consciousness.* New York: New York Review of Books, 1997.

Secret Book According to John. The Gnostic Scriptures: A New Translation with Annotations and Introductions. Edited and translated by Bentley Layton. Garden City, NY: Doubleday, 1987.

Seidelman, Susan. *Making Mr. Right* 1987. Produced by Dan Enright. Directed by Susan Seidelman. 99 minutes. Orion Pictures. Videocassette.

Shelley, Mary. *Frankenstein; or, The Modern Prometheus.* Edited by Maurice Hindle. New York: Penguin, 1985.

Singer, Issac Bashevis. *The Golem,* illustrated Uri Shulevitz. New York: Farrar, Straus, and Giroux, 1996.

Skinner, B. F. *Walden Two.* London: Macmillan, 1969.

Sluga, Hans. *Heidegger's Crisis: Philosophy and the Politics of Nazi Germany.* Cambridge, MA: Harvard Univ. Press, 1993.

Springer, Claudia. *Electronic Eros: Bodies and Desire in the Postindustrial Age.* Austin: University of Texas Press, 1996.

Stafford, Barbara Maria. *Body Criticism: Imagining the Unseen in Enlightenment Art and Medicine.* Cambridge: MIT Press, 1991

Tatar, Maria M. *Spellbound: Studies on Mesmerism and Literature.* Princeton, NJ: Princeton Univ. Press, 1978.

Telotte, J. P. *Replications: A Robotic History of Science Fiction Film.* Urbana: University of Illinois Press, 1995.

Tieck, Ludwig. *Der Runenberg.* In *Schriften.* Vol. 4. Berlin: G. Keimer, 1828

Villiers de L'Isle-Adam, Auguste. *Tomorrow's Eve.* Trans. Robert Martin Adams Urbana: Univ. of Illinois Press, 2001.

Warner, Marina. *The Inner Eye: Art Beyond the Visible.* London: South Bank Centre, 1996.

Weine, Robert. *The Cabinet of Dr. Caligari* 1920. Produced by Rudolf Meinert and Erich Pommer. Directed by Robert Weine. 82 minutes. Decla-Bioscop AG. Videocassette.

Whittaker, Sir Edmund. *A History of the Theories of Aether and Electricity.* Vol. 1, *The Classical Theories.* New York: Harper and Brothers, 1951.

Wiesel, Elie. *The Golem: The Story of a Legend.* Illustrated by Mark Podwal. Translated by Borchardt. New York: Summit, 1983.

Wolfe, Bernard. *Limbo*. New York: Random House, 1952.

Wood, Gaby. *Edison's Eve: A Magical History of the Quest for Mechanical Life*. New York: Knopf, 2002.

Yates, Frances A. *Giordano Bruno and the Hermetic Tradition*. Chicago: Univ. of Chicago Press, 1964.

———. *The Occult Philosophy in the Elizabethan Age*. London: Routledge, 1979.

Young, Julian. *Heidegger, Philosophy, Nazism*. Cambridge: Cambridge Univ. Press, 1997.

INDEX